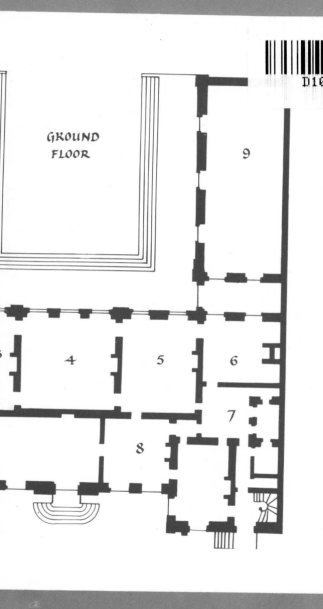

GROUND
FLOOR

9

3

4

5

6

7

8

THE
PARIS EMBASSY

THE
PARIS EMBASSY

Cynthia Gladwyn

COLLINS
St James's Place, London
1976

William Collins Sons & Co Ltd
London · Glasgow · Sydney · Auckland
Toronto · Johannesburg

First published 1976
© Cynthia Gladwyn 1976

ISBN 0 00 216640 2

Set in Monotype Garamond
Made and Printed in Great Britain by
William Collins Sons & Co Ltd Glasgow

Contents

Acknowledgements

I would like to express my gratitude to all those who have helped me in the course of my work on this book, notably: the late Mr Frank Ashton-Gwatkin; Sir Roderick Barclay; Sir James Bowker; the late Monsieur Charles Braibant, Directeur des Archives de France; the late Mr Reginald Bridgeman; Mr Thomas Cadett; Sir Ronald Campbell; the late Prince Jean de Caraman-Chimay; Princesse Jean de Caraman-Chimay; Mr Donald Castle of the D.O.E.; Mr Victor Cavendish-Bentinck; Lady Cobbold; Air Marshal Sir Douglas Collyer; Sir John Colville; Lady Diana Cooper; Baron and Baronne Geoffroy de Courcel; Mrs Crawshay; Monsieur Serge Grandjean, Conservateur des Objets d'Art au Louvre; the late Sir Hugh Gurney; Lady Gurney; Captain E. B. Haslam; the late Monsieur Louis Hautecoeur, Membre de l'Institut; Lord Inchyra; l'Institut Charles de Gaulle; Monsieur Laprade, Membre de l'Institut; Mrs Mary Lutyens; the late Pamela, Lady Lytton; Sir Fitzroy Maclean; Mr John Mallet; Mr Douglas Matthews of the London Library; Sir Clifford Norton; Sir Anthony Nutting; Lady Peake; Lady Phipps; Captain T. Powell; Sir Patrick Reilly; Sir Frank Roberts; Mr Kenneth Rose; Lady Salisbury-Jones; the late Lord Spencer; the late Sir Christopher Steel; Mrs Virginia Surtees; Mr E. K. Timings of the P.R.O.; Lady Vansittart; the late Ava, Lady Waverley; the late Duke of Wellington; the late Sir John Wheeler-Bennet; Sir Michael Wright.

Above all I must thank my husband and my daughter, Vanessa Thomas, for advice and encouragement.

Illustrations

I

The Dukes of Charost
1723—1785

The abdication of Napoleon in March 1814 left Great Britain the most powerful nation in the world. There were thus some extravagant ideas as to where the newly appointed Ambassador, the Duke of Wellington, should be housed. Up till then it had never been the custom of the British Government to have a permanent residence for its ambassadors in foreign capitals. Both the Palais de l'Elysée and the Ministère de la Marine, the eastern building by Gabriel in the Place de la Concorde, could have been rented, but were unfurnished. Other properties were considered and rejected. Then came the suggestion that the house belonging to Princess Borghese, sister of Napoleon, in the Rue du Faubourg Saint-Honoré, ideally situated and fully furnished, might be bought lock, stock and barrel. It has been the British Embassy since August 1814.

It stands high *entre cour et jardin*, with an air of remote dignity. Originally a black marble plaque surmounted with heraldry over the lofty gateway proclaimed it to be the Hôtel de Charost, for it was built by the Charost branch of the ancient and illustrious Béthune family. Louis de Béthune, nephew of Sully, the great minister of Henri IV, was declared by Richelieu to be 'the honour of his race', and was created Duc de Charost in 1672. His son married the daughter of Fouquet, Minister of Finance, whose riches incurred the suspicions of Louis XIV. Fouquet was condemned to life imprisonment, and as the young Béthunes took his side they were exiled. In banishment Madame de

Béthune practised a mystical cult, Quietism, in which she interested Madame Guyon, who became its protagonist. She also introduced Fénélon, the illustrious archbishop and writer, to Madame Guyon, who converted him. (Both Fénélon and Madame Guyon were eventually forced to recant.) However, when the Béthunes were allowed to return to Versailles on the death of Fouquet in 1680, Madame de Béthune was able to initiate the court into the new religion. Her position became so important that the Charosts were said to owe their subsequent advancement to her piety. It was her grandson, known as the Duc de Béthune and later fourth of Charost, who built the house in Paris.

At the beginning of the eighteenth century, the Porte Saint-Honoré stood at the junction of the Rue Saint-Honoré and what is now the Rue Royale, whence a more or less country road wound its way along to the village of Roule. The ground was mostly marshland with a few nurseries and gardeners' cottages scattered here and there. This was due to be developed as an important residential quarter and rich noblemen were buying plots on which to build houses. Speculators, adventurers, tradesmen were also getting their stakes in the ground and the effect promised to be that of an ugly, straggling street of mean buildings interspersed with splendid mansions. Then, in 1724, an edict went out forbidding all further work. It was not in accordance with French tradition to construct without plan, and the new Grande Rue du Faubourg had to be saved from such confusion. Only fifteen hôtels had been built of which the last was that of Charost. (Later the ban was lifted.)

On 16 February 1722 Marie Cécile Pelard, wife of Messire de la Chapelle, sold her property to the seigneur Paul-François de Béthune-Charost. The purchase price was 60,000 livres, a substantial amount for the period. The architect chosen was Antoine Mazin, *ingénieur et directeur des plans du Roi*, who had been called in to complete the Hôtel de Matignon, the 'No. 10' of Paris, when the more famous Courtonne was dismissed. Many features of the Hôtel de Charost resemble those of the Matignon.

The plans having been drawn up in April, Sieur Louis Paigneau, Master Mason, undertook to provide the masonry. The porch steps and garden steps, the walls of the grand staircase, were to come from quarries at Arceuil, the blonde stone for the elevation from Saint Leu or Montesson, plaster from Montmartre, loam from Arceuil, and the sand was to be pure river sand, the mortar two-thirds sand and one-third good lime. The steps of the grand staircase were to be in stone from Thyère and each was to be in one piece.

The estimates were then signed: Jean-Baptiste Lardin, Master Carpenter; Robert Vitry, Master Joiner; Antoine Hallé, locksmith and responsible for all ironwork; Hénin, glazier. There were estimates for gilding, bronzing, '*peinture d'impression*', marble chimney-pieces, sculpture in wood, stone and plaster. These gifted artisans completed their work in eighteen months.

Little is known of the lives of the Béthunes in their new home, though from inventories, leases and other documents we discover something of how it was decorated and furnished, the particular rooms occupied by various members of the family and their entourage. The great Hôtel must have been full to capacity.

Once inside the gateway there is privacy and aloofness from the world outside, reflecting the attitude of a rich eighteenth-century nobleman. Many times in the long history of the house it has been expedient to keep these high doors giving on to the street bolted and barred, and then those within have a sense of impregnability. Within the courtyard the walls on either side curve in a semi-circle. An open arcade on the right used to balance the existing but now closed arcade on the left in which are the kitchens. These are denoted by a finely sculptured boar being mauled by a hound above the entrance, while on the opposite side (where the stable had been), a pair of delicately carved horses prance and toss their manes.

The house itself must have been even more pleasing to the eye when the second floor was within a mansard roof and all the windows had glazing bars. The hall has more genuine features than one would suspect. These same columns, walls and staircase-well were originally marbled and had panels painted in *trompe l'œil*. The sweep of the staircase shows to advantage the ramp with its design of sunheads and lilies, very similar to that of the Matignon, but black and gold paint now covers the original steel and gilt. At the top of the stairs is a splendid oak door of a later date, carved with fasces and lightning, described in detail in the inventory of 1787.

On the two main floors of the garden side mirrored and gilded rooms lead from one to another. The Duke's *lit de parade* stood in what is now the *Salon Vert*. The Duchess slept directly below, now the Victoria Room, which is also approached by the small west staircase. This room still retains an exquisite example of Louis XV moulding, crowning the mirror between the windows. A bas-relief representing Venus and Cupid, a shell and other ornamentation has, with the cornice, survived subsequent alterations. Beyond was *le Grand Cabinet Doré à la Niche*, now the Throne Room, and enlarged with supporting columns. These dressing-rooms (one above the other on the ground and first floor) each have little doors leading to the *Cabinets d'aisance dit Lieux à l'Anglaise*. People who live in big houses crave intimate rooms and *petits appartements* were contrived by dividing some of the tall rooms horizontally. Well removed from all this luxury was the infirmary, on the street, containing two wooden four-post beds.

In the eighteenth century, the south façade remained undisturbed by the galleries which were later built out into the garden. Steps led down to flower-beds of elaborate design which filled the space in the foreground and beyond these conventional ranks of pollarded trees. A path ran down the middle of this wood to a grille and ditch which guarded the end of the property giving on to the Avenue Gabriel, where a small gate provided a useful and discreet entrance.

The Duke had created and furnished the house with that fastidious taste to be expected of the great-grandson of Fouquet. Now, in the prime of life, he held high office, while his three young sons were being moulded into worthy inheritors of the name of Béthune. But they died in early manhood, the youngest, the Duc d'Ancenis, leaving a year-old heir, born in 1738, who succeeded as fifth Duc de Charost at the age of 21. He was a greater honour to his race than the friend of Richelieu, and achieved more good than the Quietist Duchess. On his estates he abolished forced labour, built libraries, schools, orphanages, hospitals, and organized a form of health service and insurance policy. He married first in 1760, an heiress of fifteen. They had two sons, only one of whom survived childhood. Thus the future of the house of Béthune once more hung on a single thread.

The Duchess dying in 1779, the Duke married another heiress whose dowry included the Hôtel de Seignely in the Rue de Lille. The acquisition of this other magnificent house in Paris and the death of his long-widowed mother in 1784 may have decided the Charosts to move there on 1 April 1785. He let the Hôtel in the Faubourg for a period of nine years to a relative, probably visualizing that at the end of this time his son would occupy it.

II

Count de La Marck
1785—1791

Auguste-Marie Raymond d'Arenberg, born in 1753 in Brussels, of a princely house of the Holy Roman Empire, was a rich landowner in the Low Countries. On inheriting a regiment of German infantry, in the service of France since Louis XIV, he became Count de la Marck and a Grandee of Spain. He arrived at the French court in 1770 in time for the marriage of the eldest grandson of Louis XV to the Archduchess Marie-Antoinette, to whom he was deeply indebted when she became Queen for helping to hush up a duel in which he had fought and killed a fellow officer.

La Marck's marriage in 1774 to an heiress brought him a son and more land. He had a house at Versailles, and on 1 April 1785 rented the Hôtel de Charost. A number of alterations were agreed upon. Among them Bohemian glass was to replace existing window panes on the two main floors, and as the spirit of the age was already veering to simplicity, gilding was to be painted over. The vogue in France was now for the romantic English garden so the flower-beds were replaced with grass. Thus the embassy lawn dates from long before it became British property.

Two years later, on 5 April 1787, an inventory was made showing these alterations. This volume gives a detailed description of the layout of the whole house. Going through the rooms with this *Etat des Lieux* in one's hands, one can see very clearly what changes have been made and when. The décor of the central salon on the ground floor, indisputably the most beautiful of all the rooms, despite a few minor Victorian additions, dates from after this inventory was made. It is now the quintessence of Louis XVI with pilasters surmounted by Ionic capitals, nymphs with musical instruments, cherubs supporting vases, lyres on the doors, garlands, and a finely chiselled cornice. Possibly the work of Victor Louis, it is of a purity typical of this particular epoch, showing an anxiety not to be sumptuous.

Like the Duc de Charost, the young foreigner was in favour of reform. The house now became the scene of political activity, with secret meetings, for La Marck was a friend of that genius of the Revolution, Comte Gabriel-Honoré de Mirabeau. They first met at Versailles in 1788.

Elected to the States General Assembly as the representative of du Quesnoy where his wife had property, La Marck had ample opportunity to see the famous orator, who, when dining alone in the Hôtel de Charost, revealed himself to be a royalist at heart: 'Let them know at the Château that I am more for them than against them.' At La Marck's suggestion he wrote the first of those brilliant memoranda for the Court which advocated its withdrawal to Normandy, whose loyalty could be counted upon, and from where the King could proclaim the necessary reforms.

La Marck and Mirabeau were continually in touch. The latter's secretary, Jean-Joachim Pellenc, lodged in the Faubourg St-Honoré house. The Countess la Marck had moved to her estates.

In March 1790 the Austrian Ambassador, Count Mercy d'Argenteau, came to tell La Marck that at last the King and Queen would avail themselves of the help of Mirabeau, but only if the Belgian acted as a go-between. He, in turn, stipulated that the Ambassador must take part. The first meeting of the three took place in the Hôtel de Charost. The layout of the house was ideal for such a conference. On the appointed evening, Mercy drove into the courtyard while Mirabeau, given the key of the small gate in the Avenue Gabriel, walked up the garden to let himself into the house. Nobody in the ante-chamber knew he was there.

The scene of the meeting may have been the Victoria Room where, flanked by the Cabinet Doré and the central salon, the sound of voices could not have been overheard. In the dining-room Mirabeau, involved in a heated argument, had once made such a noise that a servant rushed in thinking there had been a fight.

But the King and Queen were still suspicious of the man who was proposing to help them. La Marck was aghast when Louis XVI stated that everything Monsieur de Mirabeau proposed doing must be told to his ministers. However, it was agreed that the erstwhile rebel's devotion to the royal cause should be put in writing. The letter in question was so stimulating and convincing that Louis and Marie Antoinette were delighted. The difficulty lay particularly in the powerful Lafayette, who, as head of the National Guard, was admitted to the King and Queen whenever he wished on the pretext of watching over their security. Either he must be kept in ignorance of the plan or persuaded not to impede it. Mirabeau sacrificed his pride in a dramatic conciliatory letter. He tried to approach him several times and even offered to be *éminence grise* to Lafayette's Richelieu but with no success.

It was agreed that financial help would make it easier for Mirabeau to concentrate on the royal cause. At this news, the revolutionary was in ecstasy, and his cautious companion quite taken aback as he listened to fulsome praise of the King who, he was assured, would soon be seen occupying a position worthy of his generous character.

On 23 December Mirabeau gave vent to his strongest memorandum for the court. It was his forty-seventh. Eventually, Louis agreed to consider a plan for leaving Paris. Mirabeau suggested flight to some fortified town on the northern or eastern frontiers where they could count on the support of the army, but when La Marck went off to Metz to reconnoitre he learned that the troops were corrupted and the only hope lay in the civil servants of the Départements.

As the summer wore on, the Belgian found his own

position becoming difficult and, feeling that he was no longer of help to the court, planned to leave Paris. At the last moment he was persuaded not to go by Mercy, who was being transferred to The Hague. He was now the sole witness of the despair of Mirabeau at the inaction of the royal family and his sinister predictions of their deaths. 'The people will flog the pavement with their corpses' he would say. He had sent fifty notes for the court and nothing had been achieved.

On 24 March, a letter from Mirabeau was delivered at the Hôtel de Charost, written from the Assembly and telling of the impending republican regime. ' . . . I was never frightened till today . . . Oh irresponsible, quite irresponsible nation! . . . *Vale et me ama.*' That was the end of the correspondence.

The next morning Mirabeau came early to the Hôtel de Charost, obviously desperately ill. There was some Tokay in the house which he had often enjoyed and, revived by the wine, he was able to go to the Assembly and speak on a question involving the control of certain mines in which la Marck was interested. His famous voice was heard for the last time. Towards three in the afternoon, he staggered back to La Marck's room, flung himself exhausted on the sofa and gasped, 'Your cause is won and I am dead.' He was got to his feet, supported to his carriage and driven home. La Marck hardly left him. Mirabeau gave him charge of all his papers, begging him one day to avenge his memory by publishing them. They were brought secretly at night to the Hôtel de Charost. He died in La Marck's arms on 2 April. People hardly dared to look at his empty place in the Assembly and even Marie-Antoinette was seen to cry.

The ill-fated flight to the frontier was a poor substitute for the farsighted schemes of the dead man.

La Marck remained in Paris with Pellenc, frequently seeing the Queen and doing what he could for her. As the situation worsened he realized he could no longer be of help, and left for Brussels. He died in Brussels in 1833.

III

The Portuguese Embassy
1790—1792

In the late summer of 1790, La Marck had sublet part of the house, furnished, to the Portuguese Ambassador. The main building may have been divided horizontally or perpendicularly, most probably the latter. The secondary staircase goes down to the labyrinthine basement where are the vaulted cellars on which the great house rests with massive central columns reminiscent of the crypt of a cathedral. Some have high windows on to the courtyard and in one of these there is evidence of a kitchen.

Dom Vincente de Souza Coutinho had been Ambassador to France since 1772. A widower, needing a hostess, he remarried the following year a French woman. They both died in 1792.

On 20 July an inventory was made of the property of Count de Souza. By now Portugal and France had broken off relations and the Embassy Secretary had the task of dealing with the creditors of the late Ambassador, who had left huge debts. The Ambassadress owed even more to Rose Bertin, the modiste, than did Madame du Barry.

IV

Interregnum
1793—1803

France became a republic on 21 September 1792, and rough new masters installed themselves in splendid buildings designed for beauty and pleasure. The Hôtel de Charost was now occupied by a coachman, valet and butler. They brought in a merchant called Coulage, who must have found the capacious cellars excellent for his warehouse of wine and cider.

The eldest son of the Charosts was guillotined in April 1794. Suspicion fell on the Duke, whose reputation had hitherto spared him from all persecution. He was now sent to the Prison de la Force, despite violent opposition and petitions, and was only released when Robespierre was executed.

The Revolutionary Tribunal was abolished on 31 May 1795, and soon a new sort of life began. With the rise of Bonaparte those with an interest in munitions expanded their businesses. A company called Petit et Cie had offices in the Hôtel; when it failed it was succeeded by L'Entreprise d'hopitaux militaires, which did no better and angry creditors surged into the courtyard demanding payment.*

When the Consulate was formed, aristocrats were even able to get back into their houses. Charost regained his, but

---

* One little relic has survived from this commercial interlude in the history of the embassy. In 1954, work being done in the Salon Vert necessitated the dismantling of part of the wall-covering. Beneath two old wallpapers were fragments of one with a pattern of cannons, drums and tricolours.

continued to live in the Rue de Lille. He was named Mayor of what is now the seventh arrondissement and he died in 1800, having contracted smallpox from the deaf and dumb people he was looking after with his usual solicitude. He was the last of his line and he left the Hôtel to his widow.

Not ten years after the blood-letting, the youngest sister of Bonaparte bought the house. Egocentric, frivolous, extravagant, had she been on the scene a little sooner, she would have found herself on a tumbril heading for the guillotine with far more justification than many of its victims.

V

Pauline Borghese
1803—1814

Napoleon called the lovely and undisciplined Pauline 'The Little Pagan'. She was perhaps the most significant owner of the Hôtel de Charost for her furniture remains in the house, forming a valuable collection unequalled in any of our embassies. Born in 1780, she married in 1801 one of her brother's generals, Leclerc. Forced to go with him to San Domingo, she returned to France as a widow in 1803 and bought the house from the Duchesse de Charost in April.

It was nearly twenty years since it had been renovated and now basic alterations were made. There was redecoration to be undertaken, including a prodigious amount of gilding – again in fashion. Some work was done in the central drawing-room on the first floor, of which little remains except the Corinthian capitals and a chimney-piece of high quality, the work of Percier et Fontaine. In the adjoining room is another, equally fine. A few Empire motifs have survived here and there and more mirrors were placed in the main rooms to reflect and enlarge.

However, the most fundamental change made by Pauline was in 1807 when she started building out into the garden a long gallery in which to hang the Borghese pictures. Later a parallel gallery was built on the other side as a state dining-room. They were lit by skylights (an interesting innovation) across which was stretched cambric to prevent glare. These wings spoil the architecture of the south façade but proved to be of great practical use to the house when it became an embassy again. The house is the only one which has been so extended, and, as such construction was forbidden by law, Napoleon must have given his favourite sister special permission, '*le fait du Prince*', as it was called. It may also have been when she was enlarging the house that the arcade which joins the kitchen wing was filled in and the stables moved to the Rue d'Anjou, in order to convert the northwest pavilion into rooms for her vast retinue.

Napoleon, well aware that his sister could not pose as a stricken widow for long, was as anxious as she to find her a new husband. Pauline's choice fell on Prince Camillo Borghese, of a rich and ancient Italian family. He was hardly the right man for a young woman whose reputation was already notorious, but this was overlooked in their mutual eagerness to satisfy their ambitions; Camillo saw the advantage of becoming brother-in-law to the powerful First Consul and Pauline in being the only princess in the family. Napoleon agreed to the marriage, declaring that with her classical looks her destiny was to become a Roman. The contract was signed at the Hôtel de Charost on 23 August 1803. Soon news began to percolate back to France from Rome that she was already dissatisfied with her husband and wished to return to Paris. There were stories of her irresponsible behaviour, which displeased Napoleon. To stop her returning against his wishes, the First Consul even thought of buying from her the Hôtel de Charost which Hortense (his sister-in-law and the daughter of Josephine) would much have liked to have.

Pauline was forced to remain in Italy until October 1804, when her need for consolation after the death of her six-year-old son by Leclerc made Napoleon relent. His coronation was about to take place and soon her mind was full of entrancing plans for what she would wear at the ceremonies, though she resented the fact that the most important person would have to be the Empress, whose train she and her sisters must hold.

Pauline had no intellect, no sequence of thought, no conversation and her chatter was exclusively about herself. Her only interest was the cult of her body; how to satisfy it, adorn it and preserve it. There began a way of life unprecedented in the annals of the Hôtel de Charost. At her levées she walked about the room naked to be admired; a magnificent Negro carried her into her bath and lifted her out again; if the Princess felt cold, she warmed her feet in the décolleté of a lady-in-waiting, who lay on the floor. Her brother gave her an impressive household which included members of the old families of France, and wished the etiquette to be strict. She had a cardinal as an almoner and two chaplains. They can hardly have approved when she converted the Charost chapel into a billiard-room papered in yellow and silver, and ordered that the religious pictures be relegated to the *antichambre des valets*.

Meanwhile, the marital situation was eased by Borghese being given the rights of a French citizen, which kept him in France, and a military career, which kept him away from Paris. To encourage him as a soldier, the Emperor decorated him with the Legion of Honour, of which the inadequate husband became a Grand Aigle. It must have been in January 1805 that Pauline incorporated this motif in the gilded Corinthian capitals of the big salon on the first floor, the walls of which were draped with green velvet, embroidered in gold with elaborate gold trimming.

Could we see the house as it was in Pauline's time, we might be most struck by the violence of the colours. It was a flamboyant age. The Salon Ionien was hung with draped poppy-coloured velvet fringed with gold; the blue of her Chambre de Parade (the Victoria Room) may have been strong; the library (now the Ambassadress's bedroom) had orange silk, the Salon Carmelite was brown, and one of the violet rooms was contrasted with golden yellow. The floor of the State Dining-Room had thirty round rugs simulating tigerskins.

The Princess often slept in the bedroom, also blue, immediately above her impressive Chambre de Parade, preferring a small bed which Prince Clary (an Austrian visitor to the house in 1810) describes as being so low and tiny that it was almost like a child's. But he tells us that she was extremely small.

We can visualize her in those rooms and almost hear the '*Pardi*' which was her constant exclamation. Then, unexpectedly, it transpires that this exquisite Tanagra figure, light as thistledown, with feet that looked as though they had never worn shoes, had, latent in her, something of the autocratic character of her dreaded brother. Her flashing anger, self-assurance and coolness were unbelievable in someone so frivolous. That '*Pardi*' could be frightening.

The running of the Hôtel de Charost was organized with a precision almost reminiscent of Napoleonic strategy. Her orders were imperative. On Monday mornings she would go round the premises as though carrying out an inspection. Everybody must be at attention, everything in perfect working order. She examined candle-ends; saw to it that her staff had no sugar; reprimanded the footmen for talking too loud and for playing cards in their anteroom, the scullions for crossing the courtyard, '*le Suisse*', the porter, for leaving open the great doors, thus allowing stray dogs to wander in.

In 1809 letters of a secret nature were once more being delivered by trusted messengers. They concerned the welfare of Napoleon, but they came straight from the dynamic head of the new royal family himself, who was no shilly-shallying king. From the garden entrance used by Mirabeau, the short, stoutening figure of the 44-year-old master of Europe clandestinely covered the same course. He was on pleasure bent. The object of his desire was his sister's Piedmontese lady-in-waiting. It was Pauline herself who had the idea that Madame de Mathis, with her blonde beauty and a plumpness which might remind the Emperor of Marie Walewska, would make him an excellent mistress to pass the time between divorcing Josephine and remarriage. Her aim, as always, was to please the Emperor, displease the Empress and gain herself money and presents.

But the conqueror met with unwonted resistance. The Piedmontese had moral scruples. Pauline peremptorily admonished her for daring to refuse whatever the Emperor demanded of her, averring that she herself, his own sister, always obeyed his orders. Still it did not work. Madame de Mathis, of a timid disposition, had to be cajoled. It was now that Napoleon began writing letters to the Princess, 34 in all. They describe the progress of the seduction, which had grown all the more appetizing for being frustrated. Even at midnight a few lines would be sent: 'Write to me tomorrow morning what I am to say to her and if she is happier.' And the next morning at ten: '*Petite sœur.* I will come by the garden at nine o'clock.' Finally, the lady-in-waiting surrendered. 'We have made peace, *petite sœur.* Someone has been entirely amiable.'

The setting for the romance was on the ground floor. 'If she would wait for me at your *rez-de-chaussée* that would perhaps be better. I will come by the garden.' La Marck had found the privacy of those particular south rooms favourable for political intrigue. They were ideal for another sort of intrigue, having every convenience including the magnificent gilt state bed, today still the pride of the embassy. The caryatids were originally painted to resemble bronze which is still intact beneath successive layers of gold leaf, the exterior was upholstered in blue and the interior in white satin woven with gold rosettes. It stood on a dais and the gilt crown above, surmounted by an eagle, was garnished with 26 ostrich feathers. On the walls blue faille embroidered in gold was draped '*en manteau ducal à colonnes*'. The room was further enriched by motifs of gilt myrtle leaves, the emblem of Venus, which are also repeated on the bed.

But the affair never seemed to run smoothly. The mistress could be difficult at times, and the lover did not approve. That was not what women were for. 'I will not come until you think that she is no longer capricious for it tires me. I need sweetness and good-humour, not little bouts of obstinacy . . . *Adieu petite princesse.*' He held the time-honoured male view that women were there to please men, to charm them and then submit. Above all they must be docile. He would have stood no nonsense from the modern career woman.

Time was getting on. The Austrian Emperor had agreed to the French dictator's marrying the great-niece of Marie-Antoinette and the love affair became no longer interesting or necessary. On 29 January 1810 Madame de Mathis was ordered back to her husband in Italy.

Pauline had done nicely out of the affair (as indeed had her lady-in-waiting, whose husband was even remembered with a barony) and now she was ready to turn her mind to ordering resplendent dresses for the forthcoming wedding. She was to be just as impertinent to her new sister-in-law from the Holy Roman Empire, probably resenting the genuine royal blood of the Archduchess.

The prospect of ceremonies and parties in the spring of 1810 was marred by two drawbacks. Once more she must carry the train of the Empress, and her husband was rejoining her at the Hôtel de Charost. Wishing to avoid Camillo, who slept in what is now the library, she moved her gold bed up to the present Salon Vert in January, and her tulle bed down to the Chambre de Parade. From the ground floor she complained if he dared walk immediately above. She decreed that he must address her as Imperial Highness, demand an audience if he wished to see her, and pay for his meals. The Prince's distinguished title was no longer of importance to her and she said he was a eunuch. Yet, according to a little known Roman gossip, Prince Borghese also had his hour. After making some show of jealousy and indignation over the notorious infidelities of his wife, he consoled himself by flirting with the ladies of her suite, in particular Countess Cavour, so that rumour attributed to him the paternity of her son, Camillo, born in 1810, who was to become the great Italian statesman of the Risorgimento.

Pauline had a succession of lovers of all ages, types, nationalities, but if a liaison became too notorious for the liking of Napoleon, then lightning struck. One handsome dilettante suddenly found himself on the Spanish frontier as a second lieutenant and another was despatched with an urgent message for Massena. Prince Clary was particularly intrigued by her bathroom, for the Princess was reputed sometimes to receive her lovers here. This must have been the large bathroom on the ground floor incorporating a section of the present Throne Room. Hung with pistachio green, the bath had a moveable cover and a day bed of lemon-wood covered with green taffetas. The furniture also included several pieces which can be recognized in the house today, such as the psyché and the dressing table by Löven now in the Ambassadress's bedroom. The greatest scandal was the rumoured incestuous relationship of Pauline and Napoleon. This may well have been true. She was a nymphomaniac and the Emperor often said that, being unlike other men, the principles of morality and decency did not apply to him.

Pauline left for a cure on 7 June 1812, little thinking it would be the last time she would see her Paris house. When the star of the Emperor began to shine less brightly, his pleasure-loving sister suddenly showed irreproachable behaviour, offering him her diamonds in a gesture to help save the disintegrating empire. After his abdication in April 1814, she was the only Bonaparte to join the defeated Emperor in his exile on Elba.

Pauline ended her life in Italy, chiefly in Rome. Surprisingly enough an aura almost approaching dignity surrounded her last days. She became reconciled to her husband, made a thoughtful will and turned to God. She died on 9 June 1825 and was buried in the basilica of Santa Maria Maggiore in the Borghese Crypt of the Capella Paolina, named not after her but Paulus V. His marble effigy and that of another great pope guard the spot where Pauline lies, as if defying a would-be lover to approach. On special occasions, the chapel is the scene of a charming rite in memory of the holy and ancient legend of Pope Liberias. Sweet-smelling jasmine is then scattered down from the cupola. It almost suggests a pleasure-dome.

VI

The Duke of Wellington
1814—1815

In an interview at Elba, Napoleon said that Wellington was *un brave homme* and that he would sooner have trusted him with 100,000 men than any of his own generals, even Soult; but he thought it foolish to send him to the Court of France to deal with those whom he had humbled. However, in that Paris spring of 1814 national prestige was forgotten. The French gave an enthusiastic welcome to the triumphant emperors and kings, field marshals and generals who were converging on Paris.

The Ambassador left almost immediately for home to be acclaimed in triumph, leaving Sir Charles Stuart, a professional diplomat, to set up his mission in his absence. Stuart had been angling for the Paris Embassy even before the appointment of Wellington; he was eventually to get it. He now became Minister Plenipotentiary for a few months. His first task was to find a suitable embassy. The suggestion that Pauline's house might be bought came from a Scottish nabob, a man of taste, who had known La Marck.

Quentin Craufurd had made a fortune in Manilla, where he also acquired as mistress an Italian dancer and trapeze artist, Mrs Eleonora Sullivan, who had had two children by the Duke of Württemberg. Craufurd settled in Paris in 1783. He was a great friend of Axel Fersen, and with Mrs Sullivan helped organize the flight to Varennes, after which they were all three obliged to leave France. Then Craufurd discovered that Eleonora, whom he had always refused to marry, was also the mistress of Fersen. There was a terrible scene, and in the end she decided to remain with her nabob.

Classed as an émigré and his possessions confiscated, Craufurd was allowed to return to Paris after the Peace of Amiens in 1801. He at last regularized the position of Mrs Sullivan. The Restoration revealed him once more as an ardent loyalist. It seems generally to be accepted that he was a secret agent of the British Government, acting for motives other than money. Uncle to a general killed in the Peninsular War, he was *persona grata* with the new Ambassador and continued, till he died in 1819, to advise Wellington on art purchases. The former trapeze artist would have been proud had she known that her grandson, Comte Alfréd d'Orsay, was to paint the only portraits of Wellington of which he seems to have approved; they made him look like a gentleman. One of them hangs in the embassy, representing him in his later years, silver-haired and benign.

Pauline was determined to drive a hard bargain, asking an exorbitant 850,000 francs and demanding to be paid in cash. It gave her satisfaction to say she would not trust the English with credit. By now the Duke felt it to be the only house ideal for his purpose. With characteristic caution, he nevertheless wrote to Sir Charles Stuart, who, with the advice of Craufurd, was undertaking the negotiations, that since it was very large and too expensive he must give up all thoughts of it. Craufurd insisted that house property was low at the moment. After much haggling the price agreed on was 800,000 francs for the house and furniture complete. The furniture was to be paid for in two instalments and the 500,000 francs for the house in four instalments, with interest. The stables in the Rue d'Anjou, a separate lot, no longer belonging to Pauline Borghese, were bought for 61,500 francs.

The sale was not completed and signed till 24 October. However, when the Ambassador returned to Paris on 22 August to present his credentials, he was able to move straight into his embassy. He wrote to the Foreign Office much pleased with the outcome of the long negotiations, saying that the purchase was a remarkably cheap one. In this same letter of 29 August he mentions that he had a list of the furniture which he would have verified by one of the gentlemen attached to the embassy. In 1959 this inventory, dated 26 August 1814, was found in the Public Records Office. It included a plan of the ground floor, the first we have which shows what structural alterations have been made at subsequent dates.* The furniture which belonged to the Princess can easily be identified, and it is absorbing to note where it was placed and with what upholstery and decoration.

Much of the contents is missing. The Empire style ceased to be fashionable and a piece in bad repair was often discarded to be replaced by something contemporary; some of it went to the sale room or to the attics To give an example of the part that fashion plays in such matters, we find listed in the inventory four armchairs painted green which had been dismissed to the *garde robe*. These must be the four Louis XVI armchairs signed Dupont. They are now stripped to their original colour and considered to be of great value. In 1814 they were not admired.

Rich though the embassy is in Empire furniture, one must regret the lost pieces. In the big dining-room were eight candelabra with Egyptian figures, sixty mahogany chairs, and three armchairs en suite for the use of Pauline and her imperial brother and sister-in-law. All these have vanished. Of six games tables, only one remains, a particularly fine Directoire *table à bouillote* which was rescued from a back bedroom upstairs in 1957 and restored.† The only bed which has survived is that of the Princess. Examination reveals that the great baldequin with the eagle does not belong to it, being decorated with different motifs and a little out of proportion for the bed.

Wellington could hardly have appreciated to the full the

* See appendix.
† As all Pauline's furniture originally bore a heart-shaped vellum on which was written the room to which it belonged and a description of the covering, the writer had this pretty means of identification put on the table.

The Entrance
The Courtyard, showing the
Chancery on the left

The Façade

contents he had secured for his country. He thought that the most beautiful piece of furniture he had ever seen in his life was the inlaid billiard-table made for Stratfield Saye in about 1840.

There is no record of where he slept but, both at Apsley House and Stratfield Saye, he preferred a small, unpretentious bed on the ground floor, near a bathroom, and as far away from his Duchess as possible. Therefore, in the embassy, he is believed to have used the Chambre de Parade of Pauline with the pistachio bathroom nearby. According to the inventory of 1814, the state bed was still in the room above and in the Chambre de Parade was placed a simple sofa bed with gilded mouldings.

His marriage to Catherine Pakenham, sister of Lord Longford, had been one of the rare mistakes made by Wellington. He complained that her mind was not that of an adult, that he could have no conversation with her, that she always believed herself to be in the right. From every point of view she was unequal to sharing his already eminent position. Many years later he spoke of the incompatibility of the Duchess to the woman-friend to whom he was the most devoted. He told Mrs Arbuthnot how nothing would have made him so happy as to have had 'a fireside at home where he could find comfort and peace'. It was sad that, with all his glory, this is what he never enjoyed.

Intimate companionship with intelligent and sympathetic women was essential to him. He needed to have flirtations, to pour out his feelings, even to write letters that were sometimes indiscreet for a man in so high a political position. It would seem that sexual relationship was reserved for professionals. Perhaps it was for this reason that he once confided: 'No woman ever loved me; never in my whole life.' The emotions of the Iron Duke were not romantic. Talleyrand, while admiring him and finding him noble, simple and like a sort of god on the field of battle, nevertheless pronounced him to be the most curious personage of the age. That formidable profile with the exaggerated prominence of hooked nose and strong chin, the hard-hitting retorts, the objective common sense brought to bear on any matter, did not reveal some very human traits in his character: he had burst into tears over the casualties at Waterloo. He burnt his violin lest it should divert his attention from the army.

His first exacting diplomatic task was to persuade the French Government to abolish the slave trade. Although the French thought him absurdly fanatical on the subject, they agreed to do so in five years' time. In the midst of these discussions, Wellington had to grapple with a lesser but more awkward incident. Talleyrand came to the embassy to warn him that the Princess of Wales, estranged wife of the Regent, had arrived in Strasbourg and that Louis XVIII wanted to know the Regent's wishes should she turn up in Paris. The Duke devised a quick though brutal solution. He sent a message to the Princess that he could not present anybody to the King of France who was not received at court in London.

Wellington was the man of the hour; he was popular, he kept open house, he was a grass-widower. Somehow he failed to establish friendship with Madame Récamier. Perhaps his approach was too bluff for the most worshipped woman of Paris. She complained that he wrote her meaningless letters. Nor can it have been his notion of 'fireside comfort' to find her salon dominated by some literary lion, leaning against the chimney-piece and holding forth. But he was welcomed by her more brilliant if less feminine friend, Madame de Staël. The Duke, seeking relaxation and diversion, thought her 'a most agreeable woman if you could only keep her light and off politics. But that was not easy.'

Other pleasures were satisfied by an infatuation for the beautiful singer, Grassini, which excited considerable gossip; she had also been the mistress of the Emperor. It amused him to hang in his room a print of her and another of Pauline Borghese on either side of one of the Pope. Then Harriette Wilson, the well-known courtesan who claimed him as an old client, set herself up in the Rue de la Paix. Riding one day up the Champs-Elysées and catching sight of her in a carriage, the Duke rode alongside to make a rendezvous for that very evening at 8 o'clock. He always maintained that he did the business of the day in the day. He arrived punctually, straight from some function, 'all over orders and ribbons of different colours, bows and stars, and he looked pretty well.' But when Harriette later came to write her indiscreet memoirs, her most famous client threatened prosecution.

More than one ambassador has had his style cramped by an inadequate wife. Naturally the Duchess expected to join her husband and she could not be staved off longer than the end of October. Coinciding with this unwelcome arrival, the Duke's enjoyment was being threatened still more seriously. As far back as June he had written from Paris to his brother, Sir Henry Wellesley, that matters there were very unsatisfactory beneath the surface and that the only security the Government had was the fear held by all classes of renewed military rule. Now he warned the Foreign Secretary, who was at the Congress of Vienna, of alarming discontent.

Lord Liverpool, the Prime Minister, received a letter from General Macaulay telling of a conversation with some reliable person who, when asked 'whether a civilized people could go to the length of arresting one clothed with the sacred character of ambassador' replied, 'Yes: not only will the Duke of Wellington be arrested but his arrest will be justified to France by your having 60,000 men in Belgium whom he is eventually to command.' Early in November the Duke reported the arrest of a general and several officers, some of them from the royal bodyguard, for conspiring against the Royal Family. He knew well that his own safety depended on that of the King, but the British Cabinet had already taken its decision. The possibility of Wellington being in peril was too horrifying to be contemplated. He might be kept as a hostage. Somehow he must be retrieved to safety, without the French taking offence or suspecting that serious trouble was feared.

Two pretexts were put forward. He could take over the command in America, where he would have full power, or he could go to Vienna to discuss with Castlereagh the Netherlands frontiers. The advantage of this second plan was that he could still remain ambassador, leaving the embassy in the hands of a chargé d'affaires.

Wellington, though alive to the danger, was in no hurry to leave Paris. He agreed that he must not be lost to his country but was determined to decide for himself what would be the right moment and manner of his departure. A succession of letters buffeted across the Channel in the autumn gales, those from the Cabinet on a frenzied note, those from the Ambassador calm. The Prime Minister reiterated that they wanted him to leave without delay, pleading: 'We shall not feel easy till we hear of your having landed at Dover or, at all events, of your being out of French territory.' They badgered him so much that, on 16 November, the Duke wrote that he would make 'immediate arrangements for quitting Paris. These will take some days.' He saw to it that they took some weeks.

Two days later he reported to Liverpool that rumour of his withdrawal had been published in the French press, creating a bad impression of relations between the two countries. 'Those who know the state of affairs consider my departure as a defeat . . . I really don't like the way in which I am going away.' The Prime Minister gave up, merely imploring the recalcitrant envoy to use his own discretion. Delighted that his departure was no longer imminent, Wellington agreed to go as soon as he could with credit to the Government and himself.

But Liverpool was again plunged into an agony of mind by an anonymous letter from 'A Loyal Subject' who had just landed in England for the purpose of delivering it: 'Unless Duke Wellington is instantly recalled . . . and in as private a manner as possible he will be privately assassinated: a plot is forming to complete the horrid deed.' The Prime Minister forwarded it to the Ambassador. At the same time he wrote to tell Castlereagh how inconvenient his absence had been, and how essential it was for him to be back in London when Parliament re-assembled in February. The only person who could take his place in Vienna was Wellington. Castlereagh took his cue and wrote to the Duke, 'Would *you* feel a disinclination ... to replace me here?' On 31 December Liverpool was at last able to write to Paris with infinite relief of how most truly grateful he was that the proposal had been accepted.

There was no doubt that the Ambassador's popularity had decreased. He was criticized for his blunt manners and satisfied smile; his nod was pronounced to be insufferable. True to type he remained impervious to the changing moods of the Parisian atmosphere.

His last despatch from the embassy was written on 23 January 1815. The next day Wellington set off for Austria leaving the mission in the hands of Lord Fitzroy Somerset (the future Lord Raglan of Crimean fame), a much liked, sensible man who had married his ambassador's niece.

On first hearing of the escape from Elba the Duke made a wrong prognostication which has often been brought up against him. He prophesied that Napoleon had acted upon 'false or no information and that the King will destroy him without difficulty'. The news that the escaped tyrant was marching on Paris flashed across Europe. On 19 March, Louis XVIII made for the north-east, and on the 20th the Emperor was carried in triumph shoulder-high up the staircase of the Tuileries.

We know when the Ambassadress left. In the accounts of the steward, Victor Tesson, we find 'By cash of Duchess of Wellington on leaving Paris March 11th to Pay Servt Books.' Charles Bagot (afterwards Sir Charles), who held the rank of Minister while acting as Commissioner, agreed to remain on as long as he could be useful in any way. Somerset was still there when Napoleon returned because he had been unable to get post horses. On 31 March he managed to leave for Ostend with the intention of proceeding with the King to Ghent. But clearly the duty of the Chargé d'Affaires was to get into uniform once more to join the Ambassador on the battlefield. Somebody else must quickly be accredited to the exiled court. Sir Charles Stuart was waiting in the wings. The hundred days gave him his chance; as envoy to Brussels he could work the two posts simultaneously. He delivered his credentials to Louis XVIII in Ghent on 1 April.

But it was the Duke who still concerned himself with the house. He wrote to Sir Colin Campbell on 12 April from Brussels suggesting that the Government instruct the firm of Clermont to take charge of it. It was far from fully paid for, and therefore could be claimed by Princess Borghese on return of what money she had received to date. 'In that case I will pay rent at rate of 2,000 pounds a year from the time I went in till 31st March when it was left by Ld F.S. and Bagot.' His plate and other belongings were still in the house and he expected these to be sent to him and all the furniture checked.

He left an unusual memento of his five months in the Hôtel de Charost, characteristically practical rather than aesthetic. He always liked to have a contraption in front of a fireplace, a pair of curtains suspended from a brass rod. Supposedly this served to conceal the empty grate in summer and was a protection against too much heat in winter. Apsley House and Stratfield Saye were well equipped with such objects. The two brass stands joined by a horizontal bar which survive in the embassy have often intrigued the curious. There seems little doubt that they were for the fireside comfort of the Duke.

VII

Sir Charles Stuart
1815—1824

Fourteen months after the original entry of the Allies into Paris, the scene was re-enacted. The great generalissimo with his uncompromising profile rode high above jubilant shouts of '*Vive Wellington*'. He had recovered his godlike image. He returned to this triumph as Commander-in-Chief of the Allied Forces. A house on the north-west corner of the Place de la Concorde was put at his disposal. (It has now been rebuilt as the United States Embassy.) In November he moved to the Palais de l'Elysée, and resumed his Parisian life with relish. Sometimes he entertained almost with abandon. Seizing Mrs Craufurd by the hand he led a Polonaise all over his house, and handed champagne to Grassini before anybody else, making her recline on a sofa raised on a dais the better to be seen. Madame Récamier, virginal on her more celebrated sofa, records that she shut the doors of her salon to him. Her patriotic sensibility was offended by the victor's rubbing in that this time he had done the job properly. '*Je l'ai bien battu*,' he told her.

Round the corner in the Faubourg the new Ambassador was not quite so happy and carefree. It was rumoured that he was jealous of his predecessor, and knew his own position to be precarious. His had been an emergency appointment and it was said that Lord Stewart, Castlereagh's brother, was pressing for the post. The two rivals were both called Charles, which must have added confusion to the situation.

Sir Charles Stuart, afterwards Lord Stuart de Rothesay, was 37, a professional diplomat, as yet unmarried, but with influential connections. His contemporaries agree that he was particularly unattractive physically, but intelligent and sensitive. Of all the ambassadors who have lived in the Hôtel de Charost there is no question as to which has been the most aware of its aesthetic merits. Stuart was a man of rare artistic knowledge and appreciation and while in Paris he formed a famous collection. He also found the city a happy hunting-ground for the *demi-monde* but he contrived to represent his country well despite his too notorious private life.

The Secretary of State arrived at the embassy on 4 July for the Peace Conference and soon was joined by his wife and her niece, Lady Emma Edgecombe, later Countess Brownlow, who lived with them and acted as companion and secretary to Lady Castlereagh. The visit of a high-ranking cabinet minister produces many an anxious moment for the Ambassador. He is responsible for the accommodation, the smoothness of arrangements, the security; and from the first influx until the sudden emptying of the house the atmosphere is exciting and inevitably tense. The strain must have been oppressive with the Castlereaghs ensconced there for nearly five months, and Sir Charles anxious above all to please his chief whose brother was a potential rival.

Emma Edgecombe has left a charming record of her stay at the embassy and what must have been the first of many conferences held there. Stuart slept on the ground floor, the Castlereaghs spread themselves on the whole of the first floor, their niece was upstairs.

There was a continual coming and going of all the eminent persons then assembled in Paris, and Lord Castlereagh gave what would now be called working dinners. In the mornings Emma sat at a little table in the small drawing-room (the Salon Jaune) dealing with her aunt's letters. The conference room was above the porch (the Wellington Room), but when her uncle was knocked down by a horse in the Champs-Elysées the meetings were held in his bedroom (the library). While waiting for the Secretary of State the delegates sometimes wandered through to the drawing-room, delighted to chat and flirt mildly with the pretty English girl.

Canova often came to the embassy and tried to influence those he met there in favour of returning to their rightful countries the art treasures looted by Napoleon. Emma saw him weep with joy when he heard that they were to be restored. The Duke, experienced in what should be considered spoils of war, came out strongly in favour of restitution. He called it 'a great moral lesson', arguing that all those empty walls and spaces would bring home to the French their final defeat. Naturally his popularity waned. He even climbed up a ladder to help take down pictures in the Louvre and, from a nearby viewpoint, watched the great Byzantine horses from Venice being lowered from the Arc de Carrousel by English engineers guarded by Austrian cuirassiers and surrounded by a hostile mob.

It was during this summer that the embassy had its first glimpse of the most delightful of all its châtelaines. A daughter of the famous beauty, Georgiana, Duchess of Devonshire, Lady Granville had no pretensions to looks herself. But she shone as brilliantly in her own particular way, with her ready wit, penetrating observations and lively descriptions which survive in her correspondence. Her brother Hart,* the young Duke, had decided to visit Paris and her husband, a former ambassador to Russia, similarly wished to see the allied armies. The three of them arrived in July.

Immediately Harriet Granville dashed off the first of her vivacious letters to her sister and confidante, Lady Morpeth: 'I take advantage of every moment to write,' and for us, too, the whole scene comes to life. She gives us a new slant on the embassy. 'I hear the society at Lady Castlereagh's is terrible, nothing but English and extremely dull.' She called on her and 'found her in the Villa Borghese forming the most complete contrast to the locale which is all Oriental luxury, she fitter for Wapping'. An excellent linguist herself, Lady Granville laughs at the mistakes made by the Foreign Secretary who 'called out to the butler: "*A présent, Monsieur,*

* His courtesy title had been Marquess of Hartington.

servez le dîner." ' She observes that 'Sir Charles Stuart is in a fever of mind which he cannot conceal from the fear of not remaining here . . . '

The Duke of Wellington was giving a splendid ball which she believes will be a 'sort of test of female character. There are bets whether a Frenchwoman can stay away from a ball but they all professed a horror of going into public.' She realizes that she has been unfair to them when only about forty Frenchwomen turn up. However, the army ensured that there would be no dearth of men and 'I found in the first magnificent room about a hundred officers but soon discovered many well-known bores under these false pretentions . . . '

She left at the end of August. She had delighted in the glitter and the fun and making her amusing little digs at everybody but 'I pine for the pure air and country life of England,' she wrote in her last letter.

By the end of November the Castlereaghs had left Paris and so successfully had Sir Charles managed their lengthy stay that he was secure at the embassy. He knew that a well connected wife would be a great asset. For months he had been courting the daughter of the Earl of Hardwicke. Though reluctant to give up his bachelor liberty, early in February 1816 he married Lady Elizabeth Yorke, plain but rich. The shy young Ambassadress was at least fluent in French.

Every successive mission has its own admirers and detractors. The most important adherents of the Stuarts were the Misses Berry, made famous in their youth by Horace Walpole. They were old friends of the Hardwickes and, having almost immediately been invited to the embassy, wrote home fulsome praise of their youthful hostess.

Her first ordeal was presentation at court for which she was to be given what was called *un traitement*, an ancient ceremonial revived for the first time since the Restoration. With a tall plume on her homely head and a long train she was received at the Tuileries by the daughter of Marie-Antoinette but, since she was too ill at ease to answer except in monosyllables, the Duchesse d'Angoulême was forced to carry on a monologue. This one-sided conversation was interrupted by the gouty King shuffling into the room, from where he delivered to his niece the expected words which had so often been heard at Versailles: 'Madame, I did not know that you were in such good company!'

Mary Berry, who saw the exhausted Elizabeth in all her finery on her return, loyally wrote home that she thought 'nobody could have called her plain', hotly denied that 'she lost her earring or her shoe', excused her excessive shyness as being merely 'a proper timidity' and compared her to a British ambassadress at the court of Louis XV, whose popularity was still legendary. The only adverse criticism the Berrys could find to make was of the embassy pens.

Lady Hardwicke, too, was in raptures over her daughter's success. Impressed by the house, the garden, the balls, the dinners, she stayed on far longer than she had intended. This must have irritated her son-in-law, who did not care for her, especially if she vented aloud what she put in a letter: 'The Duke is still here, always going but never gone. I am happy that we are still under his care.'

By the autumn Miss Berry again passed through Paris. This time a suspicion of criticism of the Ambassador creeps in, but she assures the mother that the daughter is happy, 'so never mind whether Sir C. makes you and me happy or not'.

In March 1817 the famous gilt bed of amorous memories was subjected to a new experience. On it Lady Elizabeth gave birth to a child. There was momentary disappointment at its being a girl. Added to this Sir Charles again had to put up with his mother-in-law, who arrived, pretending to be the monthly nurse, just before the event and as he was about to go into dinner. A year later the performance was repeated. These two daughters of plain parents grew up to be celebrated beauties, virtuous, charming and talented.

Like a refreshing wind Lady Granville returned to Paris in 1817 and her letters record in a few telling strokes the relationship between the Stuarts. She at once spots that there is no sentimentality between them, which may, she thinks, be the secret of their successful marriage. Where the Misses Berry became lyrical about their young friend, gushing how delighted they were 'that London has come to a proper sense of her beauty', their ecstasy was countered pithily by Lady Granville's 'Lady E. Stuart is very agreeable and aimiable, and by dint of rouge and an auburn wig looks only not pretty but nothing worse.' The writer of these caustic remarks was as frank about her own appearance. Her brother teased that his sisters had spoilt the looks of the two handsomest families in England.

Wellington continued to be the thorn in Stuart's flesh. In charge of the army of occupation he was by now supposed to be well away in the north-east at Cambrai, where he had established both his headquarters and his wife. But no, he was always in Paris, always in the limelight, behaving as though he were the envoy, even putting his signature to a petition concerning Brazil which should have been signed only by ambassadors. Stuart complained to Castlereagh, but nobody could control the Duke, and Lady Granville commented, 'Sir Charles must resign himself to play second fiddle.'

According to her the parties at the embassy were dull, but a sensational incident occurred at a dinner on the birthday of Louis XVIII to which Talleyrand, no longer Foreign Minister, had been invited. He had the habit of eating nothing till the evening when he would sate himself with wine and food. On this occasion he came out of the dining-room flushed and excited and, drawing the other guests aside one by one into the embrasure of a window, proceeded to criticize the French Government in a loud, penetrating voice. Everybody was embarrassed, particularly the recently appointed President of the Chamber of Deputies, who tried to make off. As he reached the door a now violent Talleyrand shouted after him an insulting remark about the new Minister of Police, Decazes, for whom the King had an affection which was notorious. Though there may have been nothing the Ambassador could do, it was unfortunate that this scene was witnessed by George Canning, who would replace Castlereagh, and who did not like Sir Charles.

The diners dispersed to do the rounds of the salons, and give first-hand accounts of the story. Talleyrand himself, now conscious of his indiscretion, was determined to get his own version repeated and also rushed off to a salon. Nevertheless next day he was informed that his presence at court was no longer required. When giving this order Louis asked where Talleyrand lived. The latter, on hearing of this, was said to have remarked that, even if the King didn't know, the Tsar did. It was from his house that Alexander I had planned the Restoration of the Bourbons when the Allies entered Paris in 1814.

Court mourning dashes many a diplomatic rout. In January 1819 there was to be a ball for the Duke of Gloucester to celebrate his birthday. The party was imminent when an ill-timed message arrived announcing the death of the Queen of Württemberg. Elizabeth, while conceding that it would be sadder if it were the young Queen who had died, was alarmed at the possibility of its being the dowager, the Princess Royal, eldest daughter of George III. She wrote to her mother with simple eloquence of the consequences. 'In that case we can have no ball, and shall be in black gloves again, so that the shoes which should have danced will be old, and the meats – baked or boiled – will furnish no supper tables.' Then, before the letter is finished, the more tragic but welcome news reaches her that it is, after all, only the young Queen who has died and, obviously relieved, she ends, 'How hard-hearted it seems to dance.'

She was soon to feel more sorrowful about a mourning which engulfed all France. On 13 February 1820 the Duc de Berry, second son of Charles X and hope of the Bourbon dynasty, was assassinated at the opera. The unpopular government of Decazes fell. Chateaubriand said his feet had slipped in the blood.

Sir Charles enjoyed his grosser desires with no attempt at

discretion. For a while in 1822 Chateaubriand was Foreign Secretary. In *Mémoires d'Outretombe* he gives a portrait of the Ambassador which shows to what extent the latter had become careless of his reputation. Chateaubriand, having lived in England as an émigré, was in a position to observe that Englishmen, so formal at home, loved to lead a disorderly life when abroad. The Ambassador would call on him at all hours, in boots, dirty and dressed like a brigand, after having been round the boulevards visiting women whom, said Chateaubriand, he paid badly and who called him 'Stuart'.

In 1822 Lord Londonderry (Castlereagh had succeeded to his father's title) killed himself and George Canning succeeded him. From now on the Stuarts were anxious as to their fate. By December the following year Elizabeth was properly disquieted by gossip in the English newspapers that Lord Granville was going to The Hague 'on his way to a more brilliant post'. There could be no doubt as to which that post would be so she ended her letter home on a defiant note. 'We have no intention of making room here. Sir Charles gets deeper and deeper into business every day.'

He was now seriously concerned by the unexpected dilapidation of the house. Nearly ten years had gone by since Wellington wrote to Castlereagh that it was in excellent repair. During this time little had been spent on it. Apart from normal maintenance all that had been necessary was the buying of suitable furniture to make the state dining-room easily converted into a chapel on Sundays, the placing of the royal arms over the gateway, and the adaptation of the north-west pavilion for the use of the Embassy Secretary.

Suddenly it became evident that all was not well with the fabric and that, in particular, the work done by Pauline was gimcrack. The Lords of the Treasury, alarmed and incredulous at the report of the French experts, sent out the architect Robert Smirke to give an honest account. The necessary repairs, he told them, would cost £3,000. By the time the horrified Treasury approved this sum Sir Charles had heard that he was to be replaced by Lord Granville.

Canning, brilliant, civilized, witty, was a friend of Granville's since Oxford days. He had been in love with Harriet's aunt, and he knew the worth of Harriet herself. In judging how excellently they would represent their country in France he also knew that Granville would carry out his foreign policy.

By the middle of June 1824 Harriet was privately told what was in store for her but also that the move must appear unpremeditated. This was the reason for their being first sent to The Hague. She wrote confidentially to her brother of 'her dread of all the worries and duties of Paris, late hours, *grande parure*, visits, presentations, all my favourite aversions. Then comes the thinking Granville will prefer it, that my children will have better masters.'

Canning had every reason for removing Stuart, who was unpopular not only with his own monarch but with the government to which he was accredited. Even the French Ambassador in London had suggested it as a means of better understanding. The long-awaited opportunity came with the death of Louis XVIII. It was Granville who was sent out on a special mission of condolence to the court of the new king, simultaneously with the announcement of his appointment to Paris.

Stuart showed reluctance to go. When his successors were about to arrive, quantities of packing-cases containing the fruits of years of discrimination and flair, were still blocking anterooms and passages. But 'We hear the house will admit us,' wrote Harriet to her sister.

The house was ready to admit this ambassadress with open arms.

VIII

Viscount Granville
1824—1828

Granville Leveson-Gower was loved by two of the most delightful women of his time. Both were gifted letter-writers who have perpetuated his memory.

The youngest son of Earl Gower (later Marquess of Stafford) was born in 1773. With his background, some ability and great amiability, he was destined for politics and diplomacy. His looks were comparable with Antinoüs, though not everybody admired him unreservedly and it was said he was 'too much of a fair, soft, sweet sort of beauty'.

There are some who, discovered through correspondence or memoirs, enchant us as compellingly as they did their contemporaries. Such a person was Harriet, daughter of Earl Spencer and wife to the Earl of Bessborough. Of all the men Lady Bessborough loved, the one that most mattered to her was Granville, yet, she admits, he was probably the one that loved her least. She first saw '*gli occhi azurri*' at Naples in 1794. Beneath his portrait she wrote, 'Those eyes where I have looked my life away.' She knew from the start that the scales were tipped against her, he was twelve years younger than her and must marry. She tried to change passion into friendship: 'It is almost as affectionate, more equal, more lasting' and she told him she was 'passed *l'âge des amours*, and, thank heaven *au port*'.

She was by no means in port. We would know more of this great romance had not Castalia, the over-scrupulous widow of the 2nd Lord Granville, while bringing to light the lovers' correspondence, expurgated and destroyed

Lady Granville

Lord Granville. Detail from *The Trial of Queen Caroline* by Sir George Hayter

Lord Normanby by Alfred d'Orsay. Photograph by English Publications Ltd.

letters which, in her opinion, the writers would not have wished their descendants to see.

Lady Bessborough had four children by Granville, two of whom survived. They were given the name of Stewart, after Granville's mother, and their birth and upbringing have been wrapped in mystery. They believed their father to be their guardian.* Lady Bessborough was anxious as to their fate when Granville should marry, and suitable brides were discussed. There was a girl they called The Pearl, which shows they knew her worth. This was Lady Bessborough's 24-year-old niece, named after herself, and nicknamed Hary-O (pronounced Har-yo), who could be relied upon to be kind to the illegitimate children who were her first cousins though she resented the intensity and notoriety of the long affair with the man she herself loved as fervently. Harriet Cavendish, plain and unworldly, was an exceptional young woman, spirited, witty, shrewd. Though essentially warm-hearted, her perspicacity could be penetrating and not entirely without malice. Her marriage with Granville took place at the Devonshires' villa at Chiswick on 24 December 1809, and at the age of 36 the experienced lover settled down to be a faithful husband who gave his wife unceasing happiness as long as he lived.

By the time they were about to move to Paris in 1824, Lady Granville had been married fifteen years. She was 39 and had five children. Like other ambassadresses, she studied the plans of the house which she at once perceived 'seems an incomparable one'. It is The Pearl who now comes into her own. Reset in the Hôtel de Charost, she still glows for us in her letters which give the best descriptions of the house, French society, English visitors and the life of an ambassadress in that embassy. Let us follow Lady Granville from the moment of her arrival in Paris.

---

* The girl, Harriette, was born 23 August 1800 and died as Lady Godolphin on 28 October 1852. (Her husband succeeded as 8th Duke of Leeds in 1859). There are affectionate letters (some censored with scissors) to her from Lady Granville. The date of birth and upbringing of the son George has not been traced. He died in 1870.

'How shall I begin, where shall I begin, dearest of sisters?' started her first letter from the embassy, written on 20 November, two days after her arrival. She got her first impression of the house with the bright sun of a cloudless Paris autumn streaming in on the enfilade of south-facing rooms. She spent that evening 'exploring and admiring' and being enchanted with everything. Then the gilt bed received the most conjugal couple who had yet lain on it.

The next morning was devoted to something which this ambassadress did not enjoy: choosing clothes. A complete trousseau was ordered in a vain attempt to transform the homely Englishwoman into something more Parisian. The dressmakers and modistes arrived early, 'Mme Herbault in one room, Mme Guérise in another. The result is that I am already half an *élégante*.' The expense was a worry to her. She could not compete with her predecessor, who had been given £1,000 a year by Lord Hardwicke to spend 'in bedecking herself'. Still she believed that 'save the wig, my success would be *à la longue* as unbounded as hers. I am so anxious to do well that I hope I shall, but some of my duties are difficult to me. To avoid intimacy of communication, to have a degree of repelling civility of manner, to have no preferences and create none, all this will rub my back up the wrong way, but I think over my part so much that I must end by learning it.'

Those *élégantes* got her down. 'But, O Lady Morpeth, it is the woman made by Herbault, Victorine and Alexandre, the woman who looks to see if you have six curls or five on the side of your head, the woman who talks, dictates, condescends, sneers at me . . . It is odd that their effect upon me is to crush me with the sense of my inferiority while I am absolutely gasping with the sense of my superiority.'

There is no mention in her letters of an insult to her husband which must have struck deep. On arrival the new Ambassador was to be honoured with a grand ceremonial reception at court. Then he was informed that the *traitement* was indefinitely postponed because of mourning for Louis XVIII. This thin pretext deceived nobody. It was plainly a deliberate slight to Britain, whose attitude over the independence of the Spanish colonies in South America angered France. Charles X, not intelligent like the late King, had learnt nothing from the Revolution.

Canning wrote to Granville calling the affront 'saucy'. This same letter (23 November) reveals much about the Ambassador. It is the first of many containing not merely advice but precepts which an experienced diplomat of 52 should hardly have needed. Granville, smiling and sanguine, was capable of omissions, carelessness and laziness. Canning's criticisms are written with such good humour, as from one old friend to another, that they could only be accepted in the same spirit. Evidently the Foreign Secretary preferred to have a man of this calibre in Paris rather than somebody with a stronger personality who might act without instructions.

Already in his first conversation with the King, the Ambassador had failed to make clear an important point by omitting a key word, and when he wrote of the 'specific' policy of the Tsar instead of the 'pacific' policy, Canning advised him to read over his despatches before signing them. Also they were too short and did not always make sense. One report 'leaves me at the conclusion entirely uninformed whether you accomplished the object stated at the beginning'. Then, 'the perpetual recurrence of dinner is exceedingly distressing. But did it never enter your mind that you might evade the force of that not unexpected impediment by beginning to write at a time of day when it does not usually present itself? Try that device.'

Canning would have liked to go over to Paris himself; instead he sent his wife. Mrs Canning was a very intelligent woman. She got down to work with French politicians and reported it all to the Secretary of State with more clarity than Granville.

The Ambassador and Ambassadress were at last presented at court with full honours. So much depended on how this long-postponed *traitement* went off that Lady Granville wrote, 'I feel as if I were going to be hung, and all my reputation turning thereon.' In her new court dress (which she feared was too short at the sides), with her hair dressed by Frédérique and extra diamonds borrowed from the royal governess (which apparently was quite usual), she was encouraged when complimented by Granville, who never can have doubted that his own good looks would stand out over everybody. A female compatriot of Harriet's was astonished at her metamorphosis. 'My dear Lady G., when I recollect you at The Hague, dressed like a housekeeper. Forgive me – just like a housekeeper.'

By early new year she 'pines for Lent, exactly in proportion as the *élégantes* dread it'. One of her letters ends, 'Wishing you no dinner, no ball, and a good night's rest, I remain, beloved Lady Morpeth, etc.' She was 'not young, not handsome', and for her particular nature the strain of Parisian society was severe.

Lord Granville, so lax when reporting on French politics, suddenly showed an almost fierce energy about the deplorable state of the embassy. He sent a despatch to the Foreign Office which, for clarity and forcefulness, was exactly what Canning had been asking for in another field. Nothing had yet been done since Smirke's report. Nor did it appear that his attention had been called to the state of the furniture which was 'not new' when the Hôtel was bought. It was already out of date. In January 1825 another architect, Lewis Wyatt, was sent out, who heartily agreed that the furniture needed repairing and replacing for which he estimated £7,996. On top of this was the £14,601 to put the house and the stables in order.

Hitherto the custom had been for the Government to supply each ambassador with royal portraits and services of silver, in varying quantities, which remained his property when he retired. By Granville's time they had become the property of His Majesty's Embassy and the silver sent out was thus inscribed. It was now that the fine *surtout de table* was acquired, since erroneously believed to have been bought with the house. It is '*Restauration*' not Empire and possibly was bought by George IV. It is listed in detail in a shipment from England in August 1825, from the Lord Chamberlain's Office. Only an epergne is now missing.

The possibilities of work at the embassy seem to have gone to Wyatt's head for he envisaged building a chapel at the bottom of the garden at a cost of £3,000. The souls of the British colony were neglected, since the state dining-room, where church service was held, could only seat 300; tradesmen and servants were not admitted and a girls' school had been turned away.

Even apart from the proposed chapel, Wyatt's excessively high estimate was badly received by the Lords of the Treasury. They decreed that the embassy must be sold at once. But Granville was in a fighting mood and showed ingenuity and sense. After making enquiries he was able to write: 'I have been told here that the French architects quite chuckle at the exorbitancy of the charges which the English architect has agreed to pay for the execution of the intended repairs.' He pointed out that the cost of renting a house of equivalent importance would, in the long run, be far greater than keeping up this valuable freehold. He wrote with authority for he had undertaken to rent Marshal Soult's house for six months from 2 April while the necessary work was being carried out at the Hôtel de Charost. The Treasury gave in, but allowed only £7,000 for the restoration and £5,000 for the refurnishing. No chapel was to be built. The local architect chosen for the work was Luigi Visconti, who later designed Napoleon's tomb in Les Invalides and the new wings of the Louvre. He had little scope for grandiose schemes in the embassy under the suspicious eye of the British Treasury.

Concurrently with this wrangling the Ambassador was engaged in a private dispute over book-shelves ordered by his predecessor, just before he left, for his study and anteroom on the first floor. Stuart being gone, Granville was expected to pay for them. He protested. Not having strong literary tastes he had no intention of sending for his books from England and therefore the conversion of these rooms into libraries left him with rows of empty shelves. The shelves were removed.

Visconti made an imaginative innovation by glazing in the broad terrace which flanked the garden side and the two galleries. It spoils the south façade but has proved of tremendous value for, as the ground floor rooms give on to it, there is seldom congestion even at the largest gatherings. At the time of its inauguration it was a magnificent conservatory filled with flowers in all seasons. Within the house much was altered. The Chambre de Parade was no longer a bedroom. The state bed was redone in fashionable straw colour. The central drawing-room on the first floor probably still had Pauline's green velvet for it was referred to as the Salon Vert. New furnishings and furniture were bought.

When the account was sent in it far exceeded the estimate. The Treasury was irate. Profuse apologies from ambassador and architect failed to appease them. The affair smouldered on till June the following year when finally Granville offered to settle the matter by buying some of the furniture himself: he was prepared to take £1,500 worth. His offer was immediately accepted.

This disagreeable business did not spoil Granville's enjoyment of his sumptuous house, nor was he rattled by further reprimands from his old friend at the Foreign Office in whose letters could now be detected a note of exasperation. His despatches were not long enough, his private letters were careless and the handwriting too bad to show to the King – 'all Kings are particular about handwriting – ' he failed to collect news, he gave an impression of being above his work. Even intemperate Sir Charles was held up as a good example. After he had held the post for a whole year Canning was beseeching him, 'Pray, pray, my dear Granville, take a little more pains . . . put it in my power to do you service with the King, and let him see that you are on the alert.'

Then there leaked into the press the extraordinary story of a duel fought, without seconds, by one of the secretaries, Major Cradock. Canning calls this 'the practice of ruffians, long ago exploded in England, and, I had supposed, in civilized Europe'. It was Granville's duty to report the matter to him but he dryly remarked, 'I have not the benefit of your opinion.' Cradock was recalled but got himself back to Paris by the following autumn.

The redecorated embassy was opened to the *monde* in January with a huge ball. 'Three salons *au premier*, five whist-tables in the salon vert, écarté, newspapers and books of prints in the State couleur de paille bedroom. A buffet below in the first dining-room till supper. At one the large dining-room open with hot and cold supper.' It was a brilliant success. The conservatory was particularly admired, where flowers, divans and chairs were conducive to flirtation. Everybody was excited about this innovation and at other balls complained that there was no conservatory.

At last the Duke of Devonshire was coming to stay. Hary-O hoped he would arrive in time for a concert. 'I have been arranging it with Rossini already – four hundred people in my great room and all the best singers.' She wanted Hart to send her some of the products of Derbyshire which were the rage at that moment. 'They asked me mints in a shop the other day for two hideous bits of the old purple spa, set as candlesticks.' This was the now much valued blue John. He came in March, this kind, gentle, deaf man. The most eligible bachelor in England must have had his reasons for not marrying. Light-hearted with joy Lady Granville wrote to her sister, 'You cannot conceive, with all your powers of conception, I beg your pardon, what a delight it is to me to have him. He allows my little pretention of comparing my villa in the Faubourg St Honoré to Chiswick. And, dear sis, if you could see me at this moment! I am writing in the end of the conservatory. Behind my soft comfortable divan is a little grove of orange-trees and lilacs, a large basketful of moss and violets upon the table, and, all along the gallery I look down, every flower of the spring.'

Hart took her to a nursery garden, and 'aware of what the beauty of the conservatory is to me, and how it enlivens the Saturday mornings and concerts to have *élégantes* over-shadowed by camelias, etc., he has spent an enormous sum ordering me the finest plants you ever saw. The *pivoine en arbre*, double red camelias – I am pleased beyond diamonds.'

Up till now her brother had not been particularly interested in flowers or shrubs. Inspired by the embassy conservatory he became an enthusiast and, while still in Paris, appointed to the post of head gardener at Chatsworth a young man of 23 whom he had talked to when walking in the gardens of the Horticultural Society, which adjoined Chiswick Villa. The shy Duke was to have a lifelong friendship with Joseph Paxton, who became an important Victorian figure and an architect as well as a landscape gardener.

Lady Granville was lyrical about her creation, and her name was now made as a successful hostess. Yet there was always a certain casualness about the way the embassy was run. She was allowed to get herself into full court dress adorned with all her diamonds at five in the afternoon and drive in style round to the Tuileries only to find that she had come the wrong day.

The person who should have seen that such mistakes did not happen was George Stewart, seldom mentioned because of his illegitimacy, but loved by the whole family. He acted as private secretary to his father. While glittering parties were being held in those grand drawing-rooms, high up on the second floor was another little world controlled by strict nurses and governesses. In the rooms overlooking the courtyard lived the children who, on moving to Paris, were seen less and expected to behave better.

To a difficult, plain, young girl life in this palatial house seemed fraught with injustice. Even Lady Granville, seen through the eyes of a misunderstood daughter, becomes someone different: her observation too keen, her wit too derisive. Georgiana, the second child, was fourteen when she came to the embassy. She was born with a passionate temperament which she had not mastered even in middle life when her mother wrote, 'Georgy likes storm so much better than calm – high wind, a troubled sky, a rough sea.' She contrasted unfavourably with her elder sister, Susan, whose sweetness and delicate health made those in authority cosset her. Nor did the rigid French governess, Mademoiselle Eward, show any comprehension in managing the unco-operative, unattractive pupil who was accused of being glum and cross.

Austerity was considered good for the young: a fireless bedroom in winter, dry bread, milk and water for breakfast and supper, with a more substantial meal allowed only in the middle of the day. No wonder Georgiana stole chocolate, though her father, always desirous to please, secretly gave her sugar candy.

Fortunately there came a secret compensation. Georgiana discovered the ecstasies and agonies of love. Her mother, who loathed Byron as well might the embarrassed cousin of Lady Caroline Lamb, had unwittingly awoken this desire in her daughter by reading aloud *Childe Harold* and *The Corsair*. By good luck the books were left in the schoolroom. Surreptitiously Georgiana looked at his picture, read the account of his life in the preface, was upset to learn that he was irreligious and had not died good. But her imagination was fired. She blushed, she palpitated whenever his name was mentioned. Driving out in the carriage she fervently hoped that they would pass by the Avenue Biron; even to see the great French name which resembled his in sound, if not in spelling, written up at a street corner gave her a happy throb.

After about a year this unrequited romance gradually burnt itself out. Had Lady Granville known that Georgy had but recently recovered from a fantasy love affair with Byron she might not have allowed her to be closeted over the keyboard with a young Hungarian, Franz Liszt, the composer of magical music. He taught her his compositions, running round the room stopping his ears at her mistakes; then the pupil begged him to play to her instead. Such showers of notes, such heart-melting airs may well have stirred her.

While escapist day-dreams were being woven in the schoolroom, in the salons below Lady Granville was objectively dealing with the present. To a capital such as Paris her compatriots travelled almost continuously. The great Sir Walter Scott was given a splendid reception. Not only were the Granvilles fervent admirers of his novels; his letter of introduction had come from Windsor. The *élégantes* crowded round him with 'Ivanhoe. Ah!' and 'Dear Sir Walter, it is your imagination which I love.'

In contrast, the advent of Lady Jersey was something to be dreaded. She was nicknamed Silence because of her talkativeness and was likened to a watch with the mainspring broken. 'Is Paris on the way to Vienna?' anxiously asked Lady Granville of her sister, and suggested all manner of things calculated to put her off coming. 'Tell her that Herbault (the fashionable milliner) is dead, that the Jesuits have forbidden women to talk, that I am grown beautiful, that there is not a Whig in Paris, and anything you can to ward off from us this calamity.' When the Jerseys arrived Harriet made a supreme effort to control her feelings and was satisfied that she had shown perfect civility. Granville praised her for it. But obviously Silence sensed underlying mockery for she accused the Ambassadress of neglect, unkindness and rudeness.

It got Lady Granville into a state of worry, on top of which her conservatory was proving too expensive and Granville was blowing up for an attack of gout. To be worried, she told her sister, was 'an unfortunate condition attached to existence,' and she almost began to wish that she was as insensitive as Lady Jersey. Granville was never worried. The smiling serenity was not even ruffled by a further irritated letter from Canning in July 1826.

This time the trouble was that information concerning talks recently held in Paris by the Russian Ambassador, Pozzo di Borgo, reached the Foreign Secretary through the British Minister in Madrid and was apparently unknown to our ambassador in Paris. Canning wrote, 'Surely you might find some channel of information as to these proceedings. See how awkwardly the knowledge of them coming from other sources contrasts with your contemporaneous reports of Pozzo's confidential professions.'

For a long time the Secretary of State had wanted to go over to Paris himself; now he probably felt it was high time he did so. He arrived with his wife towards the end of September to be warmly welcomed. The Ambassador was probably thankful to have the burden of diplomacy taken away from him for a while. The visit was a success in every way. Almost at once the Foreign Secretary was writing to the Prime Minister, 'You see I am not idle here; and upon the whole time would be gained by moving the Foreign Office hither during the summer – one is so much nearer every field of action.' Lady Granville's long conservatory became his favourite walk while discussing affairs of state among the exotic plants.

Mrs Canning was the perfect guest. She stayed in her room all morning and liked to go to bed early, while the men got down to serious matters at male dinners. There were parties almost every day and, to make them decorative and amusing, Lady Granville did not fail to invite those famous *élégantes*. They raved about the Foreign Secretary. He was *superbe* and *magnifique*. He, enchanted, called them dear delightful women.

Towards the end of October the Cannings returned to England. Six weeks later the Secretary of State delivered his most celebrated speech to the House of Commons in which the phrase: 'I resolved that, if France had Spain, it should not be Spain with the Indies. I called the New World into existence to redress the balance of the Old' gave violent offence to the French. Their anger was such that Lady Granville prepared herself to be cold-shouldered everywhere she went. Privately she felt that their friend had gone a little too far.

When emotions had calmed down somewhat and the situation was better understood, the French Foreign Secretary made a courageous and friendly statement towards England in the Chamber of Deputies, whereupon he at once became the butt of his countrymen. The Ambassador showed his habitual slackness in failing to inform the

Foreign Office of this amicable gesture. They got the news all right but again it was through another source: the Rothschilds.

With anti-British feeling rampant it was almost a godsend that the Duke of York should have died early in the New Year of 1827. It meant court mourning and a reprieve from going to balls. Lady Granville gloated that, by the time they and their household had got out of black, Lent would have begun. It was at the state funeral of the Duke that Canning caught the cold from which he never fully recovered. In the spring he became Prime Minister but, mistrusted by some, he had difficulty in forming a ministry. The strain of this, on top of his already impaired health, was too great. Devonshire lent him Chiswick Villa, and there he died in August 1827.

Nowhere could the news have been received with more sorrow than in the Paris Embassy. The Granvilles were broken-hearted; they could think and talk of nothing else. Granville also knew that political changes in England might affect his career. In January the ministry of Lord Goderich was dissolved and the Duke of Wellington became Prime Minister: nevertheless Granville was allowed to remain on in Paris for the present.

During this time the buoyant spirits of Harriet revived. Life must go on and she describes it with her usual verve. 'I must try and amuse you,' she writes to her sister, thinking of all sorts of absurd gossip, social and political, to tell her. 'Lord G. looks over my shoulder, don't approve at all, says I must not send such nonsense. I say I must . . . I say you never show or repeat such stuff as I put into my despatches, so after a hair-breadth escape my letter goes into the bag instead of the fire.'

By early June 1828, Granville knew that his departure was imminent. His wife began packing, paying bills, burning papers. She described a lovely Paris midsummer eve when they took the letters brought by the courier to 'read beneath the conscious moon, the garden bright with lamps, sweet with orange flowers'. Yet the bag did not contain the expected letter from the Foreign Secretary, Lord Aberdeen, that Stuart was to be re-appointed ambassador. 'We cannot remain here long, but until the official announcement nothing can be settled.'

By 7 July Lord Aberdeen, Wellington's Foreign Secretary, had still not announced Stuart's appointment 'but the diligent young Lord has written himself to say that he shall be here in a fortnight'. (Sir Charles had taken the opportunity of being related to the previous Prime Minister, Lord Goderich, to claim a peerage, and was now Lord Stuart de Rothesay.) After a hectic week of farewells and packing, the Granvilles were ready to leave for Devonshire House.

From an empty Salon Vert Hary-O wrote her last letter. 'Remember that somebody said, "Whatever you do, do" which is just what I think wanting in this *siècle*. Granville is very sorry, but sorry like an honest noble-minded man – no repining, no irritation. He stands by his own conduct, without one shade of bitterness or unfairness. In short, I think more highly of him than of any human being – happiness enough for any woman, Lady Carlisle.'*

* Her sister was now Countess of Carlisle.

IX

Lord Stuart de Rothesay
1828—1830

The second term of Lord Stuart in Paris was to be less successful than the first. He was always a controversial figure, ambitious, independent. He had not been liked by the French Government, nor by George IV who, in the early 1820s, had urged his recall from France and then, with typical weakness, wished to rescind it fearing criticism from the influential Stuart partisans.

During these three and a half years away from the embassy, Stuart had had a difficult time with a Foreign Secretary who did not trust his ways. The retiring Ambassador had first been offered the Governorship of Madras. He pretended that it was the Governor-Generalship of India he was expecting, conduct which Canning described to Liverpool as 'of a piece with other trickeries he is practising'. In the end he was sent on a mission to Rio de Janeiro, where (and Canning made it very clear) he was, with Portuguese credentials, to handle negotiations connected with the independence of Brazil. Stuart far exceeded his instructions by taking it upon himself to negotiate a Treaty of Commerce, the terms of which were published prematurely in the Rio newspapers. Canning refused to ratify the treaty.

Eager to get back to his former post, Stuart arrived with his wife, his pretty daughters in charge of a lenient governess, and his packing-cases. The house, having been overhauled, was in excellent condition but the place had been much pulled about, not in accordance with his taste.

Immediately he demanded the replacing of those book-shelves which had already been the subject of acid correspondence. Then he eyed with distaste the furniture of Granville's choice. The latter had taken some of it back to England but the bulk remained. It was customary for an outgoing ambassador to send in a bill to his replacement covering furniture and fittings which he had been obliged to acquire. Stuart scorned to buy these unworthy objects. Granville complained to Aberdeen, who advised Stuart to settle. In the end he did so but not without being unnecessarily offensive about 'the Granville sticks', which he promptly sent off to an auction room. The friends of the Granvilles were up in arms and the Stuarts found themselves unpopular.

Lord Palmerston, who had already resigned from Wellington's government, came over to Paris in January 1829 and recorded that 'Lord Stuart has not succeeded since his return here. When he went, people all thought him gone for good, and out came all sorts of stories about him; and those who had made free with his name are shy of his society.' This is corroborated by Charles Greville, the diarist. 'Lord Stuart de Rothesay is sent back to Paris, though personally obnoxious to the King and universally disliked.'

There followed an unfortunate incident which further increased the Ambassador's unpopularity. It would appear that he was let down by his attaché, who did not keep a proper watch over the diplomatic bag. Certain favoured British residents and visitors were allowed to use it; it was an economical way of sending letters and, as they avoided the censor, they could write freely. The French police were not to be done out of their information. They bribed the Chancery servant who received these letters and taught him how to get at the contents without damaging them. The man soon discovered that it was also lucrative to keep copies for himself of the more scandalous bits of news in order to blackmail the writers, and some letters outspokenly critical of the French Government appeared in a London newspaper. Lord Stuart had difficulty in living down the subsequent scandal, which shook the confidence of the British colony.

Lady Stuart bravely carried on with plans for a grand entry she was to make at the ball given by the Duchesse de Berry. This has been the subject of a curious inaccuracy. Several English writers state that the watercolour by Eugène Lamy is of the staircase at the embassy, whereas it is of that at the Tuileries.

Scandalous incidents dogged this ambassador. No sooner had he recovered from one than another cropped up. *The Times* of 3 October of this same year came out with 'A report taken from the French papers about packages addressed to Lord Stuart marked "Saddling, carpets and malt liquors" which, when accidentally opened at the French Customs, were found to contain "muslin and silk manufactures".' On seeing this, Lord Grey, then in opposition (and in Northumberland), wrote to his great friend, Princess Lieven, the highly intelligent wife of the Russian envoy to London, asking for gossip about this ambassadorial smuggling. The Princess, an arch-intriguer, sent back the required information, adding, 'It appears to me that Ld A[berdeen] would not be sorry if S[tuart] were to have somewhat of a discomforture.' Thus did the leader of the opposition discover what the ministers were thinking.

The embassy can never have looked more magnificent than in the time of Stuart. Permanent pictures were lacking there and his collection was superb, as was his furniture. He enjoyed living in style and could afford it: on the staircase hung his embroidered red damask ambassadorial panel: the rooms were brilliantly lit regardless of expense: on grand occasions his footmen wore the early eighteenth-century full dress liveries which, together with his plate, he had lent for the Duchess of Richmond's Eve of Waterloo ball.

The summer of 1830 brought a change of King in both England and France. George IV died and Charles X abdicated. The reactionary policy of the latter ended on 25 July in a brief revolution and on the 30th placards appeared in favour of the Duc d'Orléans, son of Philippe Egalité, as a 'Citizen King'. Louis-Philippe was proclaimed on 7 August.

In this crisis Stuart once again acted without the knowledge of his government. He sent Cradock to urge the abdicating King to depart slowly and to leave the son of the Duchesse de Berry in France, and then sent him to Louis-Philippe, advising him to carry on the government. Wellington, accustomed to unquestioning obedience, wrote to Aberdeen referring to certain diplomatic changes about to take place: 'But I am haunted by a much more important arrangement than all this. I mean the removal of Stuart,' whose despatches were 'more unintelligible than ever'.

However, in November the Tory government was defeated and William IV sent for Grey. When Stuart heard who was to be Foreign Secretary he is said to have told his wife, 'Palmerston is in, my dear, and we are out.' Granville was reappointed to the embassy and once more the outgoing Ambassador spun out his departure, not even answering his successor's letter asking when it would be convenient to take over. The wife of the secretary, Mrs Hamilton, was made to write to Hary-O urging delay in coming. 'Yet go we shall,' was the spirited comment. Finally the Stuarts were obliged to clear out but they lingered on in Paris for several weeks.

Lord Stuart was not to be pitied in retirement. He was planning a remarkable building on his Hampshire property by the sea. A windfall came to him in the shape of a Gothic ruin which he found being demolished while journeying through Normandy. Lady Stuart had turned a blind eye to her husband's infidelities, but when she found the cliffs piled up with the Manoir des Andelys she was properly angry. All this was at her expense. The connoisseur arranged his *objets d'art* in the fantastic castle and ended his days enjoying his great collection.

In July 1949 Christies conducted an important sale at Highcliffe. One item, Lot 417, had no business to be there at all. Stuart had gone of with Granville's despatch box.

X

Earl Granville
1831—1835

The Granvilles sailed from Dover on 2 January 1831, having been assured of a calm crossing with just enough wind to steady the ship. But the packet was named the *Duke of Wellington* and, reflecting the dudgeon of its namesake, gave the Canningites a terrible tossing of three hours. Everybody revived after a good night at Calais, and before resuming the journey Hary-O wrote to Lady Carlisle in tearing spirits. 'Going abroad, anyhow, anywhere is such a lark; not more, nor less, but a lark. Neither comforts nor grievances are as substantial as in England.' She almost did not want to arrive, but of course she was enchanted when she got back to the house.

Evidently it was one of those winter days which give a promise of the warmth that is to come. The Ambassadress walked through the familiar salons to the scene of their intimate gatherings. 'The room, the green beauty, looks just like its old self, with the sun broiling upon it.' She complained that she had grown older and flatter in London. She was now in her mid-forties, and increasingly preoccupied with her husband's health. A little of the bubbling exhilaration had evaporated but there was many a flash of it.

Her first duty was to have the attachés to dine. She was always kind to these young men whom she made feel at home, took to her box at the opera and had to dine twice a week when the bag went. But she would not tolerate casual behaviour. When young Blount perceived his Ambassadress in her carriage from the top of an omnibus, and thought he should not raise his hat to her from such a plebeian vehicle, she sent for him next day and ticked him off. She was even more annoyed when he went to the opera in what he described as compromising circumstances, and threatened to send him back to his father.

As for Hamilton, whose wife had been made to write that letter urging the Granvilles to delay coming, he was 'not of the slightest use in any branch of diplomacy,' and tiresome Mrs Hamilton, prejudiced in favour of the Stuarts, was interfering again. She had the impertinence to hint to the Ambassadress that what would console her predecessor, still in Paris, 'would be being considered as a cut above the general society here, first in all times and places . . . and, in short, would like to enact with me ex-Queen and *régnante*'. Lady Granville bore with Lady Stuart kindly; for she was quite helpful with her good French. Lord Stuart seldom appeared, saying that he was prowling about among the dowagers. More likely he was prowling on the boulevards.

Contrary to Lady Granville's expectation the Citizen King made it known that he wished for great elegance in society to encourage the silk weavers at Lyons. The Ambassadress, asked to make herself *bien belle* for her presentation at court, had no need to borrow jewellery this time; her brother had lent her the magnificent Devonshire diamonds, so she was 'very fine, in a grey satin gown, my diamonds which make my fortune and a Herbault all feathered and bowed – very fat, but squeezed into a tournure [corset]'.

With her husband welcomed back and valued in France, herself once more in the house she loved, the Ambassadress should have been happy, but she was obsessed by the need for economy. Why this had become acute in their second term is not clear. She began to fear criticism at having to retrench, especially as her first big ball must be given at 'half-price', which would contrast unfavourably with the splash made by the Stuarts. It was the lighting that depressed her, and Granville behaved like any husband, not caring 'a straw about the thing looking less well than formerly. I find to my shame that I have not a mind that can raise itself above dark rooms and an ill-lit ball.' It may have been her bad cold that put her in low spirits. 'Do you see me, Lady Carlisle, in my dressing-room – harts-horn and oil on the chimney, cloves in a saucer, a piece of flannel airing at the fire, Michaud . . . and Richard arranging *paravents* in the bedroom to keep out the blustering wind?' Granville, incapable of unkindness, consented to more lighting and even dancing in the central drawing-room as well as in the ballroom.

This spirited ambassadress need not have worried about the success of her parties for they were reputed to be exceptionally brilliant. Invitations were sent to a wide range of politicians, officials, the indispensable *élégantes*, musicians, writers, artists who all jostled against industrialists and families of the emerging bourgeoisie. Sometimes there was music or a play in the ballroom. But it was the conservatory, still an unprecedented marvel, which gave scope for all sorts of fantasies. At the King's Birthday Ball she hid the lamps behind flowers to provide opportunities for tenderness among the waltzers. Though delightfully dark for romance, it was more so for crime since eight burglars in faultless evening dress profited by the occasion by lurking there till everybody came out to watch the fireworks when they planned to snatch the women's jewellery. Fortunately, they were observed. Thackeray describes a rout when the conservatory was transformed into a banqueting-hall. 'In a word, Albion did the thing very handsomely.' For her carnival ball this wise hostess provided extra good food for those who talked but didn't dance. 'But oh! dearest, the numbers, the Carlists, the *Libéraux*, the hideous, the anxious. Well, there are always the Miss Levesons.'

The Leveson-Gower girls were grown up and Mlle Eward dispensed with. In absence this strict governess had become benevolent to her rebellious pupil and was the recipient of her confidences. Georgiana was finding the sudden transition from schoolroom into society perplexing; she was expected to help entertain and much that hitherto had been sternly forbidden was insisted upon, such as animated conversation at meals and staying up late. Yet the mornings were still Spartan with tea and butterless rolls for breakfast and study afterwards. Suzy was more like her handsome father with his 'cloudless radiant nature . . . Dody is a dear girl too,' but had no pretensions to prettiness. She was considered piquante; we hear of her 'making her play on a pair of attachés', flirting in the billiard-room, dancing in the conservatory, which rang with laughter.

Granville was working with unwonted application. The relationship between him and Palmerston was excellent, the latter putting in a postscript: 'I cannot refrain from saying how much we all appreciate the admirable manner in which you execute our instructions,' and 'You have done capitally, and the successful result of our efforts is most satisfactory.' Left on his own Granville was instinctively a diplomat of appeasement. On 1 April the Secretary of State replied to a private letter from him advising England to give in to the French claim to a town on the Belgian frontier; the wise answer of the statesman was that a weak policy never settles matters.

Lady Granville, proud that her husband was appreciated, resented his slaving away with little help from his staff. At last a charming bachelor of 32 joined the family circle; he was to have a career of a brilliance such as could not have been expected from the other disappointing attachés. George Villiers, future fourth Earl of Clarendon, was sent to Paris on an Excise Commission and was instructed to put himself 'on a friendly footing of confidential communication with Lord Granville'. The Ambassadress was delighted to report how Suzy had sat between him and Lord Rivers at dinner and had talked almost entirely to Villiers, 'whose agreeableness is entraînant to the greatest degree.' She foresees that 'he will be popular beyond measure; he is in bad health but gay and more agreeable than anybody'. A few weeks later this praise is qualified by 'charming though he is [he] does not dance or talk to any one but married ladies of distinction and therefore is no lark for us'. Hopes of her daughter's progress with Villiers must have been dashed when she got wind of his spending much of his time in the company of

Madame de Montijo, half-Spanish, half-Scottish, whom he had met a few years before and for whom he had a tender attachment. Indeed so intimate was it that he was seldom actually seen in her crowded salon. She was the mother of the future Empress of the French.

However, the eldest Granville daughter could be relied upon to do the right thing; the Salon Vert was the scene of her marriage to Lord Rivers in February 1833. After she had left for her honeymoon her lonely sister rushed up to 'our room' to pour out her heart in an emotional letter to Mlle Eward, for she herself was in love with an unsuitable *parti*, a cornet in the Blues, of landed gentry, but without means to support a wife. Fortunately Alexander Fullerton reminded her kind uncle of his mother, Georgiana Devonshire, and he made the marriage possible by giving financial aid and talking round the Granvilles; it took place, also in the Salon Vert, in July. The new son-in-law was quickly removed from the army and converted into a competent attaché.

Yet another pair were married at the embassy in 1833. In the autumn Georgiana's now celebrated piano teacher was best man to Berlioz, the French composer. Six years before Lady Granville described to her sister the wild success of the English players at the Odéon and of how everybody was moved to tears by the performance of a beautiful Irish actress, Henrietta Smithson, as Ophelia. Though the Ambassadress criticized her for being ungainly and having 'the vulgarest pronunciation and gesticulation', Berlioz, passionately in love from the moment he first saw her, could only think of her as romantic heroine. By the time they finally got married his Ophelia was penniless and crippled. On 3 October the two brilliant composers and the poor bride grouped themselves for the wedding in the state dining-room. Three years later another ill-fated marriage took place there. Thackeray, then living in Paris, married Isabella Shawe, who later became insane.

Marriages were at this time performed by Bishop Luscombe, who had been embassy chaplain since 1828. In

1833 he got permission from Granville to purchase land in the Rue d'Aguesseau, just across the Rue du Faubourg, on which to build an embassy church. The Bishop undertook to raise £2,000 in £100 shares for which an interest of 5 per cent was to be paid until the debt was discharged; he was to fit it up by voluntary subscriptions, and charge £1 annually for a seat, but reserve some free seats for those who could not afford to pay. Palmerston sanctioned this scheme on condition that suitable accommodation should be reserved for members of the embassy and that all arrangements should be approved by the Ambassador. There is no record of when the church was completed.

This spring her husband's health and other worries brought home to Lady Granville the precariousness of happiness and she began to suffer from *angst*. She confided to Lady Carlisle, who understood what happened when 'nerves take dominion . . . I have a new fear is the constant move of my mind.' However, by the autumn she had discovered a most sensible cure. With 'energy and resolution' she faced these fears, told them they were unreal and found that they vanished. Recovering her old gusto she encouraged her sister to do likewise, urging 'society, interests, amusements, change of scene . . . ' but not St Leonards. 'Paris, Lady Carlisle, Paris.'

On 15 November 1834 William IV astonished the whole of England by dismissing the Whigs. Palmerston wrote off next day to his brother, William Temple, Minister at Naples: 'We are all out; turned out neck and crop; Wellington is Prime Minister and we give up the seals etc to-morrow . . . I shall now go down to Broadlands and get some hunting.' Politicians in opposition did not then need to have recourse to memoirs, journalism, or merchant banking.

Lady Granville was, of course, amazed at the news but, contrary to some opinions, believed that the new government would last and that 'the Duke of Wellington will hoist the most liberal sails, eat back all his words, every possible measure, Church and State, do as he has done before.' Her own feelings at leaving France were mixed for she longed to see her family again but 'Granville likes being here, so I wish it . . . ' Conjectures began as to who would succeed the Granvilles, who were packed and ready to go directly the new appointment was announced. They left on 15 January. Wellington was Foreign Secretary, so it was almost inevitable that he would offer the embassy to his brother Henry.

XI

Lord Cowley
1835

Lord Cowley had had an unusual experience for an ambassador; he had been imprisoned in the country to which he was now accredited for nine months in 1794. While he was bringing his widowed sister back from Lisbon, their ship was attacked by a French frigate and they were taken to Quimper, from where they had an adventurous escape.

Henry Wellesley was the youngest of the five remarkable sons of Lord Mornington and his strong-minded wife. Lady Mornington was furious when Henry, at the age of 30, married Lady Charlotte Cadogan. She was justified in her objections for, after presenting her husband with three sons and a daughter, Lady Charlotte eloped. Henry Wellesley got £20,000 damages and remarried. His second wife, a daughter of Lord Salisbury, was considered far more suitable.

Born in 1773, he began his career in the army, but changed to diplomacy. After spending some time in India with his brother, Lord Wellesley, then Governor-General, he returned to England and became a Member of Parliament. For many years he was envoy to Austria and he was created a peer in 1828, reviving the name of his grandfather, Colley or Cowley, who had changed this for Wellesley or Wesley on succeeding to estates.

Lord Cowley arrived at the embassy at the end of March 1835 and presented his credentials on the 30th. Hardly had he performed this ceremony than he found himself in a highly awkward situation; his government fell on 8 April.

In Bruton Street Hary-O was dashing off letters to her brother about the new appointments. It was not certain that Palmerston would get Foreign Affairs. That was on the 12th. On the 13th: 'Of course you know that Lord Melbourne is to declare himself Premier in the House today . . . He [Lord Palmerston] talked most openly, told me there was a report that Johnny [Lord John Russell] was to be at the Foreign Office. He looked much *ému* when he said it and added "this I cannot believe". Then he muttered, "I suppose I shall shortly be there myself," and then loud, "in which case I hope you will instantly prepare and pack up for Paris." ' The atmosphere was becoming electrical. Palmerston threatened not to serve in the government at all unless he became Secretary of State and Lord Wellesley thought of challenging the Prime Minister to a duel because he had only received a court appointment. All ended well. Palmerston was back in the Foreign Office and the Granvilles got ready to return to Paris.

Lord Cowley left the embassy on 13 May. It must surely have been the shortest mission on record.

XII

Earl Granville
1835—1841

'It looks so like what always was,' writes Lady Granville on 29 May, the day of their return to Paris for the third and final term.

There was, however, a new attaché, Henry Greville. Within three days he was highly popular with his Ambassadress, not only for his amiability to her but for the help he gave her husband with efficiency and hard work in the Chancery, yet with the proviso: 'If he could but become a Whig and hold his tongue, he would be a model.' He was the younger brother of the better-known Charles Greville and he, too, kept a diary.

The Ambassadress resumed her old life; visits began, invitations poured in, Paris was 'awfully hot and gay'. She was glad to get back to the house and garden and gives a charming picture of herself staying at home one evening while her husband is on a round of ministerial visits, the family all out, she at an open window with 'the orange flower smelling too strong, the nightingales singing too loud, and this in the midst of a city is delicious'.

Remembering how thoroughly the embassy had been overhauled, improved and redecorated but ten years before, since when about £500 had been spent annually on maintenance and furnishing under the supervision of a local architect, Silveyra, and that there was a huge staff of well-trained servants to keep it clean, it is amazing to find, in July 1835, Granville asking for an estimate to be made 'for rescuing the hôtel from its present degraded state'. Incited by the Ambassador, Silveyra composed a report which was unlikely to go down well with the Treasury. Palmerston, who only the previous year had decided that the house and contents deserved to be insured for £27,000, now declared that the expense of it was out of all proportion to its value. It had cost nearly £33,000 since becoming British property: it must be sold. For the second time the axe was poised. But Granville won again. In June of the following year the Secretary of State authorized the expenditure of 40,000 francs for general repairs and decoration, and 20,000 for new copper roofing, on condition that the latter came from England. As often happens, far more work was done than originally anticipated; it took two years. The stables were put in order, the kitchens rebuilt, the drains relaid and the garden walls raised (the old height can still be seen). Surely ordered by the Ambassadress was the early cast-iron fountain placed on the terrace outside the conservatory: a little boy standing on a shell holding a fish from which water gently plashed. She could hear the sound as she wrote her letters home in the Salon Vert.

'Do you see me? . . . Can you see us?' is a favourite beginning to her family as her pen races along trying to catch up with her eager thoughts. We see her. With Balzac at the opera, 'a fat red man whose locks flow,' who imagines Lady Jersey to be the '*vrai type de l'aristocratie Anglaise*', at the first performance of *Esmeralda*, an unsuccessful opera by Ambroise Thomas, beautifully produced 'But oh! the music! the tune the old cow died of throughout, grunts and groans of instruments and voices'; analysing the unpopularity of Lady Harriet Baring against whom 'the world is upon its guard, gun cocked, to be in the proper attitude for receiving the shot it always imagines her about to fire, and then it is such a shot when it comes, so direct and so piercing'.

Most enjoyable of all is when she sets the scene for us in the Salon Vert, the heart of the house. Here she writes her letters, however full it may be of family, friends and attachés. She must catch the post bag but she knows her sister will think she should be looking after all those people: 'Can you see us? I fear you will not approve. The green room. Granville and F. Lamb in two fauteuils opposite the fire. Lady Elgin and Dody on the green couch in a theological discussion . . . Mrs. Lambton with all the attachés about her.' And again, 'Five o'clock – Oh, how difficult to write! Look at the Green Room – Lieven and G. whispering; Lord Bristol rising in his stirrups and clearing his throat before them but they don't seem to perceive him': then an evening after her own heart when a cold and a rash on the tip of her nose prevented her from going to the Duc d'Orléans' ball at the Palais Royal: 'You can have no idea of my present comfort with a cup of tea, blazing logs, not a sound or wheel to be heard, whilst at eight o'clock Harry, Heneage, the Fullertons and Granville were all adorned and armed for the ball . . . Georgy was in a blaze of jewellery. You know Alexandre. When she proposed adding a little branch of diamonds to her coiffure, he said: "*Avec une pareille magnificence, notre pensée doit être la simplicité*," and rejected her plan.'

Personages who have become familiar to us flit across the scene for the last time, trenchantly portrayed. The final telling sight of Lady Stuart is of her coming to call at the embassy on a warm day 'in a fuss . . . Betty is puzzled, opens her mouth, looks like a very hot red and white spaniel . . . sitting upon her hind legs in great distress.' Her vexation was understandable. She and her husband had come over to Paris for an occasion of historic and artistic importance: the Château de Versailles, rescued, redecorated, altered, even added to, was opened with a great fête in June 1837. The theatre was done up in the heavy colours then admired. (One hundred and twenty years later it was restored with exquisite taste to its original eighteenth-century fairy-like glory of blue and gold and inaugurated for the state visit of Queen Elizabeth II.) Distinguished foreigners, including the Stuarts, had been asked to the banquet of 1500 in the Galerie des Glaces; but 'the day before received formal printed un-invitations, desired to consider their formal invitations as *nuls et non avenus'*, because too many had been asked.

On 20 June Palmerston wrote to the Ambassador announcing the death, that morning, of William IV. The fresh era which had begun in England was full of promise: it appealed to Harriet, who wrote excitedly to Hart, '*avide* for news, devouring newspapers, gasping for letters . . . for it is history, fate, romance, all in one. Everything is new, nothing to be calculated upon. Such a little love of a Queen!' Then she adds, probably thinking of the scandal over Mrs Norton, 'Lord Melbourne must take care to throw a something paternal into his manner.' Lady Carlisle's daughter, Harriet Sutherland, became Mistress of the Robes. 'Does the Duchess think the Queen cares about politics, and is she a Whig or a Tory in her innermost heart?'

Neither Lady Granville nor Henry Greville mention an incident at the embassy on 27 January 1838 which must have given some anxious moments. Talleyrand, feeble and just on 84, was arming Princess Lieven into dinner when he tripped over her trailing skirt and in his struggle not to fall injured his bad foot. He had to be taken home, where the Duchesse de Dino, his niece by marriage and probably his mistress, was alarmed to find him back so soon. Four months later he died.

The populace was to be treated to a superlative funeral the following year. Louis-Philippe had already pandered to the Bonapartist legend by replacing the statue of the dictator on the column in the Place Vendôme. In May 1840 he sought to further his own popularity by asking England for permission to dig up the Emperor's coffin from under a willow on St Helena in order to re-inter it ceremonially in a magnificent tomb in the Invalides. Palmerston gave consent, commenting that it was 'a thoroughly French request', and Greville writes, 'Many people laugh at it and think it is a great piece of humbug – but it is a sort of humbug which goes down here exceedingly well.' French newspapers announced that Granville had sent round circulars to all British residents recommending them not to venture out but Thackeray, still in Paris, never got his and saw the procession without mishap. The Duchesse de Dino thought everybody had gone mad; she heard rumour of a plot to demolish the Hôtel de Charost, of troops moving in, of Lady Granville being forced to flee.

The Ambassadress was secretly appreciating this wave of anglophobia: 'The quiet life we lead by the side of the storms and supposed agitation of the *siècle* is good for us all.' It was particularly good for her husband, whose health was deteriorating. Fortunately just a year earlier a brilliant young man, Henry Lytton Bulmer had joined the staff and was able to shoulder the burden of diplomacy, acting as an exceptionally able chargé d'affaires during Granville's more frequent absences.

British unpopularity stemmed from a more serious cause than the revival of Bonapartism, which had ended in another insurrection by Louis-Napoleon (the nephew of the Emperor) and his incarceration in the Château de Ham. The real trouble was over an Albanian adventurer, Mehemet Ali, who had got control over Egypt and gradually extended his rule to vast areas of the Ottoman Empire. Eventually the Sultan turned to Russia for help. Palmerston organized a concerted move of the great powers to settle the crisis but ignored France, not unnaturally because most French opinion was strongly in favour of Mehemet Ali. Nevertheless the French considered that they had received a 'mortal insult', and there were preparations for war. The trees in the Bois de Boulogne were stripped ready for the line of fortification.

For our peace-loving Ambassador it was painful to hear those insolent words *'perfide Albion'*, the sound of the Marseillaise sung with defiance outside his gate, his daughter Georgiana attacked by the mob when she drove out in the embassy carriage and the coachman dragged from the box. The strain told on Granville, who had a fall from his horse and was often laid up with gout or hobbling about on a stick.

Inexorably the expense of the house cropped up again to add to his worries. Those extensive repairs only recently completed had far exceeded their estimate. Granville apologized with his usual charm, giving the excuse that he had been much absent from Paris during 1838, therefore could not supervise matters personally. The Treasury had had enough of these futile estimates. They decided that the embassy should become the responsibility of the Commissioners of Woods and Forests, who in 1840 agreed to take it on provided they could have full power over the ambassadors. They immediately sent another well-known architect out to Paris. Decimus Burton's long report on the condition of the house and property must have come as a nasty shock, for he considered that there was much to be done. He took a poor view of the work that had just been completed, which already needed repair. 'It was not superior to that which is used in second-rate houses in London.' He had all sorts of plans for the interior, including a new Throne Room, in the present Victoria Room. He approved of the first floor rooms as being 'neat and tolerably well furnished', but most of this belonged to Granville. A much reduced estimate finally accepted early in 1841 emboldened the Ambassador to ignore the terms of the Commissioners of Woods and Forests: without their permission he bought more furniture, had repairs done, and demanded redecoration.

But this year the enchanting Granville era came to an end. In March the Ambassador had a stroke which left him partially paralysed. There appears to have been no immediate idea of retiring him; however, in August a change of government in England conveniently compelled him to relinquish his post. Henry Greville dined with them on their last evening and the next morning, 19 October, recorded in his diary, 'Put the Granvilles into their carriage with a heavy heart and a lively sense of their kindness of all kinds and with a conviction that any change must be for the worse.'

The Granvilles were genuinely beloved, and their leaving must have been one of the most moving scenes of farewell that the embassy witnessed. We can picture it. Antinoüs, elderly and ailing, precariously descending the steps assisted by solicitous hands; hovering near him his sons, legitimate and illegitimate; the warm-hearted Ambassadress openly crying; everybody waving goodbye as the carriage swept round and out through the gateway into the Rue du Faubourg for the last time. They left by train and toured Europe for two years.

According to Princess Lieven they had at one time thought of settling in Paris but it was to England that they returned, by slow stages, and there, in their house in Bruton Street, the moment came which Harriet had dreaded ever since she first loved Granville. He died on 8 January 1846. Devoted husband though he was, he had not forgotten the love of his youth for in his last illness he went through Lady Bessborough's letters, adding the dates in the feeble writing of his left hand.

Granville does not rank among the brilliant ambassadors who have served in Paris but he was a distinguished one with his 'singularly calm and clear judgment' (as Lord Dalling puts it) and his great tact and patience in negotiation.

In her radiant days Lady Granville would reiterate how happy she was: 'I cannot describe my happiness' . . . 'I enjoy my life more than I can say.' Widowed at the age of 61 she devoted her remaining sixteen years to religious thought and good works. Gone was the zest: it had died with Granville, 'adored Granville, who could make a barren desert smile'.

XIII

Lord Cowley
1841—1846

On 10 November the Cowleys returned to the embassy they had left so abruptly six years before bringing with them their daughter, another Georgiana. Clearly the atmosphere was much changed under the new regime for already by the 23rd Greville was writing in his diary, 'My life, though pleasant enough, is very monotonous, and affords little matter worth record.' To follow on an era which had been so enjoyable as that of the Granvilles was not easy, and inevitable comparisons were made, many of them to the disadvantage of Lady Cowley. The most damning indictment was that there wasn't enough food or drink.

Almost at once she made herself unpopular with both French and English. A stickler for the conventions, she struck off her invitation list the names of some of the old habitués who in her eyes were undesirable, and gave out that she would only receive English women who had been to court. Those who found themselves dropped did not hesitate to complain with malice. The gossip reached the ears of Hary-O, who could afford to be generous, saying she was sure Lady Cowley was a better ambassadress than herself. She more sincerely sympathized with her over the perpetual difficulty of getting the embassy put in order.

Decimus Burton was sent out again, instructed to produce a less ambitious, more economical scheme. He abandoned his idea of a new Throne Room, but then came the discovery that the throne itself had belonged to Granville. A new one was promptly ordered from 'A Supplier of Thrones', for which the Treasury refused to stump up. Either Cowley paid for it or Granville's was bought back at a reduced price, for the throne is now embassy property but never used. The Ambassador used to sit on it at royal birthday receptions.

At about the same time a bold scheme was suggested to the government which was sharply quashed. The two adjoining houses, then smaller buildings, on the east side of the embassy, could have been bought for the chancery and consulate for 1,326,000 francs (about £10,000 at contemporary rates). Just after the Second World War, the nearer house was acquired for the sum of £258,000.

With the New Year, Cowley faced a wave of anglophobia. The dispute over the Abolition of the Slave Trade, which had been his brother's first diplomatic undertaking nearly thirty years before, had lingered on. A treaty to settle the question was signed in London at the end of December, then suddenly the French Foreign Minister gave in to public opinion, which was convinced that it was all a trick on the part of England to get control of the seas, and refused to ratify it. When that summer the Cowleys gave their first grand ball on the Queen's birthday, the Ambassador noted in his diary that it was a great success, but the Duchesse de Dino wrote in hers that the royal princes refused their invitations 'which shows that England is no longer fashionable'.

In July the eldest prince, the dashing Duc d'Orléans, was killed in a carriage accident. It was a shattering blow to Louis-Philippe. He wrote to Victoria that if it could in any way be softened it would be by the sympathy she had given. The following year she came to visit him. It was an historic occasion. The sovereigns of England and France had not met since the Field of the Cloth of Gold, and even that meeting had taken place on what was still English soil. Cowley arrived at the Château d'Eu the day before the Queen and had a long talk with Louis-Philippe on a serious matter, namely the prospective marriage of the young Queen of Spain. The King assured the Ambassador that he had no thought of proposing one of his sons as a husband and thus reviving memories of Louis XIV. All he wanted was a Bourbon of some sort, not a German prince.

Victoria landed from her yacht on 2 September and was enchanted with everything. Part of her happiness was due to the triple relationship between the Coburgs and the Orléans. Politics were discussed in complete harmony and Victoria left well satisfied with the cordial understanding between the two countries. The return visit the next year made her even happier as the cunning old King called Prince Albert *'Mon Frère'* and said, *'C'est pour moi le Roi.'*

Yet another meeting took place at Eu in 1845 to discuss the Spanish marriage. There were only three candidates, two Bourbon cousins and Prince Leopold of Saxe-Coburg. One of the cousins was said to be impotent and the German prince was ruled out anyway, so all should have been well. But now Louis-Philippe wanted one of his sons to marry the Queen of Spain's sister. However, he assured Victoria that there would be no question of this until Isabella was married and had had heirs.

Meanwhile life in the embassy was enlivened by the arresting dark looks and gaiety of a new attaché, Charles Sheridan, grandson of the playwright. He was organizing private theatricals in the ballroom, aided by Henry Greville; scenes were given from *The School for Scandal,* with a cast which included three of the author's grandchildren, Charles himself acting Charles Surface, and his sisters, the Duchess of Somerset and Lady Dufferin as Lady Sneerwell and Mrs Candour.

With Lady Dufferin came her nineteen-year-old son from Oxford. Fifty years later when he was ambassador in Paris he recalled how, at an embassy ball, his handsome young uncle with his Sheridan effervescence and his fatal hectic flush had sat in one of the drawing-rooms, the centre of an admiring crowd who could not tear themselves away to dance. Two years later, at the age of 28, he died of consumption. We know where this took place for Sir Harold Nicolson as a small boy had it pointed out to him by his governess. In this room, immediately to the right of the front door, the writer hung some drawings by Count d'Orsay. One of them is of Charles Sheridan. His nephew, the son of Mrs Norton and Head of Chancery, died of the same disease in the same room in 1859.

The visit of a former minister, now in opposition, on a mission of goodwill, can put the Ambassador in an invidious position, and when the ex-minister is somebody as dynamic as Palmerston it is likely to be embarrassing. Hope of the Whigs returning to power in 1846 made the future Foreign Secretary decide that the moment had come to have a better understanding with the French and to dispel the image of *ce terrible Lord Palmerston*. With him came his wife, the daughter of the celebrated Lady Melbourne and widow of Lord Cowper. Her looks and intelligence were a great asset to her husband and this remarkable pair, no longer young, made a stir wherever they went. They arrived for Easter, staying at a hotel in the Rue Castiglione.

If their coming was awkward, it was made more so by it being put about that the Palmerstons intended to ignore the Cowleys altogether and would ask Sebastiani, a former ambassador in London, to present them at the Tuileries. However, they were duly presented by the Cowleys, who, as Lady Palmerston could now write home, 'were very cordial and amiable and their feathers quite smoothed down'.

The Palmerstons proceeded to bring off a triumphant visit. Inundated with invitations they dined at the Tuileries, at the embassy, with Guizot, with his 'Diplomatic Sibyl' Princess Lieven (Charles Greville wrote that she and Lady Palmerston were 'dear friends who hate one another cordially'), with Thiers, the Prime Minister, who gave them such a magnificent party that Princess Lieven was annoyed that no adverse criticism could be made. The impression made by Palmerston was phenomenal. Even the Duc de Richelieu, famous for disagreeable remarks, joked with her, 'You mustn't think that people hated you all that in the past or that they like you now as much as they give you to suppose.'

Ostensibly on friendly terms with Palmerston, the Ambassador must secretly have been longing for his departure for, spurred on by success, he was behaving with irregularity. His letter of congratulation to the King on his third escape from assassination was considered an impudence on the part of a former minister and he had even implied to Guizot that the Peel government was cracking up and a change would soon take place.

He was right. Lord John Russell came into power at the end of June and Palmerston was back at the Foreign Office. Cowley sent in his resignation. He was now an infirm 73. Like many another diplomat who has been posted to Paris he could not envisage living elsewhere and moved to a house in the Place Vendôme where this much liked man died the following April.

XIV

The Marquess of Normanby
1846—1852

Rarely can an ambassador have taken up his post in more exceptional circumstances than those which awaited Lord Normanby. On 24 August when he presented his credentials the King expressed the wish that he should regard himself as '*un Ambassadeur de famille*'. Then, only a few days later, there came a piece of news which scandalized Europe and infuriated Britain. At midnight on 28 August the Queen of Spain announced her engagement to the impotent Bourbon suitor and, simultaneously, that of her sister to the Duc de Montpensier, son of Louis-Philippe. The elder Greville wrote in his diary that this was 'a great damper to the Queen's *engouement* for the House of Orléans', while the younger, more bluntly reflecting the indignation of England, wrote, 'we have been what is vulgarly called "done" by the French in this affair'.

Guizot's lame excuse was that, as Leopold was still a candidate, France was absolved from keeping her word. But such double-crossing was so out of character for the Foreign Minister that there were some who sensed the guiding hand of Princess Lieven. It wrecked the Entente Cordiale and contributed to the downfall of Louis-Philippe. Victoria rose magnificently to the occasion. 'Do not mention it to anyone,' wrote Palmerston to Normanby, 'but the Queen has written the King of the French a tickler in answer to a letter he sent her . . . '

Born in 1797, Normanby succeeded as 2nd Earl of Mulgrave in 1831, and was created a marquess in 1838. The

Queen, too, had envisaged him as a family ambassador. His wife, a spirited, kind-hearted woman, had been one of those ladies of the bedchamber with whom she had been so loath to part in 1839, and his brother, Charles Phipps, was private secretary to Prince Albert. Yet even with this royal backing and a successful Governor-Generalship in Ireland to his credit, he did not do well in Paris. His irresponsible character was summed up by that astute observer, Lady Granville, who, when her nephew, Lord Morpeth, was to join Normanby's staff in Dublin, wrote, 'I feel so proud of and confident in him, that he will be ballast to the light squally vessel Lord Mulgrave.'

Normanby's conceited manner was ridiculed in Paris, his knowledge of the French language was indifferent, and Guizot said he didn't understand the idiom. The Secretary of State complained his despatches were full of irrelevant matter, his private letters too numerous and his beautiful handwriting difficult to read. From the start Ambassador and Foreign Minister were at loggerheads. With good reason for disliking and mistrusting Guizot, Normanby made no attempt to mend the rift between the two countries. On the contrary, he confided in Thiers, saw opposition journalists, and did not frequent Princess Lieven's salon.

In November Henry Greville was back in Paris on a visit and called at the embassy where, recapturing memories of those halcyon days of the Granvilles, he 'felt very strange in that old house surrounded by new faces'. He found the Ambassador in a predicament over the presentation at the Tuileries of the Duchesse de Montpensier to the Corps Diplomatique. In the absence of instructions from England, Normanby himself had to decide whether or not to attend and, still smarting from the behaviour of Guizot, chose the latter course. This uncompromising handling of the situation caused a sensation. A few days later he sought to excuse his rudeness by writing to the Foreign Minister explaining that he had understood the ceremony was one of congratulation on the Spanish marriage, in which he felt he could not take part. He now asked for a special audience in order to be presented to the Montpensiers. Of course, Madame de Lieven saw the letter and told Henry Greville that it was far too long, and badly worded.

Henry Greville left, and early in the new year his brother Charles came to Paris to reconcile Normanby and Guizot. Arriving in the morning to stay at the embassy he was immediately handed by his host a box containing all the papers about the Spanish affair, and by the afternoon he was already in session with the Princess, who complained of the 'greenness' of Normanby, of his mistakes, of his taking advice from the wrong people. From there he went to Guizot, who criticized Palmerston fiercely. Then it was the turn of Thiers, who told him not to believe what Madame de Lieven said.

All hope of re-establishing the Entente Cordiale had to be abandoned while our ambassador remained on excellent terms with the ex-Prime Minister and on no terms whatever with the present Foreign Minister (now virtually Prime Minister). The obvious solution was to replace Normanby but this might have been taken as an admission that Guizot's treachery was condoned. Nor could he be recalled for a short period because the Chargé d'Affaires, William Hervey, and the Foreign Minister would not speak to each other.

Greville returned to England early in February having failed in his mission and 'leaving the Embassy in certainly a very painful and unbecoming condition'. A fortnight later he was writing in his diary: 'Matters get blacker and blacker at Paris and Normanby has got himself into a deplorable fix . . .'

When Greville wrote these words he was still ignorant of a new blunder which had just been perpetrated by the Ambassador. Dalling called it 'a great . . . and vulgar error which was quite unaccountable in a man of such high breeding'. The feud was at its height when a ball was given at the embassy to which Guizot received an invitation. Then he heard that his card had been sent by mistake. This was justified by Normanby on the grounds that the Foreign Minister boasted he had only been invited by order of the British Government, who did not approve of their representative's quarrel. But it was the Ambassador's French which added fuel to the flames for he confused the word '*méprise*' (mistake) with '*mépris*' (contempt). Guizot referred to the insulting incident in the Chambre. Normanby was not only criticized but ridiculed in Paris, and a duel was talked of.

Palmerston reprimanded the Ambassador for his appalling tactlessness and by early March could at last write, 'I am very glad you have arranged your differences with Guizot.' He generously told him 'that it is the duty of ministers to support those who are acting with them and to back them up well through the difficulties to which they may be exposed'.

With the vendetta patched up Normanby settled down to a more peaceful time. However, he did not have long to wait before Guizot fell from power. His reactionary policy, backed by Louis-Philippe, which favoured the emerging rich middle-class industrialists and ignored the exploited workers, was really responsible for the outbreak of the revolution of 1848.

When the Reform Banquet, a weapon of political propaganda by which it was hoped to achieve a change of ministry, was prohibited from taking place on 21 February the people were stirred and the National Guard could no longer be counted upon to support the government. A shot from an unidentified marksman wounded an army officer, who ordered his soldiers to fire on the crowd. There were shouts of vengeance, 'death to Guizot', and barricades were hastily put up all over Paris. The mob battered on the railings of the Tuileries and the King scuttled through the gardens to the Place de la Concorde, hailed a cab and escaped to England. Guizot and Princess Lieven also fled there, she disguised as the wife of the English painter, David Roberts.

In his almost indecipherable handwriting the Ambassador kept an hour by hour account of events. At last he was on good terms with a Foreign Minister, the poet Lamartine. His wife remained at his side, calm, courageous, comforting, and he was proud, too, of his attachés. Police or troops could no longer be counted on for protection, 'so we have nothing to trust but our strong gate and "*le droit des gens*".'

After an election in April the Provisional Government was replaced by a Constituent Assembly too moderate for the hungry, discontented people and towards the end of June fighting broke out in Paris with bloodshed and atrocities. Normanby persuaded his wife to go to Chantilly. When she was able to return, she travelled by omnibus with twelve other passengers. This was regarded as a great hardship, but 'Lady Normanby has shone on this as on every other occasion.'

It was the victor of Waterloo who, knowing the French character, now wrote, 'France needs a Napoleon! I cannot yet see him . . . Where is he?' He was in London, still exiled. The glamour of the Napoleonic idea was easily fanned to enthusiasm in the confused political state of 1848. Fortunately the pretender bore the name Louis. The romantic poets had written of his uncle: '*Toujours lui! Lui partout.*' and '*Parlez-nous de lui, Grand'mère.*' When pictures were displayed with just the word '*Lui*', people saw the double meaning and felt they had found their lost leader. In September he was elected to the Assembly and in December was sworn in as President for four years, an oath he was soon to break.

With him came his English mistress to whom, during a night of love at St Cloud, he swore what she always referred to as 'the holy oath' which she maintained was a promise of marriage. This also he broke. Harriet Howard was the daughter of a horse-coper and her face was as pure as a cameo. She had been presented to the Prince in London by Count d'Orsay, fell in love, set up house with him, espoused his cause, financed his schemes, and now lived discreetly across the road from the Elysée with her own illegitimate son and two of Louis'.

From the first Normanby did not get on with the Prince-President, but both he and his wife struck up a lasting friendship with their beautiful compatriot. Through Miss Howard Normanby must have fancied he could wield influence. Shortly after this, Lord Malmesbury, now in opposition, came to Paris and breakfasted with the President, who confided that the Ambassador was intriguing against him. He believed that Normanby was carrying on a private correspondence with Prince Albert. This special relationship the Normanbys had with the court could be useful even for matters unconnected with politics. The Ambassadress, despising the gilt empire fire-dogs which adorned each hearth, ordered eight massive black cast-iron fenders complete with sets of fire-irons from Mellon in the Rue St Denis. One of these remains in the Victoria Room. She was dismayed when Mellon presented a bill far higher than anticipated, but after much wrangling the Office of Works paid up. They could hardly have done otherwise. Lady Normanby was able to arrange that four such fenders would be highly welcome at Buckingham Palace, where Decimus Burton considered them appropriate as they were 'of rich and handsome character'.

During this period some work was done in the ballroom by Hittorf, architect of the Gare du Nord, but with Burton continuing to advise; it included opening the south wall on to the garden with glass doors. Altogether the improvements to the room were of such importance that the Ambassador decided it must also be made convertible into a chapel for use on Sundays. It may be wondered why it should be necessary again to hold services in the embassy when there was the new church over the way, but this was now owned by a clergyman called Chamier, who, for some reason, did not become the embassy chaplain.* In the second

---

* After Chamier's death, the embassy discovered, too late, that the church had been put up for sale and already bought for the United States by a remarkable member of the American Colony, *le bel Evans*, dentist and loyal friend to the Emperor and Empress. He had not been aware that the English wanted it. When approached by the Ambassador, Earl Cowley, Evans behaved admirably and handed it over at once, Clarendon having guaranteed the necessary money. On 3 May, Cowley informed the Foreign Secretary that 'the chapel in the Rue d'Aguesseau has reopened today as the Chapel of the Embassy'. And thus it remained till 1970. In 1971 the building was pulled down to be rebuilt with amenities for Chaplain and congregation.

Lord Cowley's time there was even a suggestion, quickly discarded, of building a chapel in the embassy courtyard.

By 1851 Louis-Napoleon had only one more year to run as President and was not eligible for re-election. Having failed to alter the constitution by legitimate means he decided to achieve it by force. His object was to get the presidency for life and to recreate the empire. The *Eminence Grise*, who schemed and successfully brought off the plot was his half-brother, Comte de Morny, son of Hortense by the Comte de Flahault, himself an illegitimate child of Talleyrand. The day chosen was 2 December, the anniversary of Austerlitz and the coronation of the Emperor. Morny planned the take-over while Harriet Howard pawned and sold her jewels and mortgaged her property to give her lover ready money. The deed was done swiftly at night. Resistance was firmly dealt with: civilians shot in the streets, deputies arrested in their beds, rebels sent to Devil's Island. Morny, cold and cynical, was satisfied with the way his plot had been carried out but the Prince, sensitive of his reputation, never ceased to regret it. Years later, when suffering from his traumatic moods of depression, Empress Eugénie would say that the *coup d'état* was his Nessus Shirt.

Scandalized, Normanby believed that no country would recognize the dictator. His Foreign Secretary had no such scruples and, without consulting sovereign or cabinet, praised the *coup d'état* to the French Ambassador, Comte Walewski. The son of Napoleon I and Marie Walewska was delighted. He immediately informed his own minister, who read this approval aloud to the Corps Diplomatique in Paris 24 hours before Normanby received any communication on the subject from Palmerston. He was justly outraged.

It was now that the Ambassadress took the irregular step of entering the fray on her husband's behalf by sending an account of all that he had had to put up with from the Foreign Secretary to her brother-in-law, Colonel Phipps, who would be certain to pass it on to the Queen and Prince Albert. She sent long letters by hand as she did not trust the Foreign Office nor the post.

The Queen had had enough of Palmerston, whom she and Prince Albert heartily disliked. On 20 December the Prime Minister asked him to resign, which he did with his usual good humour. Lady Palmerston took her fall from power less well and made some scathing comments about the successor, the second Lord Granville. She underrated him. He already had experience as Under-Secretary for Foreign Affairs and, though younger than Normanby, did not flinch from telling him some home truths in a firm but inoffensive manner. In Granville the benevolence of his father was outweighed by the good sense of his mother and, seeing that our envoy was incapable of concealing his unalterable antipathy for the Head of State, he soon decided that he must be recalled. Ostensibly on leave, Normanby came over to England anticipating a lively showdown with his old enemy, Palmerston, in the Lords, but was persuaded to drop the whole matter and to send in his resignation, which was officially announced on 28 January 1852.

Eventually he was consoled with a most agreeable post. Palmerston, when giving advice to Malmesbury on becoming Foreign Secretary, had said, 'You will be struck with a very curious circumstance – namely, that no climate agrees with an English diplomatist excepting that of Paris, Florence, or Naples.' Perhaps it was due to royal influence that the Ambassador was given the legation in Florence. He remained there till 1858 when his emotional espousal of the Austrian cause made withdrawal again advisable.

His opinionatedness and biased judgement do not accord with diplomacy. But we who live in the second half of the twentieth century, when a bureaucratic Foreign Office severely discourages young entrants from having any independent ideas, may well feel a lurking admiration for Lord Normanby. There are times when our country could gain from more individuality and imagination in our representatives.

XV

Earl Cowley
1852—1867

❧

Somebody had to be found quickly for the embassy and it reverted to the Wellesley family.

Lord Cowley, son of the late Ambassador and his runaway wife, was born in 1804 and married in 1833 the daughter of Lord Henry Fitzgerald and Lady de Ros. The appointment caused some surprise for a more brilliant man was expected to go to Paris. Cowley himself never anticipated getting such an important post for, after years spent in Stuttgart with little prospect of promotion, he had thought of resigning from the diplomatic service altogether. It will be observed that he had a great propensity for resignation.

He made a welcome contrast to Normanby. He was as popular and as unassuming as his father, conscientious, cautious and appeasing; but he had to deal with a tricky political period and there were times when the burden seemed too great for him. He was assisted in his difficulties by a delightful wife. Not only was Lady Cowley's sense of humour a palliative to the often worried Ambassador, but she was a kind and experienced hostess and a talented amateur artist. They had three sons and two young daughters, one of whom, with the unusual name of Feodorewna, was one day to return as Ambassadress.

Immediately after Cowley reached Paris on 17 February, he found himself in the same embarrassing situation as his father on *his* first assignation. On the 21st, the day after presenting his credentials, Lord John Russell resigned, Lord Derby became Prime Minister and Malmesbury

Foreign Secretary. But this time there was no question of changing the Ambassador; the new government were well aware that they had an excellent representative in France and Napoleon corroborated this in a personal letter to the Secretary of State asking that he should remain.

'A strange mixture of good and evil' was Cowley's summing up of the Head of State, who, with all his charm and self-control, could not conceal the 'dark side to the picture in a revengeful disposition'. Queen Victoria, still loyal to the Orléans, and mistrustful of this new regime, was at the same time curious to hear more about it and therefore Malmesbury asked the Ambassador occasionally to send him amusing, chatty letters suitable to pass on to 'a much higher personage'. Gossip was foreign to Cowley's nature but he became quite adept. Already he was able to report how Princess Lieven had succeeded in meeting the President, and was now suspected of being his intermediary with the Tsar.

But for the moment our envoy's energy was chiefly concentrated on the house. Invariably every newcomer complains of its deplorable condition, of the bad taste of his predecessors, and wishes to change it according to his own liking. The Cowleys were no exception. During the fifteen years they were there some practical improvements were made but irrevocable damage was done.

The Ambassador began by pleading religious scruples about the ballroom-cum-chapel which had so pleased Normanby, favouring instead a dining-room-cum-chapel. His letter to the Foreign Secretary was a masterpiece. He wrote that it would be highly indecent to have divine service one day in the ballroom and dancing the next, therefore that part of the house would be lost for receptions. He won his point, but then wished to get the rest of the house done up. Malmesbury, who had recently been to Paris, was able to vouch that it was 'so indecently dirty as to render it unfit to be inhabited by Her Majesty's Ambassador'. An architect who had worked on the legation in Madrid was sent out to estimate for the alteration of the state rooms and to examine

The Garden Façade during the Commune, by William Simpson

The Ionian Room. Water colour by Levieil, 1959

Lord Lytton. Sketc
for the portrait b
G. F. Watts

Lord Dufferin. Pho-
tograph by H. H. H.
Cameron, son of the
great Julia Cameron

the general state of the house.

Benedict Albano was shown over the premises from top to bottom by Cowley himself and by the end of August produced a lengthy report of all that was wrong and how it should be remedied. Some of the facts brought to light were startling: vermin overran the buildings, mice and maggots were discovered in the ambassadorial bed, ants swarmed over the food put on the dining-room table, and from the cesspool in the basement there emanated 'a strong offensive effluvium'. Albano's estimate for putting the whole place in order was so high that in August of the following year the question of the expense of the house was brought up in the House of Commons and all the unsavoury details made public.

Indignantly Decimus Burton rebutted one by one the points made by the insignificant little man whose report reflected on his efficiency. Burton had been responsible for the embassy for ten years from 1840, but in January 1851, when he was about to make his annual inspection, he had received an order not to do do, since when it had been in the hands of the local architect. Dilapidation was to be expected in a house 120 years old but it was 'in a respectable and becoming state both of repair and decoration' when he last saw it in 1850. He rightly made short shrift of vermin and ants, which were the responsibility of the inhabitants of the house, and he found it unaccountable that any family allowed such an extraordinary state of things to exist. There had always been a rat-catcher and he reminded the authorities that as there were no sewers in Paris the larger houses depended on their own cesspools, which must be emptied regularly. All this was printed in a White Paper which made unpleasing reading for both families concerned, particularly for the Normanbys. In the end the weight of Malmesbury and Cowley carried the day, and the Commons voted the necessary money.

Already Albano had got his fell hand on the furniture. He mercilessly overhauled what he chose to keep of the Empire chairs by lowering the seats, fitting them with springs, adding castors and putting iron backs on couches, thereby altering their proper proportions. He decided what new furniture must be bought, how much of the old was worth restoring and selected what should be sold. The sale, for some reason, did not take place till 1858 and the list of objects makes harrowing reading. Fifty-five mahogany chairs must surely be what remained of Pauline's sixty dining-room chairs, the sort of thing that Decimus Burton had described as of 'mean appearance'. Included in the condemned items were quantities of other 'old' chairs, armchairs, sofas, firedogs, gilt stools, and the baldaquins. They went for £50 and some of the things were just thrown away. This stuff may have been in bad condition, but its chief fault was to be out of fashion.

The Cowleys, 'to their great inconvenience', moved temporarily up to the second floor to sleep in clean iron bedsteads while Albano wrought havoc below, Victorianizing anything he could find.

At some time, not specified, the bedroom of the Ambassadress on the first floor became a sitting-room and the boudoir beyond it her bedroom; evidently this change had taken place before Albano made his report. He gave the Cowleys contemporary twin beds, above which he suspended a baldaquin 'with a very good cornice' which he rescued 'from the filth of the *garde robe*'. Possibly this explains why the design of the only baldaquin left in the house does not accord with the only Empire bed above which it now hangs. He does not mention Pauline's bed, nor the eagle, which may still have been in the attics or vaults, cluttered up with lumber of every description amidst the ghastly smell. The Ambassadress's bedroom was now red and the adjoining sitting-room was decorated with a brilliant green flock paper bordered with black which can still be seen in places under the present silk covering. This room now became, and has remained, the Salon Vert, while the central drawing-room, the Salon Vert of Lady Granville's time, was changed to yellow. At least Albano spotted the great door at the top of the grand staircase as 'a very fine specimen of solid oak carving' from which he removed numerous coats of paint, but he failed to appreciate the steel of the balustrade, which he painted black. Gas was installed and to hide the pipes many old mouldings were destroyed. Some unforeseen expense was incurred when the Ville de Paris demanded that the ancient parapet and ditch which still protected the farther end of the garden be replaced with railings and a lodge; for this the architect designed two lodges and a central carriage gate. Finally Albano permitted himself a flight of fantasy above the main entrance: from England he ordered a gas apparatus for illumination 'representing Her Majesty's initials, supported by a wreath of roses, shamrocks and thistles, and surmounted by the English crown'. It cost £40, and, on extra-special occasions, there could be added a Star of the Garter, which was only a few pounds more. The effect was resplendent.

That the end of the Second Republic was imminent was clear to Cowley on his arrival: the President behaved and was treated as though he were a reigning sovereign, by April he was holding all functions at the Tuileries, in October came the announcement from Bordeaux that he would accept the imperial title, and on 2 December, after a plebiscite, he was proclaimed Napoleon III outside the Hôtel de Ville before unenthusiastic crowds. The Emperor showed his desire to be on good terms with England by opening the first ball of the Second Empire with Lady Cowley.

The question of his marriage was now much discussed. He was angling for important princesses, but at the same time pursuing Mademoiselle de Montijo. There were some who said she was really the daughter of George Villiers, now Lord Clarendon, and it was to stop this damaging gossip that the Contessa de Montijo made the unanswerable statement that the dates did not fit. Eugénie's unusual type of beauty was matched by her strange character. Louis desired her with an ardour he could hardly control and she, ambitious and with a passion only for the Napoleonic legend, proudly and chastely held out for marriage.

It was now that he showed his ruthlessness. He sent Harriet Howard off to England on a secret mission. Gales delayed her crossing the Channel, thus she chanced to learn from a newspaper of her lover's engagement and imminent marriage. She bade him farewell in a letter which was found in the Tuileries after the downfall of the Second Empire, telling him that, like Josephine, she was taking away his star. The marriage was not liked, and the Emperor lost popularity.

Clarendon, one of the most attractive and gifted of mid-nineteenth-century statesmen, was now appointed to the Foreign Office, and there began a private correspondence between him and Cowley. The perfect understanding of two friends in key positions goes a long way to ensure successful diplomacy and it is our loss that such a happy relationship now rarely exists between foreign secretaries and ambassadors.

When Clarendon took office the foremost question was that of the holy places in the custody of the Sultan of Turkey: the Russians were concerned about the Greek Orthodox subjects, the French about the Latin. The preliminaries of the Crimean War went on brewing for a year during which time there were many moments of tension between France and England. Cowley got increasingly agitated but the Foreign Secretary remained sanguine.

Early in 1854, there was reason to suspect that Napoleon wanted to please the Tsar, and Cowley wrote, 'You have no idea how the tide of public opinion is setting against us here . . . ' Then, by the end of February, he was able to report that the Emperor was now violently against Russia and ready to send a large force to the Crimea. War against Russia was declared on 28 March.

The alliance had so many ups and downs that the honest-minded Ambassador became despondent and early in 1855 thought of retiring. Clarendon dissuaded him from doing so in a moving appeal: 'I hope that as long as I am chained to the oar in this galley you will not think of being emancipated from yours . . . when I say that I feel as if I had a

brother in Paris, I cannot better describe the entire confidence I feel in you . . . '

The war was not going well and in February the Queen,
after resignations and abortive coalitions, was forced to ask
Palmerston to form a government. Clarendon remained at
the Foreign Office. Meanwhile a visit to England was
planned for the imperial couple in April. Buckingham
Palace was full of workmen so they were to be received at
Windsor, which 'is *far* better than London'.

There was a homely exchange of letters about plans, the
Empress, like any woman, anxious to know what clothes
she should bring, the Queen replying that this depended
on how long she stayed. The party left Paris on 13 April,
the Ambassador praying for a calm crossing for 'How we
are all to be sick in uniform and the ladies in smart toilettes
I cannot comprehend.' Everything went off brilliantly and
afterwards Clarendon wrote, 'When one remembers the
undisguised repugnance to the visit and to the suggestion
of the Garter, one would hardly have anticipated the
genuine warmth and pleasure with which the visit was
received and the Garter bestowed.' Victoria had succumbed
to the mysterious charm of this Frenchman who so well
understood a feminine woman. Albert cannot have been
entirely pleased; when he had first met the Emperor at the
camp at St Omer the previous December he had been
struck by his 'apparent indolence of character and marvellous
ignorance respecting many important matters'.

The return visit was to be a state occasion. The height of
summer was an odd time of year to have chosen, when the
shutters go up and Parisians go into the country, particularly
as the Queen could not endure heat. She kept her palaces
so unbearably cold that at Balmoral Clarendon once joked
how his feet had been frostbitten at dinner. However, the
royal visitors and their two elder children were to stay at the
Château de St Cloud, with its fountains and shady park.

In addition to the gloomy news from the Crimea the
letters from Ambassador and Foreign Secretary were now
largely devoted to detailed arrangements for the visit, some

of them beneath the dignity of high officials, such as how many dressers and wardrobe maids Victoria would bring and where the governess and tutor would have their meals. Then there was the uncomfortable prospect of riding in diplomatic uniform ('Have you ever tried?' asked Clarendon), the sudden scare of infection when the younger children at Osborne got scarlatina, and the belated alarm of the Queen lest she should be 'quite knocked up' if exposed to the sun. Of course 'the sacred day' must be observed but only a short sermon was expected from the embassy chaplain, who, recommended by Normanby and offering his services gratuitously, now turned out to be the paid correspondent of the *New York Herald*; 'a clergyman ought to have nothing to do with the press,' was Cowley's opinion. If Victoria went to a play it must be proper and she had better not bring the Duchess of Wellington, for at Windsor the son of Maréchal Ney refused to be introduced to the 2nd Duke and had even turned his back on him. Above all, our rules of precedence must not be meddled with. Then came the announcement, longed-for but ill-timed, that the Empress was finally pregnant and therefore could not participate in the ceremonies.

The Queen was not interested in her appearance nor did she attempt to keep up with fashion. Yet, as Clarendon wrote to his wife from St Cloud, nobody ever had such a personal success in this fastidious capital. It was not only her delighted interest in everything, proving how genuinely she was enjoying herself, which made her so popular. That famous inborn grace and dignity together with the sweetest smile imaginable, a smile rarely seen in public after Albert's death, enchanted everybody. Her splendid royal energy exhausted the Parisians. After three and a half hours walking round the Louvre, at the end of a gruelling programme, the Emperor, whose constitution was neither royal nor good, dragged his feet painfully and a fat member of his suite was heard to gasp that he would give everything – but everything – including the Venus de Milo, for a glass of lemonade. That same evening our Queen was able to dance with enjoyment and energy at a ball at the Hôtel de Ville.

It was Cowley's suggestion that if the Queen asked to see the Invalides 'it would do much towards obliterating the past'. Surely he was unprepared for her suddenly ordering the Prince of Wales to 'kneel down before the tomb of the great Napoleon', at which torch-lit sensational moment a violent storm flashed and thundered. Possibly the Iron Duke was turning in his grave. To do her justice the Queen also visited the memorial chapel to the Duc d'Orléans.

The young pleasure-loving Prince of Wales, already the despair of his father, was strictly brought up at home and even this visit was made educational under the reproving eye of a tutor, but he managed to form an unforgettable impression that this beautiful Paris was for pleasure as well as instruction.

Usually a visiting head of state returns hospitality at his embassy, but the Queen did not do so. However, she went to the Hôtel de Charost on the afternoon of 22 August after a luncheon at the Tuileries, and wrote in her journal: 'It is very pretty indeed, and newly furnished; I went over the house with Lady Cowley whose girls (pretty girls) were there.'

Apart from the strengthening of Anglo-French relations, everything had gone remarkably well. The Empress did not miscarry, Prince Albert went four times to the Industrial Exhibition, and the delighted Queen, having discovered that the Emperor 'had a charm about him that she had never met with in anybody', looked forward eagerly to seeing him again.

He had indeed used all his strange power of attraction and, as Greville says, 'she had never been on such a social footing with anybody'. In the most subtle, respectable fashion, he had shown that his feelings for her were something far more fervent than friendship. To her, 'those bright days . . . were like a vision or a dream, so lovely that we can scarcely believe it'.

Clarendon wrote to Cowley telling him how enchanted

Victoria had been, 'above all with the Emperor', and, a few days later, 'she can still think and talk of little else', and then, 'The Queen writes me word that she may often have letters and things to send and that she on no account wishes you to have the trouble of asking each time an audience of the Emperor.'

Soon after this idyll there came news of the fall of Sevastopol on 9 September but jubilation was followed by British anxiety lest Napoleon would insist on an immediate peace. The Emperor became less amiable to the Ambassador, who once more wished to resign. The Queen's reaction was, 'He is worth an army and a fleet to us,' and Clarendon added, 'a greater compliment than this has rarely been paid by a Sovereign to a subject . . . ' Cowley stayed for twelve more years and by November the Emperor was again affable.

The Ambassador was over-conscientious. The stresses and strains of his responsibilities got him down: 'I never felt so out of spirits as at this moment,' he would write, or 'I am in a great stew.' Petty things always cropped up to worry him. In the new year of 1856 he sent a tormented letter about a ball to be given for the imperial couple to celebrate a distribution of Crimean medals earlier in the day. The safety of the Emperor, the clamour for invitations, the ballroom nearly being burnt out the week before, and Lady Cowley's illness, all made him anxious. His next agitation was that the medals sent him to distribute, evidently not of the highest orders, were sneered at by the French officers as being like pieces of tinsel. 'For Heaven's sake send me silver stars for the Bath', which was his next investiture; if necessary he offered to pay for them himself. It was not the first time he resorted to this blackmail with successful results.

In the end of February, Clarendon came to Paris for the Peace Conference. He declined his old friend's offer to stay at the embassy and rented a house instead for he had also his Foreign Office work to do and had to bring 'a considerable staff'; today it seems a particularly small one, consisting of only three or four persons.

Cowley did not fail to report the Emperor's amorous escapades, going incognito to a Shrove Tuesday masked ball at a brothel, orgies with 'the men dancing with their hats on'. Even when he went away to a cure at some watering-place he was 'going it'.

The birth of the Prince Imperial put Napoleon in such a state of elation that he wanted to declare peace regardless of terms. Finally on 30 March 1856 an honourable agreement was reached out of which England did not do too badly. The Queen was so pleased that she wished to make Clarendon a marquess and Cowley an earl, honours they both declined. Clarendon 'would not change the fine historical and much-loved name of Earl of Clarendon for all the marquisates in the world' in addition to his fear that courtesy titles for his younger sons 'would be a positive injury to them in working for their bread'; while Cowley refused on account of 'his extreme poverty and . . . that an accession of rank would only aggravate the inconvenience he already experiences from being a peer'. These reasons have a modern ring about them. However, Cowley accepted the earldom the following year, influenced perhaps by Palmerston's advice that it would be a decided advantage to his daughters.

Late at night in the middle of January 1858, Evans rushed round to the embassy to tell the Ambassador of the attempted assassination of the Emperor and Empress as they were on their way to the opera. Cowley immediately went to the Tuileries. The five assassins were Italian but they had planned the deed in England and their grenades were made in Birmingham, so Britain experienced another wave of criticism, accused not only of harbouring these particular villains but also other potential murderers such as Mazzini, Ledru Rollin, and Victor Hugo, who were living there in exile. Hatred of England was so violent that French officers returned their Orders of the Bath.

In the midst of this, the embassy had to receive the Emperor and Empress at a ball in honour of the Princess Royal's marriage to the German Crown Prince. The Ambassador was in such a dither over their safety that he devised a scheme whereby the main entrance in the Rue du Faubourg, where crowds would collect and assassins lurk, should appear expectant for the arrival of the imperial coach with all the illuminations lit, while Napoleon and Eugénie would drive round by the dark Avenue Gabriel and arrive at the ball through the garden.

Palmerston and his cabinet were defeated on 20 February and Malmesbury again became Foreign Secretary. Thus the daily exchange of letters between Clarendon and Cowley came to an end. Both felt it deeply. 'For myself I am quite miserable,' confided the latter. 'After the intimate correspondence of the last five years with you, it seems like treachery to you, to Malmesbury and to myself, to continue with him the same disburdening of all my sentiments in regard to political matters connected with this country. Of course delicacy now forbids my saying one word to you upon the grave matters at issue.' For the third time he wanted to leave and once more was dissuaded. Malmesbury paid him the great compliment of saying that, as long as he remained in Paris, he didn't mind who the French appointed in London.

Anybody who supposed that the Ambassador's house was at last in good order was mistaken. Those state-rooms had only been reinstated for their original purposes and not redecorated, the Chancery had never been modernized, the roof leaked in the main building and other evidence of deterioration made it apparent that Albano employed dishonest workmen who used inferior materials. The Office of Works sent out an architect to make a survey; he declared that £20,000 must be spent. Clarendon, still in office at the time, warned Cowley that the House of Commons was 'by no means in good humour upon money matters and is wanting to show its independence . . . but truly is not £20,000 too much? Would a French architect have presented such an estimate?'

To verify the report, Monsieur F. Raveau, *Architecte de la Ville de Paris*, was called in. Among his suggestions was the complete rebuilding of the Chancery or, alternatively, enlarging that pavilion by encroaching on the courtyard. Fortunately it was agreed just to alter the interior. He planned some unquestionable improvements in the embassy, such as dormer windows in the attic bedrooms and a small dining-room to be made into a pantry and reduced in size so as to build a service staircase to the first floor.

When resignation has been refused three times, the resigner feels pretty secure of his position. Cowley was intent on getting what he wanted and he boldly informed the doubtful authorities at home that not only was he himself the competent person to decide on alteration and redecoration but that, if the estimates were exceeded, he accepted full responsibility. Encouraged by the Ambassador, the architect went ahead. The furniture was moved out, Lady Cowley and her family retreated to Chantilly, the Ambassador lived in the attachés' rooms, saying that in his younger days he would have been glad to be so well lodged.

While the embassy was being thoroughly knocked about he was seized with a fatal inspiration. It was his idea to remove the arcade on the west side of the courtyard. Carriages could turn round more easily, but the symmetry of Mazin was for ever spoilt. By October 1861 work on the state-rooms had not yet been started and Raveau had already exceeded his original estimates.

Arguments were cut short by an unexpected tragedy which brought everything to a standstill. On 14 December the Prince Consort died. Cowley, asked to send cuttings of every reference to the Prince in the French newspapers, found a melancholy satisfaction that one who had never been popular was at last admired. This was generous of him, for recently he had fallen out of favour with the court because of Prince Albert's German sympathies and violent dislike of the Emperor. The Queen was now so much of the same opinion that Clarendon, still out of office but always her confidant, warned Cowley of the coldness of Victoria towards him and her belief that he was dangerously pro-French. There must have been truth in these allegations for it was only when the Emperor brazenly lied to him over the

Italian–Austrian question that the Ambassador 'saw the cloven hoof with a vengeance'.

Cowley was hypersensitive about his unpopularity both at home and in France. When the resilient Clarendon disagreed with the Queen, he could treat it lightly: 'The Missus and I had a bit of a tiff.' He was so concerned about the Ambassador's desperation that he decided to stop off at the embassy on his way through to Wiesbaden to calm him down. Above all he wanted to prevent him from resigning, which was bound to be his reaction to his unhappy situation. The truth was that, at the moment, there was nobody as good to take his place, moreover he would forgo his full pension, and, most cogent reason of all, 'Lady C. would be wretched to leave Paris.'

The Queen remained in perpetual mourning after Prince Albert's death, but her representative in Paris knew that life must go on. By 21 January in the new year he felt the moment ripe for re-opening the subject of completing the embassy. On wide black-edged paper he wrote one of his most persuasive letters. He told Lord Russell, now Foreign Secretary, how 'when the lamented event which had filled England with mourning and dismay had occurred', it had not seemed to him a fit moment for 'projects connected with festivity and entertainment'. He now reasoned that this period of social inactivity could profitably be utilized in finishing the work. He put forward an ingenious suggestion that some valuable land in the Rue d'Anjou, which had been bought along with the stables by Wellington, should be sold and, with the proceeds, the throne-room, ballroom and dining-room be redecorated.

The ballroom hardly justifies the transaction. It was to be the great *tour de force* of the French architect and in vain did the Ambassador hold him back. The Office of Works spared us at least some of the ornamentation by firmly telling him to 'have the goodness to cut out the eight groups of figures, the four panels of trophies, the birds on the ceiling'. Raveau was allowed to keep only two bearded nude male torsos but he let himself go with ornate columns and excessive plaster-work, creating a remarkable example of that showy age, the Second Empire. Nor could Cowley ever again complain that he was unable to include his fellow country-men at his parties, for Raveau designed a removable fête room to go between the garden wings. It figures in old *Illustrated London News'* drawings, showing clusters of elegant crinolined women round Lady Granville's fountain.

Notwithstanding their titles the Ladies Feodorewna and Sophia were having difficulty in finding husbands, the elder of the two confessing to Clarendon's girls that nobody had ever proposed to her or even appeared to be attracted. Their father was showing his usual worry that they should make so little impression. With two daughters on her hands, it was natural that the Ambassadress should eye with interest the young unmarried attachés who joined the staff and lived under her roof. They occupied the two rooms on the right of the entrance and the mezzanine immediately above.

In February 1864 the younger Wellesley girl, considered the prettier of the two, married Lord Royston, son of the Earl of Hardwicke, and the Emperor and Empress came to the wedding. There remained the elder daughter. A flutter of excitement in the summer of 1864 heralded the arrival of a quite exceptional attaché, the nephew and protégé of Lady Leconfield, who had been instrumental in getting him into the Foreign Office. Wilfrid Scawen Blunt was just 24 when he came to Paris. His exquisite looks belied his virility and athleticism (he had even been a matador), and he describes himself as a 'fair-faced frightened boy with eyes of truth who blushed the colour of his red innocent hands'.

The evening he arrived, Lady Cowley took him out in her barouche with Feodorewna to see the illuminations in the Champs-Elysées. Blunt says she believed him to be rich and threw the two together. Any ambitions she may have had soon faded away for he became deeply involved with one of the most successful courtesans of the 'city of delights', a lovely Englishwoman, Catherine Walters, known as Skittles. This was the most passionate of all his affairs. She was Manon in his poem:

'I did not choose thee, dearest. It was
Love that made the choice, not I.'

But love had also chosen Blunt for Feodorewna. When the
young poet followed Skittles to London without leave, he
was swiftly removed to Lisbon.

Resentment at leaving Paris may have made Blunt bitter
about the Cowleys. He put in his diary that, in their time
and that of their successor, the embassy was known as the
British Morgue. It is difficult to believe this criticism given
other accounts and knowing something of Lady Cowley's
reputation. She was even on practical joke terms with the
Foreign Minister, Drouyn de Lhuys. Disguised as a carpenter, he called on her to measure a table which was to be
copied for the Prince Imperial. Another time, when she had
advertised for a wet-nurse for her pregnant daughter, he
dressed up for the part, stuffing himself with cushions and
applied for the job. Only after an intimate discussion on
professional details did he reveal his identity. Then there
was her amusement when Dickens, too shy to come to her
parties, agreed to read David Copperfield in the state
dining-room in aid of charity, and in the dressing-room
arranged for him behind the columns the Ambassadress
surprised him in the act of changing, and trouserless.

Clarendon was back at his old post in 1865, but not for
long and a new government, with Lord Stanley at the
Foreign Office, brought the inevitable resignation of
Cowley. The Foreign Secretary begged him to reconsider,
appealing, through Clarendon, to 'his sense of public duty'.
He relented for one more year. He was only just over sixty
but he had had enough responsibility. He was ready to go.

He lived till 1884 able to enjoy, as fully as his apprehensive
nature permitted, his often-threatened retirement and an
important inheritance of money and estates.

The difficulty had always been to find a suitable successor
for a post which, so Clarendon considered, was as good as
any place in the cabinet. The man who was most anxious to
have it was apparently out of the question. What exactly

our Ambassador to the Porte had done is not divulged. Evidently Sir Henry Bulwer had been involved in some scandal which justified his being recalled from Constantinople directly his protector, Palmerston, died.

Bulwer had been replaced there by Lord Lyons and it was the latter who was now chosen for the embassy. He was unmarried and, in Clarendon's opinion, a wife was just as necessary to an ambassador at Paris as to a parson in his parish. But then, he admitted, perhaps it was as well 'that no successor to Lady Cowley should ever be attempted'.

XVI

Lord Lyons
1867—1887

'If you're given champagne at lunch, there's a catch some-where,' was a dictum of Lord Lyons.

It was Clarendon, so debonair, who originally suggested for Paris this huge, shy, silent, over-cautious bachelor, looking like a country squire. He remained there for twenty years, longer than any other of our ambassadors.

Born in 1817, he was educated at Winchester and Oxford, and became an unpaid attaché in the diplomatic service in 1839. Posted to Athens, he was still there, unpromoted, fourteen years later when he had the courage to complain to Malmesbury. Transferred to Rome, his industry, which was his great merit, attracted the attention of Lord John Russell, who appointed him Minister to Washington in 1858, in which year he succeeded to his father's peerage.

Though fundamentally kind he was such a severe chief that his hard-driven staff, who often went without lunch, staggered, exhausted, at seven in the evening to revive themselves with the new habit of cocktails, and frequently had to return to the Chancery till past midnight. Some asked to be transferred, others broke down, and the Minister himself had a nervous collapse in 1865. By the autumn he had sufficiently recovered to accept the embassy to the Porte with the proviso that he could take two of his staff to whom he had become attached: Edward Malet, a second secretary, and George Sheffield, who ran his house.

Two years later Stanley offered him Paris. He had mis-givings, but his father had told him never to refuse

The State Dining-room, 1965

following page The Ball-room, May 1903

promotion. He arrived in October 1867 together with Malet, Sheffield and a Manchester terrier, Toby, who had won the heart of the solitary Ambassador. Their touching companionship became so notorious that the dog was the subject of an article in *Le Figaro*.

Wilfrid Blunt tells how Parisians could not resist mocking at the sight of Lyons driving out in his barouche invariably accompanied by his favourite secretaries and the dog on the fourth seat. They called Malet *le petit brun* and Sheffield *le petit blond*. Insinuations about the relationship were almost certainly unfounded. The unmarried attachés who habitually dined with their lonely chief failed to penetrate his reserve. He lavished on Toby any affection he may have longed to express. On rare occasions, the knots he had so tightly twisted for himself were unravelled by embarrassing buffoonery with the children of his sister, the Duchess of Norfolk, who often stayed at the embassy. Out sight-seeing, he would suddenly pretend to be the father of a family of tourists or, when walking in the garden, impersonate an idiot. It may have been good for his inhibitions, but it did not dispel the awe the children felt for him. His temper could be formidable when aroused. Only twice was it seen in Paris: once when his coachman appeared incorrectly dressed and again, at a review, when the Diplomatic Corps were badly placed.

He had a strong sense of the importance of representation and the embassy was run in the grandest style, even if the Ambassador was consumed with so great a shyness that, as he dared not look his servants in the face, he had to recognize the footmen by their stockinged legs. He kept the finest carriages in Paris, a good cellar though he never drank wine, an excellent chef. Some compensation for loneliness was found in excessive enjoyment of food which, together with a dislike of exercise, contributed to his vast dimensions. The farthest he was known to walk was to and from the church over the road, and even for this brief excursion away from British territory he never failed to carry his passport.

His hidebound conception of ambassadorial duties would

be quite unacceptable today: he would have nothing to do with the press, he never made a speech, he refused to undertake anything which he did not consider to be strictly part of his diplomatic business, he believed it his duty never to leave the embassy except for his annual holiday, which was nearly always spent in England and thus can have known little of other parts of France until the Franco-Prussian War compelled him to leave Paris.

The embassy must have been a dull place. His days passed with meticulous regularity devoted to duty and work. He was at his desk at nine and, with the exception of official calls, his afternoon drive and a stroll in the garden always at precisely the same hour, remained working till late. His dinner parties contained no *élégantes*, we may be sure. When alone a secretary dined with him, after which he returned to his desk.

If he required the attachés to work late, he crossed the courtyard himself to tell them, with old-fashioned courtesy, 'I wonder if you two gentlemen would make it convenient to look in this evening because I am seeing the Minister of Foreign Affairs and may require to send a telegram to the Secretary of State.' More welcome was a written message saying, 'I have nothing more for the Chancery today.' Then the young bloods could dash off to play tennis in either of the two *Jeu de Paumes* courts in use in the Tuileries Gardens, or ride in the Bois de Boulogne, or gamble, or seek those pleasures which their chief ignored. They believed he had never been in love.

The conscientiousness of Lyons forbade him delegating the smallest responsibility to others till 1881, when Thomas Legh, a young man with initiative, joined the staff. Accustomed to more interesting work in the Foreign Office, he was so appalled at the dullness of the routine in Paris that he asked Lyons if the Chancery could at least see the blueprints of the telegrams. Such daring amazed his colleagues and it was thought he would never get away with it; he was the lowest in the hierarchy, and an anomaly in being already married. Gradually, however, Legh endeared himself by faultless handwriting and invaluable assistance with acrostics. The enterprising diplomat was to write his chief's biography.

Presenting credentials at the most glittering court in Europe, where the head of the state set the tone for lax morals, was daunting enough for somebody of a retiring nature, even without having to do so, in the Emperor's absence, to a woman. He must have found himself less embarrassed when this remarkable-looking Empress showed that she was only interested in politics and held forth energetically for an hour. But the friendly relationship that had existed between the imperial family and the Cowleys was not established with the new Ambassador and when Clarendon dined at the Tuileries in 1868 he noticed that it was the first time Lyons had been invited there.

His next test was a visit from the Queen on her way through to Switzerland in August. Lyons was given a month's warning and suddenly became conscious of the shabbiness of the house. He wrote to Russell on a note which is all too familiar, of how the Cowleys had left the bedrooms in a wretched state and there was no time to put them in order even if he were allowed the money. The Clerk of the Works in Paris hastily did his best to clean and paint and polish while the bachelor drove out shopping for carpets and rugs. The visit was marred by an unfortunate misunderstanding. The Empress came expressly from St Cloud to the Elysée to call on Victoria and afterwards waited there in vain for the expected return visit. The newspapers gave out that the Queen was still loyal to the exiled Orléans.

The Ambassador's reports were able and painstaking. He noted the contrast between the glittering success of the early years of the Second Empire and the present poverty and gloom of the working classes, with the Emperor, aged, weary, indecisive, yet perpetually intriguing. The menace to France was the growing strength of Prussia and her ruthless Chancellor. Bismarck could not renounce, any more than France could accept, the unification of Germany. He only wanted an excuse for a war that he knew he could win. He got it over the disputed succession to the throne of Spain. Twisting a telegram from his King, he gave the impression that France had been insulted. The Emperor then himself declared war on 15 July 1870. Lyons believed that the Emperor had been confident he could get what he wanted without hostilities. He was now ill and in pain, so the energy and enthusiasm of the Empress stood out in contrast.

The Austrian and Italian Ambassadors planned to illuminate their embassies when the expected victories were announced. Lyons, with his usual caution, hesitated to light up Albano's patriotic decorations and received instructions from Lord Granville (again Foreign Secretary) not to do so unless the omission would cause offence. The occasion never arose for only too soon came news of reverses. When the *Figaro* came out with that sinister phrase that it was a time for calm and dignity, there was general alarm, some people panicked and fled from Paris and by the middle of August the Ambassador reported that the Emperor and the dynasty had reached a low ebb.

On 3 September came the disastrous news of Sedan and the capitulation and imprisonment of Napoleon; on the 4th, the Empress fled from the Tuileries, which an angry mob had once more broken into. She and her lady-in-waiting planned to go to London that evening and wanted one of the secretaries to meet them at the Gare du Nord and accompany them on the journey. The reliable Malet was detailed for the mission but at six the Ambassador sent for him to say that Eugénie had been forced to take refuge with Evans, who contrived to get her to Deauville and thence to England.

Ten days later another opportunity arose for Malet when he was called upon to play a role of political importance. In London Granville and Thiers had discussed the advisability of negotiation between Bismarck and Jules Faure, the Vice-President of the Republic as well as Foreign Minister, and it was none other than *le petit brun* who was selected to carry the despatch to the Iron Chancellor suggesting this. Malet had known Bismarck from childhood for his father had been Minister in Frankfurt, and on 13 September he set off with a French officer as guide travelling by train, carriage and horse. He reached the Prussian headquarters at Meaux two days later. The conqueror of France greeted him affably: 'How like you are to your mother!' Indeed he had been an old admirer of Lady Malet. He was discouraging about the despatch, and his official reply to Granville's enquiry was brief, but when he placed it sealed in Malet's hand he said, 'To you as a friend I will say one word more. If a member of the Government of National Defence chooses to come and see me I shall be happy to receive him.'

On his return the secretary was ushered into the garden where, it being his hour for doing so, the Ambassador was pacing up and down the well-kept lawn; everything stood out in sharp contrast to the scarred countryside he had just left. Next morning he was summoned by Lyons to the yellow drawing-room where he was asked to repeat exactly what Bismarck had said. Faure, who was present, listened attentively. From all this followed the meeting at Ferrières, the Rothschild château built by Paxton, where France refused to agree to terms better than those she eventually had to accept.

This same evening, Lyons took the only questionable action of his cautious career, which led to his being castigated by Peel in the Commons for having made 'an ungenerous and unmanly flight'. Along with most of the diplomatic corps, one of the exceptions being the American Minister, he and nearly all his staff removed themselves by the last train to Tours where a delegation of the provisional government was being set up. It was argued that he should not have done so while Jules Faure and some of the government remained in Paris and there was an indignant outburst from the British colony.

It was Gladstone who defended his departure in words which may serve as a guide to others in such predicament:

the primary duty of an ambassador in Paris is not to take care of British subjects but the interests of his country. One of these subjects had come round to the embassy in a fury announcing that he was a man of wealth and position and not accustomed to being treated in this manner. 'What is the use of you, Sir, if you cannot ensure my safe passage to England? If I am killed the world shall ring with it. I shall make a formal complaint to Lord Granville.'

While some were frantically trying to leave, more adventurous compatriots were arriving expressly to attend the siege of Paris. Among them were two young journalists who both became well-known Members of Parliament. Henry Labouchère and Thomas Gibson Bowles severely condemned the exodus from the embassy and were particularly critical of the Consul, Falconer Atlee, who had set himself up safely at Dieppe. Certainly the privations of the British colony were so appalling that Lyons must take the blame for not appointing somebody with proper authority to be in charge of the embassy. There was only a secretary, Henry Wodehouse, and the military attaché, Colonel Claremont.

In December the French Government was forced to move to Bordeaux with only a few hours' warning, a rush which upset the ordered rhythm of Lyons's day. He complained that he was ill-lodged, but it was as nothing compared with the hardships of the starving British in besieged Paris. On 10 December, the embassy was in charge of Edward Blount, a rich banker well known in Paris. Bowles was scathing about this appointment for all the other countries had left somebody professional in charge. At least Blount had the merit of possessing two cows: one already killed, salted and ready to eat; the other, which supplied him with milk and butter, a substantial meal in reserve. He hoped in his new position to be allowed to keep just one horse, for they were fast disappearing off the street to reappear on the table, but he was told that he had no diplomatic privilege.

Blount was formally appointed Consul on 24 January 1871 and at last got some authority. There came a letter from Lyons by pigeon, a salubrious meal literally out of the blue, but the temptation had to be resisted if a reply was to be despatched A few days later Paris capitulated and on 29 January the Preliminaries of Peace were signed at Versailles.

Lionel Sackville-West, heir to his brother, Lord Sackville, was the one member of Lord Lyons's staff who can have had no regrets about being at Bordeaux. He had an enduring liaison with a beautiful Spanish gipsy dancer who was already married when he had met her, and he was the father of four of her five children. He had bought for her a villa at Arcachon. Whether their relationship was legalized or not was nebulous. The Ambassador may have known, for the two secretive men surely understood each other. Early in March he sent a compassionate telegram to Lionel, then back in Paris: '*Votre pauvre femme vient de mourir, vos enfants vous appelent.*'

The perpetrator of this mysterious alliance himself showed a strong regard for legality when he perceived in the consular register that Blount had married Richard Wallace (of the Wallace Collection) to his mistress of 30 years. Arguing that this marriage was invalid, he promptly tore the page from the book. Wallace was forced to go through the ceremony all over again, but two other couples were never traced.

On 1 March the Parisians had the humiliation of seeing the German troops march down the Champs-Elysées and occupy the city for 48 hours. The National Assembly under Thiers moved from Bordeaux and at last, after six months' absence, our Ambassador returned to the embassy, but it was only to be for one week. During the siege, the revolutionary party had failed to overthrow the Government of National Defence but their opportunity came now. By 18 March, the Hôtel de Ville and all the right bank was in rebel hands and the next day an official from the Ministry of Foreign Affairs came to Lyons to tell him that the government had been forced to retire to Versailles. This time he hesitated to move till Granville had instructed him to do so.

He left Malet in charge. On 28 March the Commune was proclaimed.

Malet and another secretary lived in the house. Regularly at dawn they were awakened by the bombardment. Then, on 22 May, from the second floor where he slept, Malet could see the welcome sight of the *tricolor* flying above the Arc de Triomphe. During the day the battle became intense, shells flew from all directions and one hit the front of the embassy east of the gateway, knocking in the wall. Malet decided to sleep that night on the ground floor. He was awakened at five to be told that a colonel wanted to examine the position of the enemy's barricade from the street side. The garden was already full of troops, making holes in the walls. The colonel now asked that the state dining-room be arranged as a first-aid station. Malet elongated the great dining table with all its leaves as if for a banquet, and on it were placed rows of mattresses. The effect was that of a splendid hospital ward. Delighted though he was with the transformation, the thought did cross his mind of the macabre memories he would in future have at dinner parties, but only the colonel had to be carried off through the garden, dead.

That same morning stupendous crashes shook the house. Clearly the moment had come for saving objects of value. Down to the cellars, where weeping women servants were huddled, were carried archives, red boxes, ornaments and pieces of furniture. Afterwards a story went round that the only difference in the running of the embassy was that the footmen dispensed with powdered hair. This can be believed when we read of how the two secretaries ate that particular evening while the battle raged outside. Dinner was served in what looked like a robbers' cave full of loot. In the middle was the dining table, faultlessly laid, at which they sat in evening dress waited on by butler and footmen.

The embassy had been badly battered, with six direct hits, the walls pock-marked with bullets. The garden was full of strange litter, bits of missiles and masses of charred criminal records which had blown over from the burning Palais de

Justice. Malet had excelled himself and the only question was how such devotion to duty should properly be recognized. The Foreign Office wanted the VC for him but the War Office put a stop to that and, as the CMG was then only awarded for colonial services, Granville lowered the diplomatic rank for receiving the CB to that of second secretary. Thus Malet became the youngest holder of that decoration, to add to the distinction he already had of being the youngest man ever to get into the service.

The Third Republic was established with Thiers as President. The embassy was repaired and Lyons could resume his orderly way of life. However in 1874 the house entered a new phase. The second floor was now being used as a maternity ward for the pregnant wives of those immediately connected with the Chancery.

In the middle of the Franco-Prussian War, attempts had been made to introduce legislation to subject the sons born in France of foreign parents to military service by declaring them to be French. The law was in fact never actually passed and was finally withdrawn on 16 December 1874, but the threat of it was strong enough for expectant mothers, who intended to give birth in France, to wish to do so on British territory.

Only three births have been traced so far and they are all in 1874, which may have been when the threat was at its height. One of these children was Violet Williams-Freeman, daughter of the second secretary, who grew up to enchant her friends as Violet Hammersley. She remembered playing with the other embassy children in the Champs-Elysées and how one of them, whom she described as a horrid little boy, passed off false sous to the nice old woman who sold them gingerbread. Somerset Maugham could be trusted to get his own back for such remarks: he said to the writer that he and Violet used to be exactly the same age in those days but now somehow she had become several years younger. He, too, was born in the Hôtel on 25 January, of a father who was solicitor to the embassy. The last birth, that of Emily Lytton, was on 26 December, ten days after the attempted legislation had been abandoned, but probably arrangements for the event had already been made.

Another incursion disrupted the routine of the shy Ambassador this same year in April, when a grand wedding took place in the house which was invaded for the occasion by uninhibited young American women. Jennie Jerome was marrying Lord Randolph Churchill. After the ceremony there was a wedding breakfast in the state dining-room, but the custom of the day decreed that the bridal couple must eat apart in the private dining-room. They drove off for their honeymoon in an open carriage drawn by four grey horses with postilions. At the end of November, Winston Churchill was born.

There were more royal visits. We get an endearing picture of the Queen when staying at the embassy on her way to the south of France. Waddington, the French Foreign Minister, of English and Scottish descent and education, was received with the rare smile 'which lightened up her whole face'. She said, 'I think I can speak English with a Cambridge scholar.' As he came away, he found that controversial personage, the Queen's Highland servant, John Brown, lurking outside the door of the central drawing-room. Brown shook hands informally and invited him to Scotland, where he promised a hearty welcome.

1883 brought a wave of anglophobia so violent that Lyons urged the Prince of Wales to cancel a visit to Paris and Granville, who considered himself the greatest admirer of France, found it hard that 'we should have such difficult moments to pass when I am in office'. Two years later a newspaper, *La Lanterne*, falsely accused Lord Wolseley of having ordered the assassination of a French ex-Communist journalist in the Sudan. Rochefort, the author of these lies, incited the Parisian mob to make Lyons their victim. Fortunately the Ambassador was on leave but *La Lanterne* recommended that the secretaries should be strung up on the lamp-posts of the Rue du Faubourg.

The mission of Lord Lyons had a sad end. It must have been wounding to be informed, while on leave in England, that Lytton was appointed to Paris and therefore there was no need for him to return there. He used to say that he always arrived at a new post with one trunk and left with one trunk, for he never accumulated anything. But he was a punctilious man. He would have wished to bid farewell formally and see once more the house where he had plodded away according to his lights, carrying out his axiom: 'Never do anything today that can be put off till tomorrow,' and his unambitious boast, 'I always did the safe thing.'

For some while he had been interested in Roman Catholicism. He had not actually joined the Church at the end of November when he had a stroke at Norfolk House and died a week later, but he received Extreme Unction while unconscious.

There is a souvenir of Lord Lyons at the embassy and, because he was a great introvert, it remains hidden, as he would have wished. Somewhere in the middle of the lawn, beneath where he used to pace up and down, is the grave of Toby.

XVII

The Earl of Lytton
1887—1891

Lord Lytton was sent to Paris at the express wish of Lord Salisbury, Prime Minister and Foreign Secretary, because he had 'the gift for captivating individuals'. He still remains the Ambassador who most endeared himself to the French.

Distinguished and cultured, this handsome man with his dark curly hair and dreamy eyes was at heart a bohemian, and his romantic appearance that of the poet he wished to be rather than the diplomat he reluctantly was. He had the milk of human kindness, and this compassion for others was never warped by his ill-health, melancholia and a miserable upbringing. What his favourite daughter called 'his innate humility' must have prevented bitterness from taking root.

Born in November 1831, he was the second child and only son of Edward Earle Bulwer, the writer, who changed his name to Bulwer-Lytton in 1844 on inheriting Knebworth, the Hertfordshire property of his Lytton mother. The novelist, morbid and neurotic, married a brilliant Irish girl, 'wild Rosina' Doyle, who had a temperament of uncontrolled violence. He was a neglectful father and she an unkind mother. They soon separated.

The frail child, Robert, was sent to endure the harsh trials of private school where he had to spend the holidays, followed by Harrow. He afterwards conceded that at least he learnt something which prepared his sensitive nature for life. During school years he seldom saw his father, but fortunately a friend of Bulwer took an interest in the neglected boy. John Forster, a barrister and literary figure, saw to it that he had proper clothes and some money, took him to the theatre, which fired him with a love for the stage, and introduced him to Thackeray and Dickens, which encouraged his passion for literature.

Already at private school he had started writing poetry. As he grew up, to write became and remained his predominating desire. The successful author, his father, intended his son for diplomacy and, when he was nearly nineteen, sent him off to Washington as unpaid attaché to the Minister, his uncle, Sir Henry Bulwer, and subsequently to Florence.

It would seem that Bulwer discouraged his son from writing fearing rivalry, and when, in 1854, he allowed him to publish a volume of verse a pseudonym had to be concocted from ancestral connections, Owen Meredith. It was only when George Meredith objected to the confusion this caused that Robert was able to persuade his father to let him use his real name.

It is notable that Bulwer-Lytton, though held in awe, remained the idol of his son, who even copied his father's unusual style of dress. Bulwer was a dandy and it was he who inaugurated the custom of men wearing only black in the evening. With the passing of time Robert's clothes surprised people by their elaboration.

From Florence he went as attaché to Cowley in Paris and thence to The Hague. His father urged him to marry, to carry on the line. Robert longed for a home such as he had never known and in Paris, in the spring of 1864, he met a girl who, with her tall fair-haired beauty, impressed him 'with a peculiar sensation of tenderness and reverence, strangely like the atmosphere of love'. Edith Villiers, niece to Clarendon and also to Lady Normanby, was sweet and dignified but not intellectual, which made her the perfect wife for a highly-strung man with a consuming passion for matters of the mind. Though the marriage was not approved of for political and financial reasons, it took place in the autumn.

The following spring, Lytton was appointed first secretary

at Lisbon and it was that summer, when his wife had gone to England to have their first child, that a new attaché arrived. 'An intellectual honeymoon,' Wilfrid Blunt called this meeting with Robert, of which he wrote in later life, 'Neither absence, nor growing age, nor diverging political opinions, were ever able to change it from the romance it was when it first began.'

Still infatuated with Skittles and resentful of his banishment from Paris, Wilfrid was in a state of misery. Robert, who had moved to a small inn in the hills of Cintra, at once sensed that this beautiful youth was suffering from an unhappy love affair. Within half an hour Blunt realized he had found the right person to dispel his misery, for Lytton, himself so prone to black despair, yet had the gift of renewing hope in others. The older man wrote to Edith of 'a very great and very pleasant discovery' he had made. It was one which might not have been exactly a recommendation to most people in charge of a chancery: the new secretary was 'a genuine poet'. They spent three months together talking all night 'of things divine, poetry, philosophy and sentiment'.

Meanwhile Edith had a son and the delighted Robert wrote to his father with characteristic humility, 'I hope he will in after life complete my incompleteness.' Three years later this boy died in Vienna, which was the Lyttons' next post after a short spell in Madrid. When, in 1873, Robert was moved to Paris as first secretary he had become Lord Lytton, for his father, recently made a peer, had just died. His own family now consisted of two daughters and a second son, who died the following year.

Lytton was delighted to be in France. 'Certainly . . . the morsels of Paris life glitter as they pass.' But again doubt and weariness would overcome him and then he felt he was not made for society and only wanted 'to live in the country and write verses, love my friends, and do harm to no man . . . this is all I am fit for . . . When a human being gets off the right rail of life, what happens?'

What happened was that after six months in Lisbon Disraeli offered him, in 1875, a position of such magnificence that, in spite of increasing bad health, he could hardly refuse. It was the Viceroyalty of India. Four years were spent there. Informality in such an exalted status was bound to be criticized in viceregal circles, but not by the Queen, to whom he had started writing his official letters using the first person in surprising ignorance of the correct form of address. Most unusually she permitted him to continue thus.

In 1880 Gladstone succeeded Disraeli and Lytton, whose policy in India had been violently criticized by the opposition, resigned. At last he could settle down to the sort of life for which he had always longed. He returned to the ancestral home which his father had enlarged and medievalized; he was surrounded by friends and family, now happily increased by another girl and two more boys, and he devoted himself to writing. But the seven years he spent at Knebworth were also a time of disillusionment; the English climate was harsh, the English character reserved, he was constantly ill, and it all contributed to his depression. He realized how essential regular work had been to him. However, his eldest daughter, Betty, now shared the '*inneres Leben*' of this sensitive man. She became his closest confidante and companion. He wrote that 'painlessness in love' could only be obtained in a harmonious platonic relationship such as this.

In December 1887 Lytton was sent to Paris. Salisbury told the Queen that what we needed in France was good information: 'There is no competitor for the appointment.' Lytton was 56 and still looked remarkably young and handsome. When he left England he was in particularly low spirits, caused by an accumulation of unhappy circumstances: Betty had just married, he was feeling ill, and he was in love with Mary Anderson, an American actress of 28, whose talent and beauty had taken London by storm. But she wanted marriage with her distinguished admirer, not an affair.

So it was a sad, sick man who arrived at Paris in bitterly cold weather on 22 December. The drive from the station along slippery roads in the state coach attracted the sort of attention he disliked, and when at last they reached the embassy it was to find the building encased in scaffolding and the ground floor stacked with vanloads of packing cases from Knebworth. On top of this the Board of Works' architect broke the news that dry rot had been discovered and several rooms could not be used. Not for the first time did an ambassador complain, 'When I shall be able to open, for official receptions, the doors of this disorderly house, heaven only knows.'

An excellent dinner revived his spirits but the next day came a summons from the Queen to cross the Channel all over again and kiss hands at Osborne. She was annoyed that he had not done so before leaving England but Salisbury had insisted that the new Ambassador should be present at the Presidential New Year's Day Reception. These extra journeys in bad weather made him ill and on his return he was only just able to stagger out of bed to present credentials at the Elysée, fortified with doses of laudanum and cocaine.

The Lytton era was short and not distinguished by any outstanding political event but it was brilliant and unforgettable. This highly temperamental Ambassador came to the embassy like a bright light after the subfusc years under Lyons. Certain conventional members of the Chancery found the change too startling. At first they could not quite understand such an unusual head of mission with all that artistic brilliance, bohemian friends, and fancy clothes. Then there was his indifference to formality. He would not hesitate to stop the ambassadorial carriage outside a *pissoire* if he so desired, and his staff must have dreaded a repetition of what once happened at a Viceregal banquet in India when, to relieve the tedium, he had put the dog on the table.

The house was now noisy with the lively Lytton family, who all talked at once and never listened. If Lord Lytton was in a mood to be silent he sat brooding alone, and it was up to his wife to make gracious amends. But when he was elated his exuberance was un-British, he sparkled, kissed women's hands, danced untiringly, fell in love. Once he was even foreign enough to describe how lovely his wife looked, glimpsed through the door of Pauline's bedroom as she sat in her hip-bath in front of the fire.

No one could question the perfection of Lady Lytton as ambassadress. She was grand-mannered. Her strong sense of duty made her struggle unceasingly to control her unaccountable husband and, since he was the kindest of men, his love affairs were generally abandoned when she protested too much.

If some of the embassy staff were slow to recognize his merits the French were in no doubt. Brought up in the tradition of Versailles, where Louis XIV had made a nucleus of all that was brilliant in France, art was considered an essential part of life. The French immediately saw that this ambassador was an exceptional man and he was warmly welcomed into the world of the intellect as well as that of diplomacy. Blunt says that he was more than popular, he was beloved. The Foreign Minister, Flourens, esteemed him highly and his wife, a perceptive woman, understood his complicated character. He confided in her about his dual personality, his happy self full of hopes and his sad poetic self.

Presumably the image of Mary Anderson began to fade for he started to enjoy himself. He was entirely at his ease in a Latin country, but he would have been happier in a small apartment on the Rive Gauche, with no fixed engagements. Sometimes he felt ashamed of not appreciating the luxury of the embassy.

'*Les bons dîners font la bonne diplomatie*' is a maxim of Talleyrand's to be remembered in embassies. Lytton secured the best chef in Paris and, a few weeks after his arrival, profited by his wife's absence in England to give a dinner after his own heart. It was entirely male, 'a single petticoat would have spoilt it all'. Though the guest of honour was the Foreign Minister, politics were not even mentioned, for the Ambassador had selected guests who would enjoy discussing the subjects which interested him most. It was a resounding success from the moment they entered the house and were given that radiant welcome which was so great a feature of his charm. He described it all to Betty: 'The new cook, who was on his mettle, surpassed himself. The conversation was brilliant, the lead being taken by Sardou [the dramatist] who is quite the most fascinating talker I have ever met. It was well sustained by Coppée [the poet], I throwing in only a word now and then to keep it going, and Lesseps [the diplomat responsible for the Suez Canal] furnishing the texts.'

The guests went home ecstatic and it quickly went round Paris that the British Ambassador was the only person who knew how to give a delightful dinner. In fact he was such a success that he wrote to Lady Salisbury how 'all parties and classes continue to be overwhelmingly civil to us, and I feel rather alarmed at the excess of their civilities'. Not only was he popular with the French and the press, he was equally so with his own compatriots. The President of the British Chamber of Commerce was the one-time acting Consul of the Siege of Paris, now Sir Edward Blount, who records that the British colony was 'a body very hard to please'.

Always Lytton found time to write. His poetic inspiration was prolific, and since he almost thought in poetry it was believed that his despatches were first written in verse as this medium came to him more easily than prose. Inability to abridge his writing was a Lytton characteristic. Lengthy political screeds went off to Lady Salisbury as well as to the Secretary of State, and soon after his arrival in Paris he urged his 'dear chefesse' to come to stay 'when the chestnut-trees bloom in the Champs Elysées, and the voice of the *café chantant* is heard in the land . . . to revisit the theatres and studios of this delectable city'.

Intimate feelings, impressions, ideas on all manner of subjects were kept for the understanding mind of his eldest daughter. Reading *Manon Lescaut* set him off on a dissertation on the 'mystery of passion', an enigma which absorbed him and showed he must have had poignant experience. Only Shakespeare 'who touched all chords' understood.

After the almost daily luncheon parties and when he was not going to the Chamber of Deputies, making official calls, or learning the talk of Paris in crowded salons, he spent the leisure of the afternoon more intimately. In the green room of the Comédie Française he had made friends with some of the more distinguished actresses, of whom the one that charmed him most was young and lovely Mademoiselle Brandes. Sometimes his afternoons were spent most properly just walking in the Bois de Boulogne with a daughter and the dog.

Lytton was a devoted family man, yet his youngest daughter was obsessed with shyness of him during the Paris years. Emily was born soon after the death of his second son in 1874 when it was fervently hoped that the next child would be a boy. That she should not be aware of this disappointment, Lady Lytton spoilt her; but when they moved to the embassy the harried Ambassadress discouraged her from clinging. Emily felt unwanted and resolved never again to show her feelings to anyone. Thus easily are inhibitions formed. Georgiana Leveson-Gower had discovered happiness in fantasy; Emily Lytton found it in a living form of which her parents knew, though they did not realize the depth of her feelings nor their reciprocation. She corresponded with a clergyman living in the remote Norfolk village of Booton. He was seventy-one, she thirteen.

The Reverend Whitwell Elwin, an interesting and erudite eccentric, had a compelling attraction for the Lyttons. Booton was the Mecca to which their eyes were constantly turned. The highlight of their summer holidays was to go there. The Ambassador was delighted to leave the pomposity of diplomatic life to stay with whom he called 'the last true man of letters', where the talk was on a high intellectual level and the atmosphere tranquil and informal. Elwin would sit in his green velvet chair and assume the role of a priest in his confessional. His forte was forming the characters of young girls. They were his 'blessed girls' and undoubtedly there was a mutual attraction.

Emily became the blessed girl *par excellence*. In his hands he held the taut threads linking him with this temperamental family now living in the embassy. Regularly a spate of letters left *la ville lumière* bound for the sleepy East Anglian backwater. They came from the Ambassadress confiding her worries over her husband's love affairs, from the Ambassador complaining of his wife's attempts to change his bohemian ways, and from the bruised heart of Emily, the young girl.

With shrewd psychology he urged Emily to write about herself. Headed by a highly-strung poet such an emotional family could hardly be harmonious for long and she was inclined to dwell on the more discordant incidents. The rector's method was not to rebuke but to soothe and encourage. He gave her a beautiful example to emulate; he quoted Wordsworth's 'A perfect Woman, nobly planned', which instantly appealed to her.

The old clergyman must have ruminated with interest on some of the things she revealed about his friend Robert, who sometimes mocked at sacred subjects and admitted to being a fatalist who did not believe in the efficacy of prayer. He learnt, too, how the atmosphere changed when Betty came to stay, bringing with her a sunshine which dispersed Lytton's melancholia. When father and favourite daughter were engrossed talking her mother was ignored, 'pushed into the background'. Sometimes when Emily wrote to him she had the illusion of actually sitting close up to the green chair, 'Only I can't feel your hand which is the best part of your talk'. From the bleakness of Norfolk the eccentric old priest had kindled a flame in the girl's heart which must have warmed the cockles of his own.

Various accounts from other members of the family show them all in a more harmonious light, including Emily herself, who looked like her mother and whom her father wanted to 'come out' at fourteen. Neville, the second boy, was probably the most like him. When he was discovered mixing water-colours with toothpaste to paint a portrait of Disraeli to hang in the embassy, Lytton decided he should take up art as a career. He proudly wrote to Betty, 'Neville is becoming a sort of Wunderkind – paints in oils, plays the flute [he was having lessons from the first flautist of the Opéra Comique], and has established quite a social reputation for *esprit.*'

A visiting ambassadress, Lady Paget from Vienna, was amazed at the way the Lyttons took no advantage of privilege. They went about in ordinary cabs at night, at the theatre they sat in the stalls and balcony instead of in a box, the daughters even travelled third class and went in omnibuses. Coming from the strictest court in Europe she imagined all this was because they lived in a republic, but really it was the Ambassador who liked it that way.

Their guests were often as unconventional. A strange trio came to stay: Wilfrid Blunt with his wife, Lady Anne, whom Lytton describes as 'looking more grotesque and wigged than ever', and their daughter Judith, 'a handsome ill-dress'd very shy young giantess'. The main interest of Lady Anne, the granddaughter of Byron, lay in her Arabian stud. She was said to go up to bed all ready, even booted, for her morning ride. The only child of this marriage had been encouraged in boyish pursuits and Emily, paired off with her, appealed to her old clergyman in dismay when she found that she was expected to shoot and wrestle, activities not in accordance with his Wordsworthian image of woman.

During his four years in Paris, outwardly so brilliant, Lytton's health deteriorated. In 1889 he had a serious operation of which his wife was not told till it was successfully over. 'I have at least looked close into the great facts of sorrow and death,' he wrote. 'My life, though externally much favoured by fortune, has been familiar with pain of all sorts, and I keenly realize the contrast . . . between the importance of the individual itself and its unimportance to Nature.' After this sad letter it is good to know that in August he went to recuperate in the bracing air of Dieppe, then the summer resort for the intelligentsia and the world of fashion, and was sufficiently recovered still to find enjoyment in life. He saw there friends, actresses, painters and writers, and he admired 'an accomplished pretty little lady *de la haute*', Mme de Greffuhle, soon to be immortalized as the Duchesse de Guermantes by Proust.

But back in Paris weariness overcame him again and he felt, like Falstaff, 'I would it were bed time, and all were over.' As the end of his life approached, he became more despairing, more introspective. He admitted that he was changeable as the wind, and an enigma even to himself with 'half a dozen persons in me, each utterly unlike the other – all pulling different ways, and continually getting in each other's way – and I don't think anybody else knows all of them a bit better than I do myself.' He ends a particularly long outpouring to Betty with 'But O my dear alter ego, enough and too much of this egotistical psychology!!'

At least he had some pleasure this last summer at the embassy in the giving of a brilliant party, the organizing of which was something so much to his liking that it must temporarily have snapped him out of despondency. Two plays were performed in the ballroom by a distinguished cast from the Comédie Française, which included his favourite, Mlle Brandes. Betty describes it: 'The actors beamingly happy, the company very smart, very gay, very appreciative. The house, decorations, the food and all other accessories got up with the beauty and refinement of a Louis XIV Fête. After the performance thirty privileged persons, including the actors, crept up the back stairs to supper in the big drawing-room on the first floor.'

When she went to bed dawn was peeping through the shutters. In the garden 'A still grey quiet light was over everything . . . the birds were singing lustily. The contrast of the quiet and stillness of the morning after our desperate efforts to amuse ourselves wildly was soothing and saddening.' It had been Lytton's swan song on a perfect mid-June night of *la belle saison*, for after this his health started breaking down irrevocably.

A long-standing wish to go to Bayreuth was fulfilled late in July. He was already too worn out to enjoy Paris 'with its clever people and clever talk, its good cooks, its esprit, its amours, its well-dressed women and witty men,' whereas at Wagnerian opera 'At once you are safe in the very heart of the world of dreams.' This was followed by a holiday in England and his last visit to Booton. Elwin urged his seeing his doctors. They wanted him to give up Paris at once and to keep him under observation, but he insisted that he would benefit from the care of his family and the comforts of the embassy and, he adds, almost apologetically, that clairvoyants had told him that he would live long.

A rough crossing made him worse and he arrived desperately ill. From his bed he was still capable of doing some work, and of writing. Friends visited him, Lady Salisbury stayed, and Oscar Wilde, who spent that autumn in Paris, often sat with him where he lay 'in Pauline's beautiful room'. Blunt came to bid a tender farewell, aware that he would never again see the man he so highly valued. He died on 24 November.

There is a tradition that Lytton was in the Salon Vert on a sofa (which is still in the house) writing a poem, when he suddenly had a stroke and fell back without a sound into the arms of his wife. He was the second ambassador from Britain to France to die in Paris; James Beaton of Balfour, Archbishop of Glasgow, known as Jacques de Béthune de Balfour, ambassador for 42 years of Mary Queen of Scots and James VI and I, died there in 1603.

Lytton, who had always shunned pomp, was given a spectacular farewell, the like of which had not been seen since the state funeral of Victor Hugo. The Elysée flag was at half-mast, troops lined the streets, pavements and windows were crowded, shops were shut. In the British church the whole intellect of Paris was said to be gathered. The procession to the Gare St Lazare was preceded by cavalry, infantry and a band and followed by relatives, officials, diplomats, and no less than three thousand persons on foot.

In adversity Lady Lytton behaved with splendid dignity. She was very poor after the failure of some investments.

The Queen, in a moving letter of admiration for her forti-
tude, offered her the post of Lady of the Bedchamber, which
gave her an interest and helped her financially. Her devotion
to her husband was such that she got someone to take her
to see the woman who had most inspired him, Madame
Navarro, as Mary Anderson had now become, and sent her
children to her every year.

Edith Lytton lived to be 95, retaining to the end her looks
and beautiful manners.

Emily had a stormy passage before she settled down.
Blunt, who modelled himself on the morals of *Les Liaisons
Dangereuses*, was still strikingly handsome at 53, and great
strength of mind would have been needed to resist the
prowess of such an experienced admirer. His daughter
claimed that his eyes were hypnotic and glittered with
double lights. (These show in portraits and photographs,
but the present Lord Lytton thinks that she added the
phenomenon with white Chinese ink.) A dangerous flirtation
with Emily went on for three years concurrently with his
other renowned affairs, till Judith learnt of it and enlightened
her as to his wickedness. Neville married Judith (who
inherited the Barony of Wentworth), and their son, in
whom is combined the heredity of Byron, Blunt and
Lytton, is the present earl.

The tragedy of Robert Lytton was that he was not a great
poet, a fear which constantly haunted him. Yet Blunt
foresaw him taking his place next to Tennyson and before
Browning. He considered his letters as good as Byron's and
Shelley's. Lytton made his name in the career which had
been thrust upon him. Nature endowed him with skill in
negotiation, which is the art of diplomacy, and his genuine
interest in people enabled him to obtain 'good information'
for his Secretary of State. Had his four years in Paris
coincided with one of those inevitable recurring phases of
anglophobia he might well have weathered the storm more
successfully than many far cleverer men.

It is again Blunt who, in a few words, evokes an affectionate memory of his old friend: 'It was but a passing glimpse,

but I like to recall it and the picture which remains in my mind of him as he sat writing, with one hand busy with his work, and his other caressing his black poodle's head. There was something typical in the attitude and the act.'

XVIII

The Marquess of Dufferin
1891—1896

It was difficult to follow Lytton.

Lord Dufferin, a cultivated man of great charm with an impressive diplomatic and Viceregal career behind him, lacked the glamour and endearing human qualities of his predecessor. Unlike Lytton, he was wiry and athletic and had had a devoted mother. He reciprocated her love with chivalrous fervour which coloured the whole of his life and was the key to much in his character.

He was a small man with distinguished looks inherited from his Linley ancestry, for he had the same Latin colouring and poignant delicacy of beauty as can be seen in the portraits of this remarkable family. Dufferin states that his Linley great-great-grandfather was a musician 'who had to earn his bread by the exercise of his profession'. The musically gifted Thomas Linley, the son of a carpenter, left descendants only through two of his daughters. The elder, Elizabeth Ann, the exquisite singer, became the first wife of Richard Brinsley Sheridan, and their grandchildren were another bevy of beauties of which Helen Selina Sheridan was the eldest daughter. To her son she was the ideal of womanhood. Lord and Lady Dufferin were not of this opinion when, at the age of seventeen, this 'granddaughter of a playwright' attracted the admiration of their only surviving son, Price Blackwood. However, they married in July 1825 and, to escape the Dufferins' disapproval, left the same day for Italy where, in Florence, in June 1826, Frederick Temple Blackwood was born.

When her husband, whose only interest was the navy, went off to sea, Helen Blackwood spent most of her time with her married sisters in London. These dazzling Sheridans with their wit and Irish lack of inhibition took London by storm, Benjamin Disraeli particularly admired the grass widow, and, since her son knew her to be pure as the driven snow, it must have been distressing to him that a persistent rumour should name Dizzy as his real father. An olive complexion and a rich musical speaking voice not unlike that of the statesman seem to have been the only foundation for the story.

Price Blackwood died soon after succeeding to the barony, and the fifteen-year-old Dufferin left Eton for six months to be with his mother in Italy. This period remained in his mind as something particularly precious. Also at Castellammare was the misunderstood son of the Marquess of Tweeddale, the Earl of Gifford, who went sailing with Dufferin and on shore confided his unhappiness to the sympathetic widow.

After Oxford, where he was President of the Union, Dufferin settled down with his mother in Ireland and London. But he showed no inclination to play a part in politics; he dallied, yachted and hunted. The name of his ancestral home was not pleasing to the ear so Ballyleidy was replaced by the more euphonious Clandeboye and the place vastly improved regardless of expense. On a high point of land he built a tower in honour of Helen Dufferin in which hung golden tablets inscribed with verse eulogizing her perfections.

He was very charming with his almost feminine manner, old-world courtesy, gentle lisping voice and Irish gaiety. Yet the mercurial Sheridan blood had been much watered-down. He was conventional and minded intensely what people thought of him.

In 1860 he was sent as British representative on a commission to Syria for which his mother joined him, after which he became Under-Secretary for India. Then came the offer of the Governorship of Bombay, which he refused because his mother's health could not have stood the climate. At this point Helen Dufferin must have realized that the time had come for her to withdraw from the scene if he was to have the brilliant future she envisaged for him.

That romantic figure, Blunt, could speak with authority on love, and his analysis of Dufferin's temperament is interesting. 'He trifled with women rather than made love to them.' His mother was the one passion of his life. She arranged his marriage and 'he accepted it as he would have accepted anything else at her hands'. The ideal wife had been maturing close to Clandeboye. The daughter of a distant relative, dignified, virtuous, she could be counted upon to devote her life unquestioningly to her husband and guard him from anything which might upset him.

Surprising news was in store for those who had followed with interest the engagement of Dufferin. Exactly ten days before his marriage to Hariot Rowan Hamilton in October 1862, his mother became the wife of Lord Gifford. The two couples made an odd pattern of age-groups. About the same number of years separated Dufferin from his mother as from his bride, while his stepfather, a dying man, was but four years older than himself.

Though Dufferin understood the compassionate motive for this brief marriage (which may also have been to encourage him to do likewise) it was not an episode that he cared for. He was too conventional not to mind the talk to which it gave rise.

Helen Dufferin died in 1867, too soon to see her son attain high office but with the satisfaction of knowing that he was founding a large family. In 1871 he was made an earl in anticipation of becoming Governor-General of Canada, where his amiability and talent for elegantly-phrased speeches made him as much liked as did his lavish hospitality. When appointed Ambassador to St Petersburg, he entertained on such a scale that it was said to be more like a court than an embassy.

By now he had made a name as an appeasing negotiator. After Constantinople came the crowning point of his career when, in 1884, he went to India as Viceroy. He enjoyed the splendour of his exalted position, for he was at his best in ceremonial which he carried out with impressive gravity. His great achievement as Viceroy was the annexation of Burma, for which he was created a marquis.

He did not wish to remain his full time in India and asked for Rome as his retirement post. The appointment was highly popular, but signs of age were creeping up on him. His eyes gave trouble and he was deaf. In 1891 he was made Warden of the Cinque Ports, a pleasant sinecure for an elderly statesman. Then with Lytton's death there came, on 10 December, Salisbury's offer of 'the great prize of the diplomatic profession', which he accepted. He was 65. With Paris his successful career seemed to reach a turning point; the tide ebbed, and the last ten years left to him were a sad regression, ending in calamity.

The two unmarried Blackwood girls had no need to turn to a Byron or an Elwin. Their interests were entirely centred on their happy family life, the pivot of which was their father. Dufferin's eldest daughter was married and he frequently wrote to her, admitting to minor irritations, which he resented because they affected his dignity. His wife's protective wings could not shield him from the unforeseen. In one of his first letters from Paris he tells of an incident which evidently rankled: 'I have now got through all my official visits, and my official reception – a tiresome affair in uniform.' The word 'tiresome' suggests something had gone wrong. Lord Dufferin excelled in ritual for he was something of an actor. Still extremely good-looking, with the agile figure of a much younger man, he looked superb in uniform on which the highest decorations in the land, artistically arranged, proved how well he had served his country. Yet on this particular occasion his public image had suffered. In order to make the most effective impression on President Carnot he had learnt his speech by heart. Unfortunately he forgot one word and, afraid of altering the text which had already been handed in, was forced to refer to his paper. It was as well he did not attempt to think of a synonym. In India he had been known to temporize for several days in search of the right word when sending telegrams.

Sir Henry Durand, Foreign Secretary at Government House when Dufferin was Viceroy, has left far the best and most just appraisal of his character. The elaborate manner, the eyeglass, the blarney, were all apt to give an impression of affectation which belied his shrewdness and good sense. He had a hasty temper which was soon over. His staff were devoted to him. His real weaknesses were extravagance, sensitivity to criticism, especially from the press, and a strong dislike of detail. Anything he considered unimportant he brushed aside. During his last twenty years Dufferin relied heavily on a devoted private secretary, James Macferrar, who dealt brilliantly with those affairs which could be classed as unworthy of his master's personal attention. He had perfected an imitation of the Ambassador's handwriting to such a degree that he was able to write and sign his letters.

In *Helen's Tower* Sir Harold Nicolson gives an amusing sketch of staying in Paris at the age of five with his uncle by marriage. His mother was the younger sister by seventeen years of Lady Dufferin, of whom she was somewhat afraid. The small boy was quick to observe the veneration his uncle inspired in those around him, which was particularly noticeable in the behaviour of his aunt. She stopped speaking the moment he appeared, and flushed with shy pleasure at the gallantry of his compliments.

With such an example of deferential homage set by the Ambassador's most intimate companion, it followed that persons of all ranks in the embassy were on their mettle to see that he should never be contraried. When Harold arrived home from a shopping expedition to the Grand Magasin du Louvre with a large gaily-coloured balloon and inadvertently let go of the string, consternation was great as it rose up and lodged against the ceiling of the grand staircase. His horrified governess, Miss Plimsoll, summoned the footmen, who summoned the steward, Mr Nowell, the highest in the hierarchy of personnel, and almost as grand as the Ambassador. He was properly shocked at the sight of this extraneous object high above their heads. He instructed the footmen to reach it with brooms tied together with dusters, but in vain. 'Mr Nowell himself became perturbed. "I only hope," he said, "that his Excellency will not emerge." ' However, the steward was resourceful. He attached paper darts to pins and, after a few misses, pricked the balloon, which fell to the ground to the loud mortification of its owner.

After this adventure Miss Plimsoll and Mr Nowell became very friendly. With Harold in tow he showed her round the embassy. Dazzled by everything she saw and heard Miss Plimsoll became a votary of the Ambassador, worshipping on the fringe of the sacred circle. One day Harold asked her an interesting question: 'Is Uncle Dufferin a *great* man?' She answered slowly, 'He is the greatest man in the world.' Within the precincts of the embassy this indeed was the view, but not without, where he was not merely unpopular with the French, but actively disliked.

It was understandable, because much of his famous administrative career had been directed against their policy. The French believed they had been tricked by him in Syria, in Egypt, in Burma; they had not forgotten an association with Bismarck; and they suspected that he was going to undermine their hopes of a Franco-Russian alliance. Finally, just as he arrived in Paris, the British concluded an agreement with Siam without consulting France. This great gentleman who above all wanted to be liked, was denounced in *Le Figaro* as 'that acute and dangerous man', a wounding indictment to somebody hypersensitive about his reputation.

The calumnies about Dufferin were so rampant that early in 1893 he determined to refute them in a speech at the British Chamber of Commerce. He did not consult the Foreign Office but they afterwards agreed that something had to be done. He referred to the enormous sums of money which supposedly had been given him to corrupt French politicians and prevent the Franco-Russian alliance, and concluded with a sentence typical of his style: 'The fact is that since I arrived in Paris I have not spent a sixpence that has not gone into the pocket of my butcher or baker, or that harmful but necessary lady, the avenger of the sin of Adam, whose bills every householder who values his domestic peace pays with alacrity and without examination – I mean the family *couturière*.' The speech was accepted as humorous and 'gentleman-like', and a few months later a man was tried and condemned for forging embassy documents purporting to prove the bribes given by the Ambassador. The whole story was ridiculous and soon died down.

Even then Dufferin was not liked. His personality did not appeal to the French. When he smiled 'his slow, his almost silken smile', as Harold Nicolson put it, it failed to get the desired response. Nor was the detached Viceregal bearing of the inwardly shy Ambassadress admired. In August 1893 Blunt notes in his diary: 'My news from Paris is that Dufferin has undoubtedly been a failure there; he is too fond of paying little insincere compliments, and his wife is too ungenial.' This unpopularity is corroborated by Walpurga Lady Paget, who went to a luncheon in Paris where the only person to speak up for our ambassador was the artist who had been commissioned to paint his portrait, Benjamin Constant. 'All the other Frenchmen seemed to dislike him superlatively.'

At least in the large British colony the Dufferins were held in great esteem. In this sphere Lady Dufferin was at her ease and shone, as she had in India, as the guardian angel of the poorer residents. On their behalf she busied herself organizing bazaars and private theatricals. Getting up these plays, acting in charades or even just putting on fancy dress produced an unsuspected side of her personality. Like Lord Lyons, she seemed delighted to cast aside her protective armour directly she had the opportunity of impersonating some other character. The dignity melted away, she became excited, even frivolous.

Edward Blount was so deeply impressed by the great interest she had for her compatriots that he goes so far as to

The Garden,
1957
The Staircase,
showing the
Louis XVI
door, 1957

The Hall, May 1903, showing the original doors and handrail

state that 'the social functions of the Embassy were probably never more perfectly fulfilled' than in the time of the Dufferins. He also admired an ambassador whose most embellished rhetoric was delivered at the annual dinners of the British Chamber of Commerce. At that of March 1894 Dufferin embarked on the then state of Europe and the importance of England and France putting aside those differences which occasionally caused quarrels. He declared that the joint course of the two countries was comparable to 'a mighty river which rushes with unrivalled majesty along its appointed way', diplomatically ignoring those moments when the waters of the great river blended so unharmoniously that it seemed about to form a delta.

This speech was approved of by the Foreign Office and, as he included a tactful reference to 'the well-known magnanimity of the Russian Emperor', it proved that he was not actively working against a Franco-Russian Alliance. Moreover it won favour amongst an important group, all the royalty then wintering on the Riviera. He confessed to his daughter that all his life he had been anxious to please two or three audiences whenever he made a speech, 'like the circus riders who have to stand on the backs of several galloping horses at once'.

Every year the Queen firmly left her island when the climate was at its worst and the Ambassador would be in attendance on her at Nice for about a week. He was almost the only one left of her old friends and once, when apprehensive about ministerial changes in England, she told him that she sought his advice as she would have sought that of the Duke of Wellington.

Apart from increasing blindness and deafness Dufferin remained amazingly young in body and spirit and he himself felt he had changed little since he was a young man. The eloquent blarney still flowed as gaily as ever, he was the animated centre at any gathering, he had no difficulty in rising at five for an official occasion, he rode, he cycled, he sailed his yacht on stormy seas assisted only by a single juvenile deckhand. Yet after three years in Paris he wrote to his daughter that he was looking forward to retirement. 'When the clock will have struck 70,' on 21 June 1896, he planned to end his life of public service. He made his 'last dying speech and confession' that month at the British Chamber of Commerce, excelling himself in charm and cajolery, glossing over the often adverse attitude of the press, which he called its coyness, refusing to divulge his age to the ladies present, happy to be making way for a younger man.

The Dufferins left the embassy in October 1896. The distinguished career was over and the ex-Ambassador looked forward to retirement in the shadow of Helen's Tower, devoting his leisure to yet further improving Clandeboye, reading Greek and enlarging his Persian vocabulary. Instead, he was suddenly overwhelmed by 'an indescribable calamity which will cast a cloud over the remainder of my life'. He found himself involved in a shady business deal and ruined by a venture of so proletarian a nature as the Bakerloo Tube.

He had been exceedingly rich when he came of age but, with innate indifference to money matters, had muddled his fortune away. 'Heaven knows on what,' commented Blunt in his diary, 'for he was not a gambler nor a runner after women.' His foible was a certain vanity in liking to live on a grand scale, ignoring the cost.

It was the brother-in-law of Lady Lytton, Lord Loch, who unwittingly led him into disaster by suggesting that Dufferin might augment his income by taking his place as chairman of the London and Globe Finance Corporation, the managing director of which, Whitaker Wright, was a company promoter of enterprise and ingenuity. One of the companies he promoted, the Baker Street and Waterloo Railway, did not make the profit expected. Money had to be poured in and this he took from other companies, manipulating the balance sheets so as not to reveal losses. His conduct, though probably well-intended, was certainly fraudulent.

Dufferin could never have been suspected of complicity, but unquestionably he should have made himself aware of what was going on. Had James Macferrar not died in April 1900 the chairman might have been forced to give attention to the matter. As it was, though he had become uneasy and wanted to resign, he was persuaded to remain on. Then his eldest son, Lord Ava, was killed in the Boer War and when, in December, he heard that his younger son was seriously wounded he at once sent in his resignation to the London and Globe Corporation and prepared to sail for the Cape with his wife.

When Whitaker Wright broke the news that one of his subsidiary companies was insolvent and that the resignation and departure from England of the chairman would look like cowardice, Dufferin had no alternative but to withdraw his resignation, cancel his sailing and brace himself for the worst ordeal of his life, the general meeting on 9 January 1901. The setting was far removed from those in which he had been accustomed to preside, enhancing the prestige of his country by representing his sovereign with studied perfection. Mortified, frail and elderly, he who was so sensitive to criticism was now forced to appear with Whitaker Wright before two thousand defrauded share-holders in the Cannon Street Hotel.

It was no moment for charm, but he was so palpably honourable and sorry, so badly ruined himself, that there was more sympathy shown than resentment. Next morning, however, he must have winced when he read the leading article in *The Times* which let loose a little of its famous thunder and concluded with an indictment that would have deeply wounded the expert yachtsman: 'A pilot who is unskilled and incapable of bringing the ship into port is not to be excused for accepting duties he cannot fulfil because he is ready to go down bravely with the others if he runs the vessel on a rock.'*

On 22 January 1901 the Queen died. All Dufferin's career

* Firmly believing in the honesty of Whitaker Wright he did not live to see the case tried in 1904, a sentence of seven years imprisonment passed and the sensational suicide of the prisoner directly the trial was over.

had been in her service and he wrote that he had lost a kind friend of fifty years. He himself died at Clandeboye the following January. His last year had been tragic. The fates, having showered honours on him all his life, at the very end exposed him to the glare of publicity in a less favourable light, so that the world could see the weaknesses in his character which had prevented him from attaining greatness.

During the whole of their marriage his devoted wife watched over him, bearing the torch handed to her by her mother-in-law, who really occupied the first place in her husband's heart. Hariot Dufferin did not die till 1936. These long years of widowhood were remarkable for the emergence of a new personality, relaxed, stronger, independent, remembered as an affectionate and delightful grandmother by a younger generation. Victoria Sackville-West, the wife of Harold Nicolson, wove her story into a charming novel, *All Passion Spent*.

XIX

Sir Edmund Monson
1896—1905

After the departure of Lord Dufferin the Office of Works sent out an architect, C. L. Veale, to make a report on the furniture in the Paris embassy. Nearly a century after it had been acquired the wheel of taste had turned full circle and the Empire style was again admired. Veale was deeply impressed by what he found in the house and concerned about the quantity of valuable pieces which were piled up in the attics, either because they were no longer wanted or because of their bad condition. These, he recommended, should be sent to England to be restored and used elsewhere.

In 1902 Lord Esher, secretary to the Office of Works, decided to act on this advice and use the pieces for embellishing the Foreign Office. Fortunately the Secretary of State, Lord Lansdowne, strongly objected, arguing that it would be unwise to strip the embassy and that 'fine pieces of Empire furniture would not go with the hideous Victorian decorations' of the building. Seventy years later public opinion is just awakening to the fact that these decorations, too, have their merit and deserve preservation.

The successor to Dufferin was Sir Edmund Monson. He was born in 1834 and was a distinguished scholar and a Fellow of All Souls. His first post in the Diplomatic Service was to Paris in 1856 under the second Lord Cowley, who thought so highly of him that two years later he wrote to the head of the Foreign Office, 'Monson is one of the best and most intelligent Attachés I have ever had . . . [he] does the duty of paid Attaché without remuneration. If Lord

Malmesbury would sanction the payment of a small salary to Monson I should be very glad.' This golden recommendation and his reputation for hard work led to his being chosen as private secretary to Lyons in Washington, a position which he was eminently capable of fulfilling to the satisfaction of that exacting Ambassador.

Following this promising start came a few years of posts which gave little scope for his assiduity, so, discouraged by the lack of promotion, he decided to plunge into a political career. This was to prove a disappointment and in 1865 he was back in his old profession, contenting himself with the consulate in the Azores. After a few consul-generalships, at the age of 40 he became second secretary in Vienna. Promotion was slow at this period.

In 1881, at the age of 47, he married the daughter of a South American and the British Consul-General at Montevideo. In official life wives vary between being an asset and a handicap. Writing to her grandson, the Kaiser, the Queen had once thought fit to warn him that the wife of the Ambassador she proposed sending to Berlin was 'not a *grande dame*'. She explained with candour and good sense that there might have been a choice of several *grandes dames* 'but the husbands would not have done'.

Unquestionably Monson's wife did not do. Everybody conceded that she was pretty, but she was all of a-twitter, timid and gauche. When her husband was appointed in 1893 to the important Vienna embassy, she proved herself inadequate to the role of ambassadress. The Queen herself began to have qualms as to how she would go down with the French for on 1 October 1896 Lady Lytton put in her court diary: 'In the evening the Queen spoke very kindly about our popularity in Paris, that I ought to give Lady Monson hints to help her etc.'

The new Ambassador was a tall white-bearded man, shy and unable to express the kindness in his character. One of the embassy secretaries, Maurice Baring, describes him as: 'Academic with a large swaying presence and an inexhaustible supply of polished periods.' He was known to excel in the art of writing despatches but they were so long-winded that there seemed no reason why they should ever come to an end and 'one had the sensation of coasting pleasantly down-hill on a bicycle that had no brake, and save for an accident was not likely to stop'.

Monson had a difficult mission. He took over the embassy at a moment when anglophobia was approaching danger-point. Soon after his arrival there was a retrial of the celebrated Dreyfus case, for France itself had been divided over the original verdict. An outburst of British indignation against French injustice resulted in violent hatred of England. Our still-expanding empire also aroused much jealousy and we were without a friend in Europe. British occupation of Egypt in particular irritated France. Later this same year a defiant gesture on the part of a French army officer ostensibly acting on his own initiative further fanned the flames of ill-feeling between the two countries. Major Marchand with an escort of a hundred Senegalese troops made an historic march across Africa and planted the French flag at Fashoda within the boundaries of the Egyptian Sudan, then under British protection. When ordered off the territory he refused to move without instructions from his government.

Monson complained to the new Foreign Minister, Delcassé, to be told that, as France never recognized the British protectorate in the Upper Nile, the Major's expedition was merely 'a mission of civilization in an unclaimed land'. In the end Marchand was recalled but indignation on both sides was so great that there was talk of war. Salisbury, writing to the Queen of the violent jealousy of both Germany and France, admitted that whereas in Germany the Queen's personal influence with her grandson was a strong defence, 'in France we have no such protection'. Neverthe-less he discounted much of Monson's nervous apprehension because: 'Sir Edmund always tends to be a prophet of evil.'

He was not entirely satisfied with our ambassador who, at the beginning of this year, had delivered himself of a lengthy flow of oratory which received wide publicity and was furiously criticized. Again it was at the British Chamber of Commerce, with its audience largely composed of loyal compatriots, that Sir Edmund aired his views on Anglo-French relations without consulting the Foreign Office. Free-wheeling downhill on his bicycle it was a pity that the Ambassador did not crash before he reached his peroration which was directed against French officials and press. He ended: 'I would earnestly ask them to discountenance and abstain from the continuance of that policy of pin-pricks.'

The country whose goodwill he had been appointed to cultivate, was stung to fury. Indignant headlines blazed across the newspapers retorting that this was typical of British arrogance, that it amounted to a declaration of war, that the only thing for France to do was to strengthen her fortifications and build more cruisers. The Foreign Minister was urged to ask the Secretary of State whether it was on his instructions that his Ambassador fancied himself authorized not only to represent the Foreign Office but to direct French foreign policy, and the majority of the French Cabinet pressed for the recall of Monson.

There were plenty of francophobes in England to applaud 'the Pin-pricks speech' as it was now called. Even *The Times* backed it up, because the foreign policy of France had a tendency to thwart us 'not in pursuit of any solid French interest, but merely for the love of annoying us'. Others were profoundly shocked, and Salisbury can have been far from happy for an ingeniously-worded communiqué was issued from the embassy stating that 'the Ambassador's idea has not been understood, or was not presented with sufficient clearness'. It ended by assuring the French that Sir Edmund would never think of giving offence. Thus, rather lamely, the incident was closed.

During this diplomatic storm, Maurice Baring, the son of Lord Revelstoke, arrived at the embassy. He found the work boring. The younger members of the staff had to copy out despatches, register them, put them away and decipher telegrams which sometimes arrived at night. The Ambassador remained a remote figure the other side of the courtyard who never came into the Chancery and conveyed his displeasure in a memorandum in red ink sent over in a red box. Much of the time was spent in dull protocol, going to funerals, meeting people at railway stations or dealing civilly with all the cranks who called at the embassy. However, one evening a shocking piece of news burst on the world and it was the newly-arrived attaché who happened to be on duty and answered the telephone: he was told that President Faure had suddenly died.*

Dullness prevailed within the embassy but the Chancery was a particularly brilliant one. Baring, witty, poetic, pure, lived in a dream-world of 'bright adventure', forever evoking legends of chivalry and glamour. But sometimes this guileless man was prompted to behave with the absurdity of a clown. Possibly this was more an outlet for suppressed emotion than ordinary high spirits, such as the time he went berserk in the Chancery. During a friendly argument with another junior secretary he threw an inkpot at him, the shot was returned. The black ink exhausted, they started on the red, carrying the fight down the stairs, into the courtyard, right out into the Faubourg St-Honoré, where even the embassy walls got bespattered. After the battle the culprits were appalled at the mess, their dread being lest by some ill-chance the Ambassador might for once decide to look in at the Chancery.

In October 1899 the South African War was declared and anti-British feeling reached its zenith. Even the aged Queen, always a respected and popular figure in France, was now abused and ridiculed, and when the Prince of Wales spent a night at the embassy he was hissed in the streets. In April 1900 he refused to attend the Paris Exhibition, at which he was to open the British Pavilion, because he feared the mob might insult him.

* Faure died in compromising circumstances in Josephine's blue and silver salon at the Elysée. The hastily summoned priest anxiously asked, 'Est-ce-que Monsieur le Président a toujours sa connaissance?' to which the huissier gave the memorable reply, 'Elle est déjà partie par la porte de service'.

The heir to the throne had always been interested in Foreign Affairs but it was not till he was 51 that he was given possession of the gold key used by his father to open the Foreign Office box. In January 1901 he succeeded to a country enriched by a vast empire but intensely unpopular in Europe. During the years he had been deprived of responsibility, he had travelled much and had become a cosmopolitan man of the world with a far greater knowledge of foreign countries than most royalty. Of all the official papers he now had to read, the Foreign Office despatches were those which most interested him and he also liked his more important ambassadors in Europe to keep him even better informed by writing him private letters.

Edward VII gladly turned his attention to France. The impression made on his adolescent mind nearly fifty years earlier had never faded. Frequently he had been back there, privately as well as officially, and all his sympathies were with that country. Convinced that the present animosity between England and France must be replaced by cordiality, he decided to try to win over the French people through his own tact and charm.

He laid his plans with skill and in the face of no enthusiasm from the Secretary of State, the Foreign Office, or the Ambassador to France. In the spring of 1903 he sailed off on the royal yacht, ostensibly to pay visits following his accession to the kings of Portugal and Spain. Instead of taking with him the obligatory cabinet minister he chose an under-secretary in the Foreign Office, Charles Hardinge. When Lansdowne objected to his not being in the government the King insisted that Hardinge be raised to the rank of Minister Plenipotentiary. One of the new minister's functions was to write the King's speeches. Only after they were well at sea and telegrams had to be deciphered did the King's private secretary, Frederick Ponsonby, discover that their journey was to finish up in Paris.

Not much time had been given to make the necessary preparations there and agitation and apprehension seethed within the embassy. The quiet scholarly way of life of

Monson was rudely disturbed, and Lady Monson dithered with nerves. In addition the house was by no means in a fit condition to receive the Sovereign. Even the furniture was not considered suitable, so an English architect who lived in Paris was called in to advise.

Vye Parminter swiftly transformed the interior by eliminating some of the contemporary pieces from Maple (who had opened a branch in Paris), which had cluttered up the ground and first floor rooms since the arrival of the Monsons. Parminter had the unusual idea of filling the empty spaces abhorred by Edwardians by borrowing quantities more Empire furniture from the French *Garde Meuble*. In photographs taken at the time many of these pieces can be recognized as being now at Compiègne and elsewhere. The architect was entirely satisfied with the result and 'the State Bedroom, in particular, was rendered exceptionally handsome'. The wallpaper was replaced by red silk of the same design as is now in the room, and further embellished with a tapestry, a portrait of the Emperor of Austria, an important writing table, fire-dogs and screen all from Fontainebleau. Ornamental handles were put on the doors of the royal apartments, shades on all the chandeliers (now lit by electric light), antimacassar lace on the Empire furniture. The rooms were further crowded after the fashion of the day with a profusion of flowers and plants and in the hall a jungle of greenery soared up the sweep of the staircase. The *marquise* or glass porch was hung with velvet, there were electric illuminations for the street and garden, and a shed for the guard was built in the courtyard. The Treasury considered the expense of all this 'extraordinary' but agreed that it had to be met because it was on account of the King.

Part of the trepidation over this visit arose because the Monarch was not always easy to deal with. He had, on attaining authority, developed into a serious character with a strong sense of duty, anxious to do the right thing and ready to rely on his advisers. Kind, intelligent and intuitive, he had a winning charm which he knew how to use with the instinct of an artist. But he was also apt to get bored or irritable or suddenly flare up in a rage. Angry explosions of this sort were best countered with extreme tact and firmness, for he respected those who stood up to him.

The King had little in common with Monson, nor was Lady Monson the type of woman who would please him. Maurice de Bunsen, an able diplomat, had recently returned to Paris with the rank of minister. He thought the Ambassador looked ill and had little work left in him. The minister was invited up to Balmoral to discuss the matter and his young wife was deputed to help Lady Monson. She kept a diary of the royal visit.

It has been said that 'every May belongs to Paris', and on a glorious spring afternoon, the King arrived at the Porte Dauphine station. He drove along the Avenue du Bois (now renamed the Avenue Foch) and the Champs-Elysées, which were lined with troops and crowded with people. It was an anxious moment as the whole scheme could easily prove to be a blunder. There were cheers, but they were said to be in honour of the President, and clear cries of '*Vivent les Boers, Vive Fashoda!*' An even older hatred was revived with '*Vive Jeanne d'Arc!*' Impervious to all this, the King behaved with amiable dignity, smiling and saluting as though he were being acclaimed as the highly popular friend of France and conveying the impression that he was very happy to be among these critical people.

As the procession approached the Faubourg St-Honoré the excitement within the embassy became intense. The wives were gathered at the Chancery windows having been told they would not be wanted at the house. Then, just as the guns started to boom, Lady Monson panicked, changed her mind and sent a message that they must all come over at once to help receive the King. Nothing could have been more awkward for the wife of the minister. She was in deep mourning and black was a colour not favoured by royalty, she was in an old dress and she was pregnant. She tore off her crêpe veil, somebody lent her the regulation white kid gloves, somebody else a fur to hide her condition and they all scuttled across the courtyard just in time. Just in time also to persuade the Ambassadress to go down the steps to receive the King and kiss his hand there rather than to stay at the top. 'We convinced her that this must be done,' wrote Mrs de Bunsen in her diary.

It was at once evident that the Monarch was in a bad temper. He had been upset by the fact that the French soldiers failed to present arms. No one had thought fit to warn the King that in 1902 the French Army gave up presentation of arms except in the cavalry. (This regulation remained in force till 1914.) Directly he entered the hall he brusquely said to Sir Edmund, 'See the President off!' though, according to the de Bunsens, Loubet gave the impression that he expected to be invited in; he then asked to have the staff presented to him, saying that he did not know a single one, and retired into the drawing-room to have tea. It was an unpromising start to the visit.

After dinner they sat among the plants in the gallery waiting to go to the theatre. Suddenly the King got irritable, petulantly supposing that somebody would tell him it was time to go, and when the arrival of the President was announced he became furious because he had not been informed that it was the President himself who would be coming. He said, with truth, that 'things were disgracefully managed'. The whole party drove off to the Comédie Française to see a play called *L'autre Danger*, which Mrs de Bunsen disliked because it was about a daughter who falls in love with her mother's lover.

During the interval the King suddenly began to win through the wall of antagonism, doing so entirely by gallantry which he instinctively knew would not fail. He insisted on mixing informally with the crowds in the foyer to the alarm of the police, and when he perceived a well-known actress, Jeanne Granier, he went straight up to her, kissed her hand and told her how much he had admired seeing her act in London when she represented all the grace and spirit of France. This charming gesture gave great pleasure to those who heard it and was repeated throughout the theatre.

Next day at the Hôtel de Ville he made a brief spontaneous speech, not composed by Hardinge, which unmistakably came straight from the heart. It had been the suggestion of the French Ambassador in London that he approach the people in this manner. The King told his audience how delighted he was to be in Paris '*où je me trouve toujours comme si j'étais chez moi*'. Affectionate and simple, this was Edward VII at his best. There were wild acclamations and from then on it was plain sailing.

A few awkward moments were, of course, inevitable, such as when, in the presidential box at the Longchamps races, he found himself stuck between two unattractive women, Madame Loubet and the wife of the Préfet of Paris. This he could not take. Beckoning to Ponsonby he whispered, 'Do anything that will get me out of this,' which his private secretary cleverly did by suggesting that the Jockey Club should invite him over for one race.

On Sunday the King went to the British church and insisted on sitting in the body of the church instead of in the gallery. The chairs, Mrs de Bunsen tells us, were in rags and needed re-covering. This may explain why seven Directoire armchairs from the embassy were moved over to the church and remained there, forgotten, until 1959 when they were brought back. This same day the King held an investiture. When he gave the minister the CVO he noted with approval that here was one member of the embassy making an excellent impression on the French.

On Sunday evening he gave a large ministerial dinner followed by a reception. The King was in an excellent mood and much amused when, at a late hour, Hardinge had to tell him that nobody could leave because he was sitting in the ante-room. He said he was glad of the chance of going to bed and did so at once. Next morning Mrs de Bunsen describes how they all sat in the gallery till it was time for the President to fetch the King and take him to the train.

His luck held till the last minute for no sooner had they reached the station than a terrific thunderstorm burst over Paris.

The *Entente Cordiale* was signed on 4 April 1904 in London at the French Embassy at Albert Gate. By it France was given a free hand in Morocco, Britain likewise in Egypt. Concessions were made to France in central Africa, to Britain in Newfoundland over the fishing rights, and various other differences were settled.

Peace and exhaustion descended on the embassy. The Ambassador confided to de Bunsen that the Monarch had been in a vile temper the whole time and never once thanked him for anything or expressed himself satisfied in any way. The disgruntled diplomat intended to present his letters of recall in December.

The visit, however, had been brilliantly successful. Through perseverance and personality Edward VII had deftly turned the scales. Overnight Britain became popular in France: the King was *nôtre bon Edouard,* no longer was Albion perfidious, no longer did the stage ridicule Englishwomen, and Robert Vansittart, the new resident clerk, was the first Englishman elected to the Jockey Club since Fashoda.

The King had seen only too clearly what he had all along suspected, that Sir Edmund was not the right man for the then most important diplomatic post. The 70-year-old Ambassador retired with a baronetcy on 1 January 1905. He died in 1909.

XX

Lord Bertie of Thame
1905—1918

In the Foreign Office Francis Bertie was known as the Bull, an apt nickname for somebody whose instinct was to toss and gore people at sight if they appeared likely to give him any trouble.

He was an eccentric who ranks as one of the last of the old school of diplomats and has even been called the last great ambassador. His conception of his role was already obsolete by the turn of the century and he often amazed his own government and compatriots by the independence of his actions. Since he was the bodily representative of the King in France he disdained to consider himself an emissary at the beck and call of the Secretary of State, and ministers at the Quai d'Orsay never failed to be impressed by his forthright domination.

He enjoyed the trappings of his office as something due to his importance. He was the last of our envoys to France to have a state coach (before the First World War the German Representative was the only other diplomat in Paris to possess one) and when, in his scarlet mantle of Knight Grand Cross of the Order of the Bath and his feathered hat, he descended the red-carpeted steps of the embassy to drive round to the Elysée the bystanders in the Faubourg could be in no doubt that *la Grande Bretagne* was a great power.

Directly the retirement of Monson was announced in August 1904 the King was determined to have the embassy

Lord Bertie in what
is now the Library

Lord Derby. Port-
rait by Sir John
Lavery

The Salon Vert in Lord Lytton's time. The earliest known photograph of the Embassy, showing the Empire chairs *capitonnées*
The White and Gold Drawing-room, 1910. Originally the Salon Vert

renovated and made worthy of its new prestige. The Edwardian era was an unfortunate moment in which to turn architects and decorators loose on such a building, with no expense spared, in order to achieve the elaborate taste then admired. It cost £23,000. Vye Parminter was architect in charge; Sir Henry Tanner, chief architect to the Board of Works and a great francophile, sent directions from London and an amateur friend of the new Ambassador, George Hoentsche, advised.

Between these three much of the old character of the house was changed. It was the entrance hall and staircase which suffered most. Redecorated in what has been described as *le style Pont Alexandre*, the columns and pilasters were preserved but covered up with stuccotine simulating stonework, and opposite the front door a shallow niche was made. The iron handrail of the eighteenth century was replaced by brass, the old doors repanelled with looking-glass, the stone and marble floor which had echoed to the footsteps of Mirabeau, Pauline and the Iron Duke was relaid. More looking-glass was put in the ballroom to reflect Edwardian glitter, the state dining-room was redecorated in the early twentieth-century conception of the eighteenth century with gilded plasterwork, and a large set of imitation Louis XVI chairs was bought. One of the worst features was the fixing of gilded pelmets on nearly all the ground floor and first floor rooms, thus ruining cornices and, in the Victoria Room, cutting into the Louis XV mirror between the windows.

A lift to the second floor was squeezed into the east staircase. On the first floor the private dining-room was completely redone in order to take a set of *Leynières* tapestries which had been discovered, many years before, rolled up in Lord Malmesbury's house at the old Foreign Office.* The Salon Vert of Lady Granville was repanelled in Parminter's version of the Empire style, her galleries were stuccotined

* Before the present building was finished in 1868 the Foreign Office, which was on the same site, consisted of several adjoining houses.

like the hall, and the fountain was removed and dumped at the bottom of the garden, where it still stands not even axial with the centre of the house. Parminter then had the idea of raising the roofs of the Chancery and the corresponding pavilion. The Treasury did not object to an extra £5,000 being spent on this, but it was the King himself who cautiously suggested that a French architect should be consulted, and the scheme was abandoned.

Only five years after this extensive overhaul a new predicament arose. The Rue du Faubourg for a short while became a bus route, whereupon the house trembled violently as many of the structural timbers were defective. All the floors were taken up, which cost another £6,000. The Elysée reacted with the same alarming quiver. Madame Fallières, the wife of the then President, lunching at the embassy, complained how she and her very fat husband were even shaken in their bed. Lord Bertie's characteristic comment was that their bed must have been accustomed to tremors of another nature.

The Ambassadress who moved into the transformed house was Feodorewna Wellesley, the girl destined for Wilfrid Blunt. The impression she now made on one of the secretaries was 'a dear old thing, very ugly'. She had considerable dignity and when she entered a room, always wearing long white kid gloves however informal the occasion, everybody was aware of the fact. Attaching immense importance to the name of Wellesley, she did not bother to be a good hostess. Good-humoured, uninteresting, detached, there was but one thing which roused her to animation and that was a game of poker.

Francis Leveson Bertie was the second son of the 6th Earl of Abingdon. Born in 1844, he entered the Foreign Office at the age of nineteen. There he remained for the next forty years, having rapidly earned the reputation of being particularly able, shrewd and trustworthy. His outstanding and undiplomatic characteristic was an extraordinarily blunt manner that sometimes amounted to downright rudeness, and it was precisely this which, as he acquired more power, got exaggerated to such a degree that he became famed for his outrageous remarks.

In 1874 he married. The choice was a strange one, for his taste was for women with pretty faces who amused him. There was one son, Vere, born in 1878. At the age of 59, he was sent as ambassador to Rome, where it was found that his mocking tongue could hold its own amid the notorious gossip of Roman society. When, only a year later, the appointment to Paris was announced, fantastic stories reached the embassy of what was in store.

This original and strange man was full of vitality and extremely entertaining. Short, thickset, with curly white hair and moustache, his face was rubicund; it turned to puce when indignation was aroused, a frequent manifestation, and then his eyes blazed with fury as he let forth a stream of invective.

The junior staff grew to have an affection for their alarming chief. He would often ask them to the embassy and show them kindness. But very different treatment was meted out to senior members of the Chancery and those who worked close to him – counsellors, service attachés, private secretaries – often had to submit to tiresome bullying. It amused him to watch a man lose his temper and make a fool of himself, for he had an impish streak.

But Bertie is particularly remembered for his unparalleled coarseness. He was a Rabelaisian of the English prep school variety. It was as though, in one respect, he had never grown up, not even reaching the more mature stage of adolescence. Obscenity obsessed him, and in his collection of eighteenth-century pornographic prints the scene that interested him most was not amorous but of earthy vulgarity. The more celebrated stories about him are unprintable, some hardly recountable. This aspect of the Ambassador's character was exclusively reserved for his compatriots. The French were not even aware that it existed, with the possible exception of Clemenceau, who would have appreciated it.

That this peculiar man should have been chosen for our

most important embassy was considered by many at home to be a serious mistake, but the choice proved an excellent one for he was deeply respected in France.

It is not surprising that the Chancery was in a state of permanent agitation from the moment of Sir Francis's arrival. He could observe their movements from his study window and reprimand them if he thought they were slacking or stopping work too soon. The younger secretaries sometimes crept out of their office on all fours. They managed to get much enjoyment out of him. Vansittart describes how they worked out that the only way to handle him was to 'wear him down early by junior picador and bandarillo before the matador, or Counsellor, finished him up with the day's signatures'.

The Ambassador was continually popping over to see what was going on. Seizing one of his top hats which lay in a row on the hall table, each with a handkerchief in readiness on top, the stocky tail-coated figure with trousers pressed down the sides crossed the courtyard to appear suddenly among his staff. Regardless of their seniority he might tell them that they were burning too much electricity and, switching off the lights, leave them in the half dark; if he happened to overhear a snatch of conversation he would interject a vulgar comment; did he perceive dust on the window he wrote a lewd word in it with his finger. One day he breezed in to confront a particularly mild peer with, 'Well, my lord, did you leave her half dead?' and he once asked a secretary suffering from a cold if he had slept with a damp woman.

Vansittart found the key to his irascible chief when, to stop him telephoning him early at his flat to do commissions on the way to the embassy, he told his servant to say he had not yet come home. The success of this excuse was electric – 'We then got on like a disorderly house on fire – ' and Van discovered that this rude, coarse man had a kind heart and a respectable private life.

A young secretary, Hugh Gurney, was also one of those who maintained that the Ambassador could be tamed, and

succeeded in doing so out of sheer niceness. Soon he became
Bertie's constant companion on his afternoon walks, the
object of which was to find pornographic prints. The worst
of these hung in his study on the reverse side of those
depicting irreproachable subjects so that the room could, at
will, be made to look proper or otherwise.

Gurney was also in demand by the Ambassadress as a
card player. Ready money was necessary for those who sat
down with Lady Feo. One of the honorary attachés has
described a typical scene at the end of a grand dinner-party.
As the last guest disappeared out of view down the staircase
the Ambassador expressed his relief by dancing a jig on the
landing while the Ambassadress began to round up her
poker players and settled down to a late night's gamb-
ling.

In the summer Bertie discarded his tails and top hat for a
light grey suit and a broad-brimmed panama, the Chancery
doing likewise. He had his meals in the central drawing-
room on the ground floor. The Ambassadress went to
England and then there arrived Lady Algernon Gordon-
Lennox, sister of the notorious Countess of Warwick,
lovely and extremely intelligent. The whole atmosphere
changed, for Bertie was transformed into a happy schoolboy.
With Lady Algy he could enjoy serious conversation as well
as the racy Edwardian jokes which were bandied to and
fro, the puns, the *double-entendres*. He wrote to her every day
and left her his papers, some of which, after his death, she
edited and published as his World War Diary.

Her sister used to stay with Elinor Glyn, who then lived in
Paris, and when Thomas Powell, a young honorary attaché,
arrived to call on the authoress of *Three Weeks* he had the
surprise of colliding with his Ambassador, who had come
to see Lady Warwick. This was the sort of company of
which Sir Francis approved and he would have guffawed
heartily. There would have been no guffaw and little understanding if, when making one of his regular visits to the
salon of the well-known hostess, Comtesse Adhéaume de
Chevigné in the nearby Rue Anjou, he had run into his

private secretary calling on the brilliant young writer, Jean Cocteau, who lived in the same building.

The private secretary stood in great awe of Sir Francis. Reginald Bridgeman should have been eminently acceptable, being the nephew of the 4th Earl of Bridgeman, intelligent, efficient, an excellent talker, and a man of great charm. But intrinsically the two had little in common, and Bridgeman, despite the angry snorts of his master, moved in a set whose interests and activities were beyond the Ambassador's comprehension. He lived in the rooms immediately to the right of the front door with a private entrance from the courtyard, and here Cocteau came, staying for hours discussing art and life with his English friend. '*L'ours blanc*,' as Cocteau nicknamed Bertie, ignored the aesthetic flowering which made Paris the centre of the artistic world before the First World War. Bertie was a social snob who had no truck with such people. He was thoroughly at home in the world of the Faubourg St Germain, while in that of politics he had established his reputation as the Ambassador of the highest importance, and had already formed a valuable friendship with Georges Clemenceau, in whose rough vigour there was a counterpart of himself. The Tiger and the Bull saw eye to eye.

Well pleased with his representative, the King frequently came over to Paris or passed through, sometimes staying at the old Bristol Hotel as the Duke of Lancaster. In February 1907 he took over the entire embassy for a week travelling incognito and bringing with him Queen Alexandra. Giving but ten days to make the necessary arrangements a tactfully worded letter came from Sandringham announcing the royal intention. It was suggested that the Berties should move to an hotel, the Ambassador retaining the private secretary's room on the ground floor for his own use. The King would sleep in Pauline Borghese's bed and the Queen on the second floor.

Hitherto the Queen had never accompanied her husband on his sprees to Paris and she was enchanted to be included in this informal visit. On the arm of the Duke of Lancaster she strolled along the Faubourg, went to the theatre and even lunched and dined in restaurants. Everywhere the distinguished couple were greeted with enthusiasm and their privacy respected.

Edward VII died in 1910 and two years later, in April, the new King and Queen made their state visit to France. They formed a striking contrast to their predecessors. George V, a downright man full of integrity and goodwill, lacked the winning charm of his father, and Queen Mary's shyness made her appear stiff. Incapable of that smile that had come so naturally to her mother-in-law, she scored through brilliant inspiration. She suggested that the offering of the King to mark the occasion should be the restoration to France of the bronzes by Desjardins from the Place des Victoires. These six medallions, which had decorated the bases of the torches destroyed during the revolution, had been acquired by the Prince Regent. This magnificent gift, to be presented the night of Poincaré's banquet, was delivered to the Elysée and unpacked at the last moment by one of the presidential staff who found six busts of the King and Queen inside the packing case. There was just time to rectify the mistake. The bronzes are in the Louvre.

Sir Francis reached 70 in 1914, at the end of which year it was the intention of the Foreign Office to retire him and appoint in his place the Permanent Under-Secretary, Sir Arthur Nicolson. Meanwhile war broke out and ended a way of living of which Bertie was the epitome. On 26 July Austria-Hungary declared war on Serbia. Fulminating against Russia for the 'exploded pretension that she is, by right, the protectress of all Slavs . . . What rubbish!', Bertie urged France to curb the zeal of her ally. France argued that, if we declared our solidarity with her and Russia, Germany would not dare go to war. The Ambassador thought that the quarrel with Serbia was not one in which Britain ought to fight and that it would be difficult to arouse enthusiasm in such a cause.

Russia mobilized on the 30th, followed by Germany and France on 1 August, and the same day Germany declared war on Russia. Anguished eyes were turned towards Britain to see what she would do and the doors on to the Faubourg were kept shut lest the crowds start the old cry of 'Perfide Albion'. At 12.15 on 5 August, Britain declared war on Germany. Paris went wild with excitement. Bertie was cheered, embraced, his hand clasped, and well-wishers invaded the courtyard.

His diary shows his strange character in a new and sympathetic light. He minded the war intensely. His thoughts were continually with our armed forces and when he went for his constitutional he could not enjoy the peace of the Bois de Boulogne for thinking of the horrors going on at the front. 'How many loved ones will never return,' he wrote, 'it makes my old heart ache.' Then something of his old pugnacious self was reasserted in his fierce hatred of German aggression, and he hoped that all those responsible would be 'well hanged' at the end of the war.

Anxiety mounted when the Allies were forced to retreat from Mons on 26 August. Fighting at Compiègne was reported on the 30th and confidential papers were burned preparatory to possible evacuation. When the Government decided to move to Bordeaux on 2 September the chancery had ten hours' notice to make arrangements.

Early in December Bertie heard that the Secretary of State hoped he would remain on as ambassador for the duration of the war. A week later the Government was able to return to Paris. He lived alone with rooms shut up, objects put away, a skeleton staff to look after him and black cloth in the skylighted galleries. He now used Pauline Borghese's bedroom as his sitting-room and enjoyed showing it to people who came to see him, getting pleasure from shocking them with his comments. He had returned to a Paris of dark streets at night, early hours, rich friends living on a reduced scale and sorrowing families.

He still saw the politicians but he no longer had the position of importance he normally held and was beginning to feel out of things. Shorn of responsibility, he resented the various missions, military and otherwise, which were being set up in Paris. His pet aversion was the second Viscount Esher, who came 'in fancy khaki'. Esher had some excuse to get himself out of civilian clothes because he was Honorary Colonel of a Regiment and, as his card proclaimed, *Chef des Territorieux Britanniques*. Representing the Red Cross, he also appeared to have a somewhat mysterious position which permitted him to write on paper entitled *Intelligence Militaire*. Handsome, able and scholarly, having had the personal friendship of Edward VII, he retained close touch with George V, whom he made a point of keeping well-informed on any gossip of interest. He was forever advising and receiving confidences.

The courtier and the diplomat were the antithesis of each other: the one charming, suave, tactful, the other blunt, veracious, staunch. In spite of their instinctive mutual dislike Esher was always invited to the embassy for the Ambassador was as glad to hear the latest gossip as it gratified his guest to impart it (though in his diary Bertie took care to qualify the information with a cynical 'according to his own account' or 'he says'). Esher also wrote frequent letters with tit-bits of news which he airily begged Sir Francis not to answer. In these he relished displaying his close connection with the court: 'I avoided Windsor (on a plea of fatigue)'.

An additional reason for scoffing at Esher was his close collaboration with the new military attaché, another thorn in Bertie's flesh. Colonel Le Roy Lewis had been thrust on him, suddenly turning up in May 1915 from Buenos Aires without the Ambassador having been previously informed, so, not surprisingly, he got a scurvy reception. Promptly sent off to London for proper instructions, he had to present himself at the embassy all over again. The good-looking military attaché was a mysterious character. Able and efficient, he excelled at making arrangements for the numerous conferences that were taking place and he soon established himself as somebody who knew what was going on behind the scenes. It transpired that he had been sent to Paris because Kitchener did not like him. His new chief found him equally incompatible.

With his dander up (to quote Bertie's favourite expression), the Ambassador hit out right and left at inefficiency, mistaken policy, idiotic tactics, German barbarity, and at people who circulated balderdash. Certain cabinet ministers he held in odium, in particular the First Lord of the Admiralty, though, in a sense, he was responsible for the existence of this great historical figure. Long ago at a ball at Cowes it had been young Frank Bertie who introduced Lord Randolph Churchill to Miss Jennie Jerome.

It is difficult now to realize the extent to which Winston Churchill was criticized before the Second World War made him the man of destiny he always believed he would become. Brilliant, ebullient, teeming with ideas, he was also thought to be over-impulsive, uncontrollable, and so bumptious that Lloyd George said of him that if you threw him out of the window he would come back down the chimney. Winston now arrived at the Ritz, incognito to avoid publicity yet attracting attention, entertaining naval people and dining at the Ministère de la Marine. He did not call at the embassy, he merely sent a message through the naval attaché that he had no time to do so.

Italy entered the war in May and Bertie, who had been kept busy over the negotiations, now had even less to do. His private diary shows him finding contentment watching the changes of season in the embassy garden. Whatever the weather, his immediate reaction was the effect it must have on the men in the trenches. However, he continued to rule his Chancery with vigour. This year a new second secretary, agreeable and efficient, joined the embassy. Had the opinion of his then colleagues been sought, Neville Henderson would not, some thirty years later, have found himself in the crucial post of ambassador to Hitlerian Germany. The chancery believed he had missed his vocation since he was clearly cut out to be an excellent adjutant in a cavalry regiment rather than a discerning diplomat.

The Ambassador had reservations about him though he praised his handwriting. One evening Henderson, who believed he was doing particularly well in Paris, wandered into the chancery and had the opportunity of seeing a telegram stating that, at Bertie's express wish, he was to proceed to Athens forthwith. He had the advantage of the night in which to plan his action before the dreaded interview next morning, at which he contrived to summon up a firmness of purpose which he later failed to display to Hitler. If he could not stay on in Paris, he intended to resign from the service and join up as a private under a false name. Bertie lamely gave in, but Henderson was not invited inside the embassy for a whole year.

Though rewarded with a barony and Doyen of the Diplomatic Corps, the Ambassador was not reconciled to his anomalous position. He could only vituperate about the idiocy with which affairs were being conducted. His constant dread was mediation before Germany had been brought to her knees. He was particularly concerned because Esher went about spreading the rumour that France might seek a separate peace. Though Bertie reassured our Head of Secret Intelligence he feared that Haig, the friend of Esher, might be impressed by this story, as well as certain people in London whom he suspected of flabbiness. The Ambassador was not the only person who mistrusted Esher and his mysterious activities. That autumn a question was asked in the Commons demanding to know what department exactly he represented, which received the nebulous reply from Lord Robert Cecil that he had no definite appointment but was 'charged from time to time with particular tasks of a military character'.

In March 1917 Bertie was in bed for a month with a serious attack of pneumonia from which he recovered 'thanks to a good doctor, a good constitution and youth!'. His old friend, Charles Hardinge, now Permanent Under-Secretary at the Foreign Office, wrote to him, 'I expect you are pretty difficult to manage when you are ill as you are hardly easy when you are well.' The severity of Bertie's illness gave rise to the belief that he would be forced to retire, but when Lloyd George came through Paris in the end of April he was amazed to find him looking remarkably well and even more astonished at the disparaging manner with which he treated the editor of *Le Matin*, who was waiting to see the Prime Minister. The Ambassador boasted that he had never given an interview nor made a statement to the press and had no wish even to make the acquaintance of the editor.

In June it began to dawn on Bertie that an intrigue was afoot to get him out of the embassy and he suspected the identity of the chief instigator. Whoever came to see him at this time was grumpily received with the query, 'What is that fellow Esher doing here?' His conjecture was right. On 8 May Esher, an inveterate letter-writer, had written to Lord Derby, now Minister of War, reporting that the Ambassador no longer spoke to the military attaché, who was the only person in the embassy who knew what was going on. He even went so far as to say that, were it not for the colonel, England would be unrepresented in France.

As a result of this letter, Derby came to Paris and asked Esher whether he would object to his pressing Lloyd George to appoint him in Bertie's place with Sir Henry Wilson, Chief Liaison Officer, in Le Roy Lewis's. Esher comments, 'I am very doubtful about the wisdom of either, although Douglas Haig, who later spoke to me on the subject, urges both strongly. I should make an unconventional Ambassador, and Henry a fairly unusual type of Military Attaché.' He adds that Haig was determined on it, and 'I cannot imagine anything I should detest more. The fates will be kinder than one's friends.' For an hour Esher walked with Wilson round the Tuileries gardens, elaborating a plan which was unprecedented and hardly workable. There were to be two ambassadors: Esher was to watch over military matters with Wilson as chief adviser; the other, surprisingly enough, was to be Le Roy Lewis, charged with civil matters. Wilson states that Derby, 'primed with this scheme', was to press it on Lloyd George.

The news that the Ambassador's resignation was imminent appeared in an Exchange Telegraph Company an-

nouncement on 9 June, correlating it with an audience he
had had at Buckingham Palace two days earlier. In fact his
position was, for the present, assured. Championship had
come from an unexpected quarter, where Esher must have
counted upon support for himself. The King confided in
Bertie that the Prime Minister wished to make a change in
Paris but that he had done his best, and would continue to
do so, to put a stop to this. Paul Cambon, Bertie's equally
remarkable opposite number in London, had told the King
that he was the best informed Ambassador there had ever
been in Paris and it would be a great mistake to move
him.

On the 12th, *The Times* came out with what Bertie calls
'a very handsome statement' at the head of its leading
articles, trusting that the current report was entirely baseless,
praising his record and winding up with the warning: 'We
cannot afford to relax our vigilance or to change the guard
in positions where the most tried and trusty sentinels are
needed.' Triumphantly the Ambassador returned to his post
and, when he went to meet the King and Queen at Abbe-
ville on their visit to military headquarters in July, George V
again assured him that he would do all he could to retain
him in France.

But Esher's machinations were by no means ended. The
Secretary of State was also in Paris for the conference and
Bertie reported to Balfour, who was dining with him tête-
à-tête in the Ionian Room, how Esher had advised the
Governor-General of Algeria to discuss the Persian Oil
Concession with Le Roy Lewis because he was the only
intelligent person at the embassy. The military attaché
cultivated friends with influence and, about this time, he
was given the Croix de Guerre avec Palme, which the
Ambassador considered 'pretty hot'. The King's private
secretary, Lord Stamfordham, agreed that it was excessive
reward for somebody who had never been in the trenches.
Le Roy Lewis's private life was now the subject of gossip
for the colonel, a married man, was living at the Ritz with
a Mademoiselle Jeanne Salvarte, the ex-wife of a German

whose political past aroused suspicion.

The war went badly for the Allies in 1917. There were great reverses on the western front, a sweeping defeat for the Italians at Caporetto, and Russia began to show signs of military collapse. The grimmer the situation and the more pusillanimous the talk, the stauncher became the Ambassador. When Colonel Aubrey Herbert, who came to lunch, maintained that England could not stand another winter of fighting and made suggestions for peace which included terms with Turkey, Bertie fumed to Hardinge, 'Why is such a dangerous pacifist Turcophile lunatic in khaki sent roaming about?'

In December Esher wrote to Derby on the subject of Unity of Command on the western front. The Ambassador was advocating a French supreme commander. 'How will England and the Colonies stand it?' asked Esher. 'The sooner the snake is scotched the better.' Things were hotting up between Bertie and Esher and it was the latter who toppled first. Just before Christmas a serious shortage of petrol caused the French Government to query the list of foreigners who were allowed a car from the *réserve général d'automobiles* and to enquire what was the mission of Lord Eyscher. 'Please enable me to reply,' Bertie asked the Foreign Office, and got the same answer that had already been given in the Commons the previous year. However, Esher thought it advisable to go before a second question was put.

Under what was virtually the dictatorship of Clemenceau the war effort was pursued with tremendous energy. At last the Ambassador was satisfied and only afraid lest a change of government ruined the chances of success. The Tiger rallied the French with his great speeches, had Caillaux arrested, visited the battlefields, talked to the soldiers. He went to the battlefields so often that, when the enemy had gained some ground Cocteau said he had brought the front nearer to Paris to visit it more easily.

Air raids on Paris began in earnest in 1918 and, on the advice of the embassy architect, Bertie took refuge in the small cellar whenever the siren went, reading the newspapers and drinking his coffee where Edward Malet had once dined in style. Dauntless, disregarding falling shrapnel, the elderly Ambassador could often be seen leaving the embassy by the garden gate to go on foot to the Quai d'Orsay in order to save petrol. Once, when dining with Edward Spiers, Head of our Military Mission, an air raid started. Instead of taking shelter below, he insisted on going on to the roof where he defiantly beat a tin tray with a spoon.

On 21 March, Ludendorff launched his great offensive. The 24th was memorable for a new and sinister sound in the bombardment of Paris: it was Big Bertha, the long-range gun. The situation became critical, it was feared that the Germans would soon be at Amiens, but Clemenceau remained confident and on 26 March what he had been urging was at last achieved; Haig and the British generals agreed to unity of command under Foch.

Esher could hardly have been expected to accept what he regarded as a humiliation for the Chief, as he called Haig, and his other military friends, without making one final bid to uproot Bertie. The moment seemed particularly propitious as the Ambassador had a sudden attack of pain early in April which seemed, at one moment, to necessitate a serious operation. Esher begged Lloyd George to place our national interests in France in stronger hands. ' . . . If Milner cannot be spared, then for heaven's sake send Austen Chamberlain or any man in whom you have confidence, but of Ministerial rank.'

But it was neither illness nor Esher's hammering insistence that brought the long career of Bertie to a sudden end. The Prime Minister, with ruthless impetuosity, removed him from Paris in order to get rid of Derby from the War Office. On 16 April the King was informed of the proposed change by telephone. Greatly moved he declined to approve it until Bertie had been told and it was ascertained that his successor would be acceptable to the French Government. Hardinge, vigorously protesting against this treatment of a trusted diplomat, was then instructed by Balfour to see

Paul Cambon, and ask for the *agrément* for Lord Derby within twenty-four hours. Cambon, he says, received the request 'with great surprise and deep emotion' and, as Bertie later learnt through Clemenceau, refused to telephone to Paris as quickly as requested. At least Hardinge's protest had the effect of making 'that philosophic idler', as Bertie called Balfour, word the telegram to Bertie in highly complimentary language. Not yet fully recovered from his illness, the Ambassador was in bed when, at about 8 p.m., he learnt that his mission was ended.

Afterwards Bertie wrote to Stamfordham, 'I have no reason to complain ceasing to be Ambassador considering that I am in my 74th year; but the manner of my extinction was not very correct.' To others he snorted contemptuously: 'A gentleman would dismiss his kitchenmaid with more courtesy.'

The sequence of events was certainly rapid for the official announcement was made on the 18th, Derby arrived in Paris on the 21st, Bertie presented his letters of recall on 1 May and on the 5th, hardly three weeks after he had received the news of his dismissal, he moved to the Crillon.

Everybody, from the King downwards and including Derby, was scandalized at the harshness of the Prime Minister, and expressions of regret and sympathy poured in at the embassy. From Curzon came the assurance that 'the Cabinet as a whole had not the faintest cognisance' of it. Admittedly for some there was a certain poetic justice. It was Neville Henderson who deciphered the fatal telegram, and Le Roy Lewis who brought it up to Bertie. Those who had been badly gored cannot have been sorry when the Welsh matador plunged in his sword.

Bertie retired with a viscountcy to London, lived to see the Allies victorious but died in 1919. His widow died the following year. He was buried at Thame. His tombstone proudly records that he had served three successive sovereigns and his country for 54 years, of which thirteen had been as the King's Ambassador to France.

He was a dynamic envoy who gave the impression that

nothing awful could happen while he was in charge because he could be counted upon to prevent it. When asked why he, who spoke fluent French, had never perfected the accent, he replied, *'C'ay pour montray que j'ai la flotte Anglayse derrière moi.'*

XXI

The Earl of Derby
1918—1920

The taurine image had not departed from the embassy. The new Ambassador was said to look like a shorthorn bull.

Born in 1865, Edward Stanley was the eldest son of a second son, with little prospect of inheriting the titles, estates and vast wealth of his grandfather, the Earl of Derby. Educated at Wellington College, he joined the Grenadier Guards at the age of twenty and the following year became a Conservative Member of Parliament. In 1889 he married the daughter of the beautiful German Duchess of Manchester. Lady Alice Montague had something of her mother's aloofness, which contrasted sharply with the conviviality of her husband. They had two sons and a daughter.

In 1893, his father succeeded to the earldom and he became Lord Stanley. After serving as a press officer in the Boer War, on his return at the end of 1900 he was appointed Financial Secretary to the War Office and in 1903 Postmaster-General. While in this capacity, two years later, the genial nobleman, whose very size conveyed an impression of large-heartedness, made an appalling remark in the Commons which he had difficulty in living down. The Post Office workers had been pressing for higher pay at a moment when it was known that there would soon be an election. Stanley, accusing them of blackmail, urged that a stop be put to this 'continual blood-sucking' on the part of public servants. This came ill from a man with the richest prospects in the country and he was never allowed to forget his blunder. He lost his seat to a carpenter.

In 1908 at the age of 43 he succeeded his father. His immense wealth was derived from the land he owned in the richest, most active part of England. He was called the King of Lancashire. This prestige dated further back than the industrial revolution for in the sixteenth century it was recorded that 'with Edward, Earl of Derby's death the glory of hospitality seemed to fall asleep'. This 3rd earl changed sides three times, and the 17th holder of the title inherited the same tendency.

When the First World War was declared Derby played an active part in recruiting, with such remarkable results that Lloyd George called him 'the most efficient recruiting sergeant in England'. After compulsory National Service was introduced in the spring of 1916, Lloyd George was made Secretary of State for War and Derby Under-Secretary, and when Lloyd George became Prime Minister in January 1917, Derby got the War Office. It was the ministry he had always wanted, yet during his fifteen months there his vacillating character betrayed the confidence people had in him.

Lloyd George, steering towards unity of command, had more confidence in French military tactics than in British. In November he brought into being a Supreme War Council, which sat at Versailles and was controlled by Marshal Foch. The Chief of the Imperial General Staff, Sir William Robertson, a stolid general risen from the ranks with admirable qualities but not the vision to follow the subversive ideas of the Prime Minister, obviously had to be moved as well as Haig. Derby found himself in an awkward predicament. Swayed first one way and then another, he made successive threats to resign, once doing so three times within 24 hours. The reputation for unreliability of the big bluff Minister of War now earned him the nickname of Jovial Judas, and even his friend Haig likened him to a feather pillow which bears the mark of the last person who sat on it.

The Prime Minister perceived that the time was coming for the axe to fall on Derby but on no account did he want to offend someone whose influence on the electorate was of supreme value. He must leave the War Office for a post of dazzling glamour. Cunningly he began to tempt the minister with the possibility of his replacing Bertie. Derby insisted that he should be endowed with greater powers than those given to an ambassador under ordinary circumstances. He wished to be kept fully informed, to be able to represent in person his views to the War Cabinet and to exercise his own discretion. All this was agreed to; under the circumstances, those special powers did not carry great weight.

Delighted with the success of his manœuvre Lloyd George, waving aside protocol, wanted to make the announcement and the transfer immediate. The staying hand of the King could delay matters for only two days.

The new Ambassador could not speak or understand French but Lloyd George recommended as his qualifications that 'it would not be obvious that his bluffness was only bluff'. Behind the solid façade and convivial manner was shrewdness.

Derby arrived in Paris on his 'special mission' on 21 April and stayed at Versailles. His first letter to the Prime Minister ran: 'Here I am – but at present not what the C.I.G.S. calls "functioning" – as my credentials have not arrived . . . Any amount of food here and still many pretty women tho' most have bolted, but there are enough to make life tolerable.' Lord Derby had a roving eye. When he presented his credentials it was said that Clemenceau, who spoke perfect English, purposely made his address in French, to register his objection to the loss of his old friend.

Lloyd George had moved Derby to Paris for political reasons but the appointment was a brilliant one. Republican France at heart likes a man of high position to be a *grand seigneur*. Denied such a personage in their own administration it was a quality they could freely admire in the envoy of another power and they accorded to Derby an importance which has never been equalled. It may be difficult for our present age to appreciate the effect he had – particularly as the type no longer exists nor could it now carry the same prestige – but in 1918 it was very impressive. He was a magnifico, the summit of British aristocracy with an immense social position, the very bulk of whose figure, combined with a winning genial manner, inspired confidence. Certainly his appearance was not of the sophisticated refinement usually expected in an aristocrat of ancient lineage. Clemenceau spoke of him as that 'thickset man looking like a horse-coper'.

The embassy was run on an unparalleled scale, for he entertained so lavishly that his hospitality became legendary. Six footmen from England came over for special parties. He did everything that was expected of a nobleman of his standing: he was a superb host, he ardently admired the *élégantes*, he kept a racing stud in France and altogether his coming made such a tremendous impression on the French that they still remember his tenure of two and a half years as a golden age. His prodigality was also extended to a wide range of persons. Duff Cooper recalls how any Guards officer passing through Paris had *carte blanche* to lunch or dine at the embassy, and the wounded were invited to recuperate in the garden lying under the chestnut trees, as Cole Porter, then a young American casualty, remembered with gratitude.

Lady Derby was too stiffly Teutonic in character to appeal to the French and came little to Paris. In fact she did not appear there at all for the first six months because it was thought that, being half German, it would be more tactful for her to keep away. In her absence from Paris it was their widowed daughter, Lady Victoria Primrose, who kept her father company and acted as hostess. She was the person Lord Derby loved most in the world and when she died in the hunting field in 1927 he was shattered. Soon after Derby's arrival in Paris a badly wounded young officer in the Scots Guards joined the staff as military secretary. Malcolm Bullock was welcomed as one of the family and the following year married Victoria Primrose.

Impressing everyone with his conviviality and hospitality, Derby left the diplomatic work to be carried out by a highly competent staff. The atmosphere of tension had relaxed to normality with the departure of Bertie, enhanced by the pleasant discovery that the new Ambassador was easily persuaded to take any particular course advised by his experts, provided, of course, that there was no subsequent interference.

Bridgeman, now reappointed to Paris, revived his old friendship with Cocteau, whom even Lady Derby liked, but the most curious juxtaposition of opposites was when the Ambassador met Proust at a dinner-party. The introvert writer was a hypochondriac who dreaded draughts and would refuse to sit with his back to the window. He imprinted himself on the memory of the Ambassador because he kept on his fur coat the whole evening.

Denied a private car in Paris Esher refrained from returning there but exerted his influence by letter. He sent descriptions of all the important personalities with whom Derby would come in contact and even gave him the lowdown on his own staff. Since he was writing to an expert on the turf he described them as though they were a list of race horses. George Grahame, the minister, had 'excellent capacity', Eric Phipps, first secretary, was 'typically pleasant', the controversial Le Roy Lewis 'a certain winner if ridden on a snaffle', the rest of the chancery were 'selling platers'. As to the 'government blokes', Clemenceau was 'masterful – at a dangerous age. Life behind him instead of before him. *Capable de tout.*' The Foreign Minister, Pichon, 'would never get half round the course at Aintree', and the rest of the government were 'political hacks'.

Unfortunately Esher could not be certain that his advice would be followed. Even on a snaffle Le Roy Lewis was giving trouble and, with good reason, Derby thought he must go. (In a letter to Churchill a year later he reminds him how, soon after his arrival, the French officially asked him to have Le Roy Lewis removed as an alarmist.) Esher was wise enough not to quibble. He heard that Spiers would be military attaché so he praised him as a 'clever young fellow with a good deal of charm'. On 9 May a letter came back that the Ambassador had not yet made up his mind.

Edward Spiers (who now anglicized his name to Spears) was bilingual, brilliant and tough. He had made an important position for himself in France as liaison officer and was on excellent terms with the French Premier as well as with the generals. He was not after all made military attaché because Derby, having begun by liking him, changed his opinion after his wont till finally, in January 1919, he complained to Wilson that Spears was assuming authority where he had no right to do so. Fifty years later Spears, a Bertie man, had such a poor opinion of the ability of Derby that he was loath to concede even the impression of glamour which he had made in France.

Two months after the war ended the Peace Conference opened at Versailles on 1 January 1919 and Paris was as crowded with distinguished people and hangers-on as it had been after the Napoleonic Wars. But Derby's prestige was undiminished and the embassy continued to be the meeting-place of high personalities. Certain attempts to steal some of his thunder were speedily quashed. Lord Hardinge of Penshurst arrived in Paris, electing to call himself Super-intending Ambassador, and later in the year, when Balfour had ceased to be Secretary of State, the Assistant Under-Secretary at the Foreign Office, Sir Eyre Crowe, was sent out to take his place, dignified with the rank of Ambassador to the Conference. Both of these upstart rivals were thwarted.

The special powers which Derby enjoyed were a useful weapon against another threat to his authority. Visiting ministers and persons of importance imagined that they had the right to use the embassy staff, even the servants, for their own purposes. This was quickly stopped. No present-day envoy would dare stand up to eminent politicians in this way.

Things were less easy for him when a new Foreign Secretary was appointed with whom he had had petty differences in the past. As Minister of War he had taken Curzon to task for wasting government petrol on his

weekend guests. Then, during the excitement of the
Armistice, he returned one day from a brief call at the
Elysée to discover the embassy invaded by cheering
tommies brought there by a musical comedy actress who
ran their Leave Club. Derby arrived just in time to see
Curzon concluding a speech from the porch and being
kissed warmly by Miss Decima Moore while the soldiers
sang 'For he's a jolly good fellow' under the impression
that he was the Ambassador.

Even when separated by the Channel the envoy and
Secretary of State continued to bicker. One evening Malcolm
Bullock was handed a letter by his father-in-law with
instructions to get it off by that night's bag. It began, 'My
dear Curzon, I have always known you to be a cad. I now
know that you are a liar.' Perturbed by the opening sentence,
Malcolm consulted the minister, who advised him just to
leave the letter in the tray. The next morning the Ambassador seemed distinctly relieved to learn that it had not gone
and dictated another in a milder vein: 'My dear George,
You and I have known each other too long to quarrel over
so small a matter.'

About a fortnight after the Armistice the King visited
Paris, and a dignified member of London society, Lady
Helen Vincent, noted in her diary that the Ambassadress
was at last coming over and that her ' "*grande dame*" presence,
tact and savoir-faire would be invaluable'. Never reconciled
to the love affairs and flirtations of her husband, what Lady
Derby really minded was the serious lasting friendship he
had formed with one of the most charming and intelligent
women in Paris. There is no satisfactory expression in
English for '*l'amitié amoureuse*'. At the age of 92, frail but
exquisite-looking, Comtesse Marguerite de Mun spoke
glowingly of her old admirer. She had sensed in him something other than the *animateur*, the popular host, and had
discovered more depth and intelligence than most people
gave him credit for. At that time she was Madame Hennessy.
(Later she reverted to her maiden name.)

Derby not only admired her but had come to rely on her

advice and knew that he could count on her discretion. Their correspondence, which became a regular part of his life, only finished with his death. It is to be noted that by 1920 'My dear Madame Hennessy' became 'My dearest Madame Hennessy,' ending with 'my most respectful love and devotion,' or some such restrained expression of his affection. Thus it remained over the years. This charming friendship began soon after his taking over the embassy. Evidently he had already found relaxation and sympathy in the peace of her pretty drawing-room in the Avenue Henri Martin, where everything, like herself, was in fastidious taste, for, early in July when she, like *tout Paris*, had gone to the country, he wrote, 'I miss very much my tea with you.' He said she was 'the nicest and prettiest woman in Paris'.

A serious situation arose in 1920 over Poland in which, in the light of after-events, the French were undoubtedly in the right in helping the Poles to defend themselves against attack by the Soviet Army. General Weygand was sent out as head of a mission with Captain de Gaulle on his staff. Derby became extremely worried and confided to Madame Hennessy: ' . . . the Bolsheviks have defied us and we must do something. What can we do – we can't send troops – Winston Churchill has proposed making an ally of Germany – but still if the only available troops are the German, we may have to do so.' Recalled, reluctantly, to his post by the crisis, the Ambassador had no hesitation in telling his friend his Government's advice to the Poles to accept the Soviet peace terms was just as unwise as the French Government's recognition of General Wrangel. Anyway, he had found his own Government 'more difficult to deal with than yours', and Lloyd George – who, he said, wanted to trade with Russia in order to avoid unemployment which 'could lead to revolution' – had 'made us look ridiculous in France and an enemy for ever of Poland'.

In the middle of all this trouble the thoughts of the Ambassador were never far removed from Madame Hennessy. Among her papers was treasured a delightful tribute. Dated 13 August and written from the Ministère des Affaires étrangères, it is in the handwriting of the Secretary General and runs:

'Deux de vos amis, qui viennent de discuter cordialement de graves questions, vous envoient leurs dévoués hommages.'

Derby   Paléologue.

The term of Lord Derby finished in the autumn of 1920. He was reluctant to leave Paris and wished for an extension. However, on 21 November this fabulous era, which has never quite been equalled in the history of the embassy, came to an end. In diplomatic parlance *'une belle gare'* means an exceptional send-off at the railway station of a popular and important personage. That of the Derbys was superlative. The train drew out leaving genuine regret at the departure of a great *milord anglais* devoted to France.

It cannot be pretended that Lord Derby was an eminent envoy in the accepted sense of the term. Such a character would have been hardly necessary at that particular moment. During his first six months there the military missions played a more important part than did the embassy, the peace conference started almost immediately the war had finished and was followed by the Ambassador's conference, all of which were admirably conducted by experts. The role of Derby lay less in politics than in keeping a good relationship between the French and the English and this, at a difficult moment, he did with heart and soul and panache. Proust said of him that his 'affability is of a kind the French do not possess and by which their hearts are won'.

From Knowsley, in mid-December, he wrote to Madame Hennessy: 'The Government here have behaved very well to me, they offered to make me Viceroy of India, and when I refused they offered me one of the highest posts in the government. It was rather a tempting offer, but I refused because if I had accepted I could not have continued to publicly advocate the alliance [between England and France] and I feel it is my duty now I have begun to go on till I win. I am sure you will agree . . . How I long to be back in Paris . . . With much love to you, dearest Madame Hennessy.'

He died in 1948. The lustre of his mission to France even reached the Far East, where it was so much respected that, during the 1920s, a Japanese representative said to the Foreign Office, 'Why do you not send us as Ambassador a *grand seigneur* like Lord Derby?'

XXII

Lord Hardinge of Penshurst
1920—1922

When the 17th Earl of Derby left Paris it could be said with truth that 'the glory of hospitality seemed to fall asleep' for there followed a subdued period of two years. The embassy was back in the hands of a professional diplomat, the choice of whom was, in itself, a sort of vindication of Bertie and the shabby treatment that had been meted out to him.

Charles Hardinge, the second son of Viscount Hardinge, was born in 1858. He went to Harrow and, though he disliked his schooldays, in later life he firmly believed that the boys turned out by private and public schools would always 'lead in any walk of life and leaven the whole mass of the people'. Because of this he was convinced that the future of England was secure.

Diplomacy was a career which at that time required the entrant to have the then considerable sum of £400 and be taken on probation for two years without pay. An opportune legacy enabled Charles to enter the Diplomatic Service in 1880. The picture he gives of the Foreign Office at that time was hardly a tempting one for an intelligent young man eager for scope and responsibility. Highly-educated entrants did the work now done by clerks, typists and cypherers. They had to choose whether they wished to serve abroad or in London for there were two separate branches and this system prevailed till 1919 when Hardinge, as Permanent Under-Secretary, carried out reforms largely suggested by Sir Eyre Crowe.

Hardinge was first posted to Constantinople. Soon after

he had settled down there Lord Dufferin arrived to take over the embassy, and for him the young attaché conceived a fervent admiration. Like his hero he became Viceroy of India and Ambassador to Russia and to France but he developed into a far stronger personality who contributed work of importance and lasting value to the service. In 1890 he married his first cousin, the daughter of Lord Alington.

Hardinge's first royal assignment was to go to Bucharest to negotiate the marriage of Princess Marie of Edinburgh to the Crown Prince of Rumania. After this came an appointment after his own heart: head of chancery in Paris under Dufferin. Hardly had he arrived there than there came a request for him to return to Rumania from the homesick British Princess, who also intended to make Mrs Hardinge her lady-in-waiting. Luckily the Princess of Wales was displeased at this manœuvre on the part of a much-criticized cousin. She promptly ruled that Winifred Hardinge should be her own lady-in-waiting and the young couple remained in Paris. This connection with the court was of immense value there as it impressed the French.

After fifteen years in diplomacy Hardinge still received only £400 a year, but he was given the CB, which, he recalls, was an exceptionally high honour for somebody of his grade. When Dufferin left Paris Hardinge was made first secretary in Tehran and was congratulated by everybody except the Princess of Wales, who telegraphed, 'Too sorry to hear about Persian appointment' and refused to accept the resignation of her lady-in-waiting. Having done well there he received spectacular promotion which caused questions to be asked in Parliament. He became Counsellor in St Petersburg at the age of 40, passing over seventeen of his seniors.

Five years later he was an Under-Secretary at the Foreign Office, an appointment strongly backed by Edward VII, and that same spring there took place the celebrated journey culminating in the *Entente Cordiale*. The King now put forward his name as ambassador to Russia, in the teeth of opposition from the Foreign Office. He was only 45, and departed for his new post a Privy Councillor and covered with other decorations.

In 1906 he became Permanent Under-Secretary at the Foreign Office, an appointment which the King was keen he should accept, seeing the advantages of having an able and loyal friend in a key position. Such a promotion inevitably caused ill feeling among the more senior Under-Secretaries. The most important factor of his triumphant progress had, unquestionably, been the patronage of the King. Though it was unconstitutional, Edward VII now took him on many of his journeys abroad, at one time incurring the disapproval of the Prime Minister, Asquith. When absent from England without him he expected to be kept fully informed by letter twice a week, and at home they frequently breakfasted tête-à-tête to discuss foreign affairs. The King showed insight and judgement though not interested in detail.

Excellent administrator though he was, Hardinge was not entirely popular in the office. Tall, fine-looking, haughty, with an authoritative way of speaking, he lacked any human touch. The King thought he looked the part of a Viceroy of India, but hesitated to let him go such a distance. The appointment finally materialized in June 1910 under George V and to the fury of Kitchener, who had been so certain of the post that he had already selected his personal staff. Hardinge, now a peer, returned from the east in 1916, a sadder and even more unapproachable man for his wife had died, and his eldest son was killed in action.

Looking forward to retirement from public life, though not yet sixty, he was once more offered the Foreign Office when Sir Arthur Nicolson wished to give up because of ill-health. He found that the office had changed out of recognition, with 500 people working there instead of 150, and there was immense activity day and night. Also he came in contact with new personalities who jarred on him, particularly the Prime Minister. Lloyd George liked to run Foreign Affairs, and set up his own secretariat at No. 10, which functioned under an intelligent man with no experience of professional diplomacy, Philip Kerr. The group became known as the Downing Street Kindergarten and it was responsible for the intrigue to get rid of Bertie.

Hardinge had to endure some unpleasant publicity when the report on the Mesopotamian campaign was published and the ex-Viceroy was among those blamed for the campaign's failure. His offered resignation was not accepted but, after the debate in the Commons, Curzon came to tell him that the War Cabinet suggested he resign 'to ease the situation' of the Government. Hardinge lost his temper and, according to his version, Curzon 'slunk from my room like a whipped hound' (which hardly has the ring of truth).

Responsible for the preparations for the Peace Conference, Hardinge moved to Paris, where his opinion of the Prime Minister sank even lower. What with this antipathy and the work, he nearly had a nervous breakdown and returned to England to have a long rest. By the time he was able to resume his post at the Foreign Office an enemy of long standing had taken the place of the easy-going Balfour.

Hardinge and Curzon had begun to disagree over the Anglo-Russian Agreement in 1907, which the former had helped to negotiate, but the quarrel only became acute in 1911 when the Indian capital was moved to Delhi, leaving behind in Calcutta the Victoria Memorial Hall, which Curzon, when Viceroy, had designed and started to build, and the statue of himself which he had placed in front of it. To Curzon this seemed a deliberate affront. When they found themselves in close association within the Foreign Office, Hardinge took good care that the Secretary of State should not be allowed to forget that they were equal, on the grounds that they had both been Viceroys. Their respective strongholds were the almost identical corner-rooms overlooking the park, that of Curzon being above on the first floor, more lofty and splendidly furnished. They were connected by an old-fashioned speaking-tube down which the grander ex-Viceroy would blow to the angry resentment of the other.

Offered Paris, Hardinge confessed that his chief reason for accepting was the intence pleasure it gave him to be given the highest diplomatic post at the hands of those who, three years before, had tried to hound him out of the service. Having made his decision he had some difficulty in realizing it, for Derby kept Hardinge waiting two months longer than the date agreed upon. It was not till the end of November 1920 that the new Ambassador arrived at the Gare du Nord. With his distant manner, he alighted from the train accompanied by his twenty-year-old daughter, Diamond, who provided a lighter touch by carrying a canary in a cage.

He was the third ex-Viceroy to serve in Paris and, inevitably, he brought with him his Indian trophies. On the dining-room table was placed a large silver tiger. When Curzon came to lunch, Hardinge proudly drew his attention to this object made from silver presents given him in India which he had melted down. Curzon, delighted to get the better of his host, informed him that he had had the same excellent idea, and got five very nice tigers.

Widowerhood did not entirely account for the gravity of the atmosphere which now descended on the house; it was Hardinge's personality which was responsible. He spoke little, a fatal fault in France, where animated conversation is one of the enjoyments of life. '*Tellement boutonné,*' he was said to be, pompous, incapable of unbending even at the Longchamps races, his parties thought to be synonymous with the stiffness of the Empire furniture. The embassy had sunk into the lowest category in French eyes, dullness. It may well be wondered how Edward VII would have reacted could he have seen how his favourite Foreign Office official was conducting his favourite mission.

Fortunately there was an antidote in the shape of Hardinge's daughter. A madcap, a tomboy, clumsy in her movements, there was no doubt that Diamond was bent on enjoying things. She delighted in making jokes and playing pranks, ordering that the bread rolls for a large ministerial luncheon of *hautes personnalités* should be baked in the shape of frogs. Having perfected the knack of cracking her jaw with a loud report, it amused her to do so in public places such as the theatre.

Then Diamond had her friends to stay, and one of them brought enchantment to the embassy with her irresistible smile and rippling infectious laughter. She is now Queen Elizabeth, the Queen Mother. When the formal parties were over they pestered Nastia Cheetham, the Russian wife of the Counsellor, to take them to a more amusing place, with some of the young secretaries, such as the Foire de Neuilly, where they all had fun going down the chute in a barrel, escapades about which Hardinge was kept in ignorance.

Hardinge took over the embassy during a difficult period. Ill-feeling, which had been swamped in the non-stop conviviality of his predecessor, was now more noticeable. France was concentrating on herself, cynical, frustrated, defeatist. The war and the peace conference had wrought a considerable change in the working of the embassy for it had become a habit, never since discontinued, for cabinet ministers to travel over and see to matters of importance themselves. Since the Ambassador was on bad terms with both Lloyd George and Curzon, these repeated visits were anathema to him. He noted with scorn that the travelling arrangements of the Prime Minister exceeded those of Edward VII. Curzon must have been an unaccommodating guest with his unpunctuality and habit of upsetting arrangements, to say nothing of hurling a log in the middle of the night through his bedroom window into the garden. The host was also difficult to please. When Curzon told him that he regarded him as an element of stability and able to control the French, his reaction was 'Personally I thought this view exaggerated, but it was meant well.'

Then there was the famous scene with Poincaré, whom Curzon accused of 'abandoning' the British by withdrawing French troops from the entrance to the Dardanelles. The President in return was so rude that the Foreign Secretary had to leave the room and was given a restorative. It was left to Hardinge to patch up the quarrel, which he did, finally extracting an apology from Poincaré under threat of a collapse of the entire negotiation.

died of tuberculosis.

Gladstone, in power for the last time in 1892, appointed Houghton, aged 34, as Viceroy to Ireland, where he remained until the general election of 1895 returned a Conservative Government under Lord Salisbury. The previous year he had been created an earl, choosing Crewe as his title since he had now inherited Crewe Hall.

Eleven years passed after the death of his wife before the young widower with melancholy eyes remarried. Lady Peggy Primrose, the second daughter of Lord Rosebery, defied criticism of the disparity in years, for he was 41 and she eighteen, with the charming explanation that 'age does not affect affinity'. It was a happy marriage. Moreover, it was a rare example of perfect understanding between a young wife and her three step-daughters. They swore absolute loyalty to each other.

The political importance of Crewe was by now well established. He was never an inspiring speaker, giving an impression of aloofness, but he came to be regarded as a figure of great reliability whose advice was frequently sought, and he held successive Government posts. The Crewes had been married twelve years when they had an heir followed, a few years later, by a daughter. But in March 1922, when he was eleven, the little Earl of Madeley suddenly died of double mastoid. It was the second time that Crewe had lost a son and from this last calamity he never could recover.

Vansittart recalls that there was considerable ill-feeling in the Foreign Office at his appointment to Paris at the end of this year, for it followed soon after that of D'Abernon to Berlin. That two non-career men should be given the most important diplomatic posts was resented, particularly since Curzon defended it because 'the requisite qualities were not to be found in the Service'. Crewe knew France well, as did his wife, her mother having been of the English Rothschilds, and he was one of the few people with whom the Secretary of State got on well. In a private letter congratulating him on the appointment the King wrote with touching understanding that 'the Embassy will bring fresh interest into your lives which have been so clouded with sorrow'.

Crewe arrived just before the new year of 1923, almost simultaneously with the entry of French and Belgian forces into the Ruhr, which was the climax of a long-drawn-out dispute between us and France as to the best way to ensure against further German aggression. There followed a critical period in Anglo-French relations. The embassy was even afraid of the break-up of the *Entente Cordiale*. Crewe preserved an impassive calm. Never ruffled by any contre-temps, his gift for moderation and common sense gave him authority in France.

He played a certain part in the bitter disappointment of Curzon when he failed to get the premiership. In the spring of 1923 Bonar Law became seriously ill while abroad and was brought to Paris by Lord Beaverbrook, where it was discovered that he could only live a few months. The dying man spent an afternoon at the embassy, confiding to the Ambassador that the obvious choice to succeed him was Curzon, whom he did not like. Crewe quoted to Beaver-brook two instances when the decision of successor had been left to the Monarch. The hint was followed up. When Curzon heard that Baldwin was to be Premier, he burst into tears.

Crewe never came into the Chancery. The work was done under the efficient direction of the minister, Eric Phipps. The head of Chancery was a man with a brilliant brain. Rarely has there been found in the Foreign Service someone with greater independence of mind and judgment than Ralph Wigram. Widely read, speaking with authority, ruthless when necessary, he lived for the cause. His wife (subsequently Ava, Viscountess Waverley) was equally remarkable. The only daughter of J. E. C. Bodley, author of a classic work, *The History of France*, and brought up in France, she was of immeasurable assistance to her extremely able husband. Closeted in their apartment could be found important people who were making history. It was un-precedented for a young couple in an embassy to have made such a position for themselves. They burnt with the same flame.

In August 1926 Wigram's dazzling career was cut short by polio. Even in delirium he only thought of his work. By April the minister became concerned about the running of the Chancery and decided that his post must be filled. Ava enlisted the support of highly placed members of the French Government, got her husband to start writing despatches, and, at the end of the month, supported by two sticks, 'Wigs' was back at his post. It was a great loss to the service that his strength only lasted another ten years.

Bill (Victor) Cavendish-Bentinck was private secretary, succeeded by Derrick Hoyer-Millar, who remembers with what extreme good humour Lady Crewe greeted the occasional inevitable muddles made over arrangements, the turning up for a grand dinner of somebody of importance not expected, the sending of the Ambassador and Ambassadress out to dine at the wrong address. Invariably kind and courteous the only reproach Lord Crewe was ever heard to make was to one of the attachés known for being rather slow in his movements: 'Find the stairs trying today, Paget?'

By the time the Crewes arrived in Paris an interesting addition to the Chancery was well established. Charles Mendl was invaluable to an ambassador new to the ropes of diplomacy. He was rather an intriguer, but his loyalty was entirely to the embassy. For many years he provided a permanent thread for successive envoys, after the fashion of the Oriental counsellor in far eastern posts, a man of substance locally employed who knew the language and what was going on.

His father was a Jew from Bohemia who had arrived in England bringing no possessions. The son, handsome, attractive, was something of a buccaneer as a young man. Badly wounded in the First World War and transferred to the navy as intelligence officer in France, he was made assistant provost marshal in Paris. He joined the embassy under Derby. Given a salary and an entertainment allowance, he was the first representative of the Foreign Office News Department to be appointed and he did more than anybody to develop the post of press attaché (which he became in 1926) into the full importance which it now possesses. Mendl managed to get news as no one else did, he dealt extremely well with journalists, he seemed to be in touch with anyone who knew anything, he arranged meetings with whoever one wanted to see. His intimate lunches in his flat for this purpose were famous for he was an excellent host and a great connoisseur of wine and food. Cynical, less tarred with the official brush than members of the diplomatic staff and knowing the French well, he was a person of enormous value in the embassy and would put himself out for a new third secretary as much as for somebody of importance.

In his mid-fifties he married a rich American interior decorator living in Paris, Elsie de Wolfe, chic, vital, business-like. Charles had received a knighthood in 1924 and Elsie, glad to have a title, also liked the connection with the embassy which appealed to her in a theatrical way. She proposed marriage. The prospective bridegroom must have been a little afraid of the reaction, for he consulted Phipps, who did his best to dissuade him. The very next day the engagement was announced.

The Crewes were ever kind and hospitable to their staff, who in turn were devoted to them and proud of the impression their Ambassador made wherever he went. After the dull years of Hardinge the embassy was restored to something of the brilliance of the Derby mission, though with greater dignity, and, as with Lytton, the French appreciated Crewe's literary interests.

As elegant as the *élégantes* and with an excellent brain, Lady Crewe was a magnificent Ambassadress. Lacking any form of snobbishness and with an instinct for detecting pose, she was too genuine a person to be merely a figurehead. Being still a young woman she loved dancing and night-club life. Shyness sometimes made her a little abrupt but she did the honours of her position to perfection and her considerate manners were memorable. A young girl, some thirty years later herself to be ambassadress there, has never forgotten the kindness of Lady Crewe and her insistence that she should sit in her place in the front of the box at the opera.

When Curzon first revisited the embassy under the new régime he wrote: 'It was such a pleasure to see that beautiful house without the tiger skins, the silver caskets, the elephant tusks and common photographs of Charlie Hardinge.' He thought the place for Indian trophies was 'in some rather out of the way corner'. The butler, whom the Crewes had inherited from Hardinge, took a different view. Disregarding the magnificence of the plate, he was perpetually bewailing: 'If only you had a silver tiger!'

Soon after their arrival, and on the night of their first big dinner-party, the Ambassador went down with a severe attack of pneumonia, so Lady Crewe had to do the honours alone. Another dinner in honour of somebody of the highest importance was marred by an incident comparable to Harold Nicolson and his fugitive balloon. Just when the hall was the centre of activity with guests arriving, there was heard the ominous sound of water splashing on the marble floor of the staircase well. A steady cascade was streaming down the chain of the great chandelier. Frenzied investigation showed that it came from the bath used by the grandsons of the Ambassador just above on the second floor. The very youthful Jock Colville (afterwards an indispensable private secretary to Winston Churchill), involved but not responsible, remembers that it was the only time he ever saw his grandfather verging on anger.

A frequent visitor at this time was Lord Alington, gifted, charming and gay, who had the distinction of seeing the embassy ghost in what was still the State bedroom, but was originally the cabinet Doré. Early morning light filtering through the curtains revealed a man with powdered hair and ruffles standing by the cupboard door looking through papers. He is said to have been seen elsewhere in the house. Count La Marck might well haunt the place.

After six years Lord Crewe retired from public life. He was 70. He lived another seventeen years, always a highly respected figure to whom people turned for advice. Lady Crewe died in 1967.

XXIV

Lord Tyrrell
1928—1934

That outstanding personality, Lord Tyrrell, was certainly the cleverest and perhaps the most remarkable ambassador ever sent to the embassy. His was one of the famous names of the Foreign Service. He owed his flexible mind and sensitive antennae to his Eurasian origin, and would remind less nimble-minded subordinates never to forget that his grandmother had been an Indian princess.

His maternal grandfather, John Howard Wakefield, a lieutenant in the Bengal Army, was walking in the remote hills of Kumharsain, on the Hindustan–Tibet road, when he came upon a castle in which a princess could be seen at a window. She was said to have Circassian blood. Unable to effect an entry, the enterprising young man scaled the walls, wooed her, converted her from Hinduism and married her in 1832. The name she took on her conversion was Maria Suffolk (possibly originally Suffiq?). She was the daughter of the late Vizier of Bashahr and the ward of the Rana of Kumharsain, to whom she may have been related. Their daughter Julia married in 1864, as his second wife, William Tyrrell of the Bengal Civil Service, and an only son, William George, was born at Naini Tal on 17 August 1866.

Tyrrell's mother, a hard woman, gave him a tough upbringing. He was educated in Germany, watched over by his influential uncle by marriage, the sister of his mother having married a prominent German diplomat, Prince Hugo Radolinsky. Mrs Tyrrell spent much time in Berlin and had many friends in diplomacy so, under her influence and that of his uncle, the career of her promising boy was decided upon. Afterwards he would speak of the advantage he had had in being given such an exceptionally good education in Germany where he learnt to be bilingual, also acquired excellent French, and altogether was more advanced than the average English boys of his age. He took a distinguished degree at Bonn University and, after three years at Balliol under Jowett, tried for the British Foreign Office. Having been lazy about his examinations, he came out bottom of the list. His mother reacted with her customary severity. She refused to see him or have anything to do with him until he had reversed the order which he did, passing in first the following year. He became a clerk in the Foreign Office in 1889.

At Oxford he got engaged to the daughter of David Urquhart, sister to the celebrated don, Francis F. F. Urquhart, popularly known as Sligger, who helped to form the minds of many young men who have since had distinguished careers. She had an exceptionally brilliant brain and had become a Roman Catholic. They were married in 1890 and had four children.

Tyrrell was selected for a position of importance when, in 1895, he became private secretary to Nicolson, the Permanent Under-Secretary. After a short spell as secretary to the Committee of Imperial Defence he was sent in 1904 as acting Second Secretary to the Embassy in Rome under Bertie. At the end of the following year a Liberal Government was formed and he was brought back to become précis writer to Sir Edward Grey, the Secretary of State. He proved so invaluable that in 1907 he was given the coveted post of principal private secretary to the Foreign Secretary, where he remained till 1915. It was a position of power for which he was eminently suited and in which he made his name.

Resourceful, experienced, an intriguer, Tyrrell was the ideal man to complement Grey. Baron von Kühlmann, counsellor at the German Embassy before the First World War, wrote of him that 'he provided the greatest help and counsel to the insular English leaders, and above all to the most insular of all, Sir Edward Grey'. The Secretary of State was a distinguished country gentleman who reluctantly accepted the burden of high office. His private secretary with the Oriental appearance was aptly named the Eminence Grise, and his reputation became famous in the chanceries of Europe. He was only 45 when, in 1911, France and Spain sent troops to their possessions in Morocco to quell disturbances there and Germany nearly precipitated a crisis by unexpectedly moving a ship to Agadir. The immediate reaction of Clemenceau was: '*Je voudrais savoir ce qu'en pense le petit Japonais au bord de la Tamise.*'

For eight of the ten years Grey was at the Foreign Office there remained at his side this powerful influence. The remarkable collaboration ceased in 1915 when, not only did the eyesight of the Foreign Secretary begin to fail, but it seemed that the brilliant career of the adviser had abruptly come to an end. He had a complete collapse. His amazing flair stemmed from a highly-strung temperament, and all his life adverse events affected him so deeply that he suffered emotional upsets. Overwork and the war began to get him down and when, in February, this deeply affectionate man heard that his younger son had been killed, the strain became too much for him to bear. No longer capable of working, he was forced to retire.

From this breakdown he eventually made an astonishing recovery. He returned to serve on the committee planning the League of Nations, then to be made Head of Political Intelligence in the Foreign Office. In 1918 he was Assistant Under-Secretary and the next year at the peace conference he was fighting the policy of Lloyd George which ignored the potential danger of Germany. When the Senate refused to ratify the United States membership of the League of Nations and Anglo-American relations were at a low ebb, Tyrrell accompanied his old chief, Grey, on a special mission to Washington to try to revive friendship between the two countries.

In 1922 and 1923 he became principal adviser to the

Foreign Secretary at the Lausanne Conference. This was not the happiest appointment for Tyrrell since he and Curzon did not understand each other. Moreover, Harold Nicolson, now a bright, amusing, somewhat bumptious first secretary, appeared to impress the Foreign Secretary. Tyrrell, who never forgave anything, would have remembered old friction with his father, Lord Carnock, when he was Permanent Under-Secretary. When he himself succeeded to that post and was in a position to do so he got Harold out of the way by packing him off to Tehran (or so Harold believed).

In 1925 Sir Eyre Crowe died and Tyrrell took his place. He was not to be compared with Crowe as an administrator of a department of state. Unlike his meticulous predecessor he knew little about the internal working of the office nor did he much care; nor would he take the trouble to read all the paper that came in. In particular, it was contrary to his devious nature to commit himself to a decision in writing. Never did he put a written comment to a document; he would speak his views. All he did was to sign W.T. His private secretary once tried to catch him out by writing on a minute, 'A decision is required on this matter,' to which Tyrrell merely added, 'Yes it is.'

Both Tyrrell and Crowe, widely different in character, had been brought up in Germany, Crowe even speaking English with a slight accent. Both were prophetic in their warnings of the danger of making concessions to her. During the postwar years the Entente Cordiale had weakened and, though Tyrrell would deny that he was pro-French, it was to revive this friendship that he now dedicated his life. His policy was always 'to deal with Germany only after agreement with France had been secured'.

In 1928, to the dismay of the Foreign Secretary, Sir Austen Chamberlain, who was loath to lose his valuable adviser, Tyrrell asked to be transferred to Paris on the retirement of Lord Crewe. Then began, at the age of 62, the most interesting and brilliant years of his career.

The marked contrast he made to the previous Ambassador

at first gave rise to misgivings in certain quarters. Gone was the hospitality in the effortless grandeur of the nobleman's house. But intelligent France knew what she was getting instead, and it was soon apparent to all that the prestige of the embassy never stood so high as under Tyrrell.

He came accompanied by his daughter Anne (who acted as hostess in the constant absences of Lady Tyrrell) and her ex-governess, Mademoiselle Etcheverry. 'Mad,' as she was called, was an essential member of the household for the highly-strung Ambassador relied implicitly on her practical good sense. She also ran the house. He used the Salon Vert as his study and kept Pauline Borghese's room purely as a show-piece. Visitors, important or otherwise, slept on the second floor, as did the family. The rooms were still furnished with chintz, brass beds, stiff couches, screens and a few immense heavily framed Victorian prints.

Tyrrell was short, neatly-made, with grey hair and moustache, and rather precise movements. The sallowness of his skin betrayed his eastern blood, as did his alert amused eyes twinkling through half-closed lids and the free play of his hands. The way he ran his embassy was unorthodox. Ignoring the onerous social duties expected of him he gave few official parties, preferring to have people to more intimate men's lunches and dinners. Politicians were eager to come to these, and they became an important feature of his mission. With relish they would all sit down, study the menu ('Mad' having seen to it that the food and wine were exceptionally good), and proceed to enjoy themselves, their able host guiding the conversation into the most interesting channels. Those who never heard the conversation of Tyrrell are unable to form an idea of its brilliance. It was a tour de force, an art so subtle that Gaston Palewski (later a member of the Government and a friend of Général de Gaulle) described it as 'verbal fencing'. This dexterity of speech made him an exceptional diplomatist, enabling him to find the key to intricate situations, always with good humour and charm, never giving the impression that he was cleverer or more knowledgeable than his hearers. With him everything had to be done by personal contact, creating the proper atmosphere, discussion, persuasion, the right word in the right place. He played it by ear.

The position he made for himself was unique. Never had the British Ambassador become, as it were, the centre of the political vortex. He did not put himself out for people, it was they who came to see him. Ministers would ask his advice on private as well as official matters. His private secretary, John Mallet, remembers how frequently a message would come from the Secretary-General that he would call at such and such an hour if convenient, and how Léon Blum would drop in of a morning in his cloak and conspirator's hat.

After an important conversation, instead of writing it down, he would tell it to the Head of Chancery. Because he shunned leaving evidence he never wrote minutes, he would have the person up and talk to him. 'Never put anything in writing unless you have to' was his attitude. He could not, in fact, altogether avoid writing private letters, such as those about policy to the Prime Minister, Stanley Baldwin, whom he liked, but when Sir John Simon, whom he disliked, was Foreign Secretary, he got out of it by sending telegrams.

Occasionally the Ambassador would disappear to avoid some situation, such as the time Lord and Lady Londonderry came to lunch in order to have a look round the embassy, on which they had an eye. Tyrrell feigned a cold which kept him in bed, but as the party left the dining-room Charles Peake glimpsed him in a cloth cap sneaking out with his golf clubs.

More serious were those times when he disappeared and was not available to anybody for several days. Always extremely highly-strung, he had acute attacks of nerves when any crisis arose or something happened which upset him. He deplored all the coming and going of Ministers and Members of Parliament and would complain that the embassy had become like Waterloo Station. He retired to bed for three days when he heard that Sir John Simon had been appointed Secretary of State. On such occasions the only person who saw him was 'Mad'.

Simon became a disagreeably frequent visitor to the embassy, travelling out in the open cockpit of an old-fashioned plane, stopping at Paris to break the journey and continuing by train to Geneva. Tyrrell had a low opinion of him because he treated Foreign Affairs like briefs. Such an unimaginative approach was incompatible with the skilful tortuousness of the Ambassador. When Simon argued that two and two made four Tyrrell retorted, 'No, not in foreign politics,' and he would often repeat that misunderstandings between us and France were inevitable because our two languages were untranslatable. He was irritated and bored at having to deal with such an uncomprehending chief and did not hesitate to show it. He would openly yawn and was even known to leave conferences in the middle of Sir John's long-drawn-out perorations. Once Frank Roberts followed his Ambassador into the next room to be treated to the remark, 'The trouble with the Foreign Secretary is that you can load him but he doesn't fire.'

The Ambassador's pleasures were simple: family bridge, golf, going to the cinema, and the atmosphere was distinctly homely. Before a dinner-party Tyrrell and 'Mad' sat in the drawing-room waiting for the guests, 'Mad' knitting away at a long scarf which trailed on the floor. Charles Peake, the Second Secretary, described it as exactly like arriving at the vicarage for dinner.

Lady Tyrrell seldom came to Paris. The French believe us to be a nation of eccentrics, a characteristic for which they have lurking admiration. We are *'les originaux d'outre-manche'*. They had a remarkable example in Lady Tyrrell who, charming and exceedingly intelligent, was quite unpredictable. On her rare visits they were impressed by her excellent brain but intrigued by her behaviour. The mind of the Ambassadress was on higher things than being a hostess. She had embarked on a history of the world beginning in the year 2000 BC, ingeniously planned to inform the reader what was going on in all parts of the globe at the same time. To write this ambitious work, she would retire up a tree in

Lord Crewe talking to Sir Eric Phipps (wearing the hat)

Lord Tyrrell (on the right) and Monsieur Ettienne Flandin

The Gallery about 1910

than created and whose role was to advise, is largely forgotten. The scattered recollections of those who knew him are the only means by which we can estimate this remarkable man who more than anyone inside or outside the Foreign Office, really understood European politics, and to whom it was largely due that Franco-British relations remained on the whole good in the years between the First and Second World Wars. The lifelong opponent of the written word – 'If you put things on paper people will get at you' – left nothing to show why he had been the power behind all thrones.

Sir George Clerk
1934—1937

Conventionally good-looking, monocled, silver-haired, with a trim moustache, his tall dapper figure immaculately dressed, Sir George Clerk had all the appearance of a stage ambassador.

When his appointment to the Paris Embassy was made known, Jacques Emile Blanche, the artist and writer, remarked that it was not a great compliment to the French. In fact it constituted such astonishing luck for an amiable, easy-going diplomat for whom *haute politique* was not the main interest in life, that there were some who strongly suspected that the choice had been a cunning move on the part of Tyrrell. 'He will open up the Embassy,' he had urged, 'and entertain all the people I have failed to invite there.' He was also well aware that Clerk, though not to be described as a bad ambassador, would be regarded as a lightweight compared with himself.

He was the son of General Sir Godfrey Clerk, of Penicuik, who held an appointment at court. Born in 1874, he went to Eton and New College, entered the Foreign Office in 1899, and two years later was chosen, surely because of his eminently suitable appearance, as secretary to the Duke of Abercorn's Special Mission to announce the Accession of Edward VII to the Courts of Eastern Europe. This he carried out so well that it led to his being in attendance on Prince Albert of Belgium (afterwards King Albert) for the coronation. A not undistinguished career followed in various posts in which he showed promise and gained experience. During the First World War he was back at the Foreign Office, from where he attended conferences and, still sartorially impeccable, occasionally visited the battlefields. The impression he made at this time on the far more brilliant Vansittart was of 'one of those coming men who never quite arrive'. Eventually he did arrive and with something of a splash.

When Curzon went to the Foreign Office in January 1919 for a short while George became his private secretary and, accompanying him on his first day to the Secretary of State's room, had the privilege of witnessing his celebrated reaction to the unworthiness of the inkstand: 'This contraption, if I may say so, is merely brăss and glăss.'

In September that year Clerk got his first legation in a newly-created republic. He did well in Prague, remaining there till 1926, followed by seven years at the embassy in Angora, where he won the respect of Ataturk. That he was a very kind man is borne out by the story told to the writer by a Turkish diplomat. As a young secretary in his Foreign Office, during a moment of crisis, he somehow omitted to inform the British Ambassador that the Foreign Secretary wished to see him. When the envoy failed to turn up Selim Sarper, in a frenzy, rushed round to the embassy to find that Sir George was dressing for dinner, a ritual of importance not to be interrupted. Pleading urgency, he managed to obtain an interview and made a clean breast of the appalling blunder which could affect his whole future. To his great credit Clerk promised he would call at the Foreign Office as soon as he was dressed which he did, greeting Sarper at the door with: 'I did it for you, young man.'

In 1933 he was appointed to the Brussels Embassy. When his unexpected appointment to Paris was fixed one of the Under-Secretaries in the Foreign Office asked for leave to take the letter over to Brussels himself. Sir Lancelot Oliphant could not resist seeing the expression on the face of his old friend when he heard the news. After a few commonplace remarks, he handed the missive from the Secretary of State to the Ambassador and keenly watched the reaction. Clerk could hardly believe his eyes. About to be 60, he had imagined that Brussels would be his last assignment. Suddenly he was being offered the most splendid and enjoyable post of all.

There was a very large fly in the ointment. The Foreign Office stipulated that his wife must play her part as ambassadress to the full and he was hardly on speaking terms with her. That such a connoisseur of feminine charm could, even at the age of 24, have married somebody entirely antipathetic has only one explanation: Muriel Whitwell, a large, rather splendid-looking, unconventional woman, was said to have money. In fact she had little and the incompatibility of their characters made it best for them to live apart as much as possible. The Foreign Office would have been well advised to let him go to Paris *en garçon*, for as such he was at his best, and Lady Clerk was too eccentric to be a good ambassadress. Following immediately on Lady Tyrrell she must have confirmed the French suspicion that Englishwomen were inclined to be mad.

George was the first Ambassador since the days of the Dufferins to use the Borghese bed. His wife, like that of the Duke of Wellington, was only tolerated far away upstairs but here she spread herself and indulged in the two compelling interests of her life. A studio was contrived in one of the rooms facing north in which she painted away happily, for Lady Clerk was a considerable artist as well as a sculptress. Chagall admired her painting and became a frequent visitor to the second floor. Added to the stream of arty-looking *cognoscenti* who, as they crossed the hall and made for the lift, ran the risk of colliding with the Ambassador, were people who had come for another purpose, the halt, the maim and the blind, for the Ambassadress was also a faith-healer. Members of the Chancery forebore to let it be known if they felt ill lest she insisted on treating them. When the Ambassador took charge the cure was more effective. Once, when he heard that Charles Peake was suffering from recurring trouble from a war wound, he insisted that he and his wife should move into the embassy and be given champagne every night.

He was always generous with his champagne, sending a magnum over to the Chancery when they had to work late, and it flowed lavishly at the new year luncheon in the ballroom which he gave to the entire staff (then numbering about eighty persons). Champagne was his panacea and symbolic of his world, a dashing world of lovely women in lovely clothes, love affairs never deeply passionate, light music, dancing. At weekends he would go to the races, where his evident enjoyment made him a popular figure, or he would play golf. It was nothing for him to do eighteen holes in the morning, for lunch have double martinis, champagne, Grand Marnier, and then do another eighteen holes. Such was his notion of *la douceur de vivre* and he lived it in great style, faultlessly dressed for the appropriate occasion and never undignified. He knew that he was looked upon as a disappointment after Tyrrell and wisely did not attempt to be anything different from what he was.

It is alleged that Queen Mary once said to the King: 'They tell me that Sir George Clerk goes to night clubs.' To which the Monarch replied: 'Nonsense, my dear. It cannot be true. It's just as if you and I went to night clubs.' Completely left out of this side of her husband's life, Lady Clerk longed to go to night clubs and once persuaded Charles Peake to take her to one she had heard of. Charles drove her up and down the boulevards determined not to find it, eventually landing her back at the embassy, extremely disappointed.

John Mallet acted as go-between for the Clerks, conveying to her in more polite terms than the original message that she really must accompany her husband to some important function, getting her into the car and watching them drive off in angry silence. The natural amiability of George vanished when she was around. She invariably let him down just when he was trying to entertain with a flourish, the one thing at which, on his own, he knew he could excel. My husband Gladwyn once unwittingly became an accessory to her extraordinary behaviour. When everybody had returned to the drawing-room after a large dinner-party she discovered that he did not know a certain opening in chess. Completely ignoring her other guests she sent a footman to fetch the chess table and settled down to a game for the rest of the evening.

This was as nothing to a rout which Fitzroy Maclean remembered when he was third secretary. The Ambassadress was known to be safely away in the south of France so George decided that he would give a magnificent dinner with all his favourite people and no expense spared. Suddenly, at about 7 o'clock, into the hall walked Lady Clerk. Discovering that there was a party about to take place she proceeded to arrange it her own way, sweeping the orchids off the dinner-table to produce something more artistic, ivy from the garden hastily picked by the footmen. After dinner she decided that everybody must play a game. 'Campbell!' she shouted to the Minister, 'get the chairs,' and he and the secretaries had to heave about the heavy furniture in the order for musical chairs. When Jacques Février, the eminent pianist, was set down at the piano he started playing classical music but, to his astonishment, received a great thump on the back from the Ambassadress telling him to stop. For the first round or two the French were unable to comprehend what it was all about, but they were put on their mettle by Lady Clerk's telling them that the Turks were much better at it. They then started to play with skill and venom, and the Marquise de Ludre, a hostess of intellectual importance, missed her chair and sat on the floor with a suddenness she did not at all like. Leaving the embassy she was heard to remark that she would have preferred conversation.

The only fault the staff had to find with Clerk was that when he was needed to sign telegrams he wanted first to finish his rubber of bridge at the Jockey Club. Otherwise he ran the embassy well, kept reasonable control, supported people in difficulties and showed good sense. His excuse for not taking a greater interest in foreign affairs was: 'I've written despatches all my life and now I have a competent staff to do it for me.'

The usefulness of having a man like Charles Mendl in the embassy was evident when the Front Populaire came into power in 1936. Clerk found himself at a disadvantage because he had to admit that he did not even know the new Prime Minister, nor would it have been exactly easy for him, a blatantly right-wing figure, quickly to get on good terms with an intellectual socialist. It was to the press attaché that he turned. Charles did not fail him. He knew Léon Blum well enough to telephone him straight away in his apartment in the Quai Bourbon, for he had not yet even moved to the Matignon, congratulate him on being now 'King of France', tell him how interested his Ambassador was to meet him and, appreciating how busy he was, ask him if he would some time suggest a date. Blum dined at the embassy that same evening and the Foreign Office got a very favourable impression of the adroitness of their emissary to Paris.

Essentially a peacetime ambassador he was not the right man to represent us during the calamitous events which led up to the Second World War. He was retired in April 1937 and died in 1951. Yet he did not do so badly during those three unexpected years. He was regretted not only by the *élégantes* (who had never had it so good), by the Jockey Club and café society, but also by Frenchmen who valued his genuine enjoyment of the good things France had to offer.

During the German occupation, Prince Jean de Caraman-Chimay ran into the Duc de Magenta, who was in the Résistance, and whispered that, as he was about to leave secretly for England, he could take anything over for him if he so wished. Jean stoutly replied: 'Yes. Take my umbrella to Briggs to get it re-rolled,' but, on second thoughts, decided on something more worthwhile: two bottles of champagne for Sir George Clerk. George resisted drinking one of the bottles until the war was over and, when Caraman-Chimay made his first visit to England, the Prince and ex-Ambassador toasted our two countries.

XXVI

Sir Eric Phipps
1937—1939

'There was no mistaking the lightning in his eye. Here was Jupiter all right, even if for a change he had chosen to disguise himself as a bullfinch' – thus the third secretary, Valentine Lawford, describing Phipps's arrival at the Gare du Nord. So contrasting a figure to his light-hearted predecessor naturally inspired some uneasiness at first, but Jupiter proved to be strangely unwilling to wield his thunderbolt.

Sir Eric Phipps had an intimate knowledge of France from childhood and his appointment to the embassy in 1937 was the sixth time that he had served there. He was the son of Sir Constantine Phipps, a distinguished diplomat, and the great-nephew of Normanby. Born in 1875, he was largely educated in France and at Cambridge. His career began as an attaché to the Paris Embassy in 1898, returning there a year later as third secretary after he had passed his Foreign Office examination. In 1909 he was back in the dreaded post of private secretary to Bertie.

That year he had the misfortune to lose his wife, a Frenchwoman to whom he had been married two years. He remarried in 1911 a charming and intelligent young girl who had been brought up in France. Her mother was American and her father an English artist, Herbert Ward.

Again at the embassy in 1916, he was attached to the peace delegation from 1918 to 1919 when he became a counsellor in the Foreign Office. Transferred to Brussels in 1920, two years later he was back in Paris under Lord

Crewe, leaving to be minister in Vienna when that ambassador retired. That he did not, in 1934, get the embassy which he had always wanted, instead of the less able George Clerk, was a surprise, and his appointment to the highly important post of Berlin the year before Tyrrell retired seemed almost like a ruse to prevent his being moved again when Paris became vacant. Tyrrell used to say, possibly to justify his having recommended Clerk as his immediate successor, that it had always been the intention of the Foreign Office to send a man first for a spell in Berlin and then move him to Paris to get the right perspective of the two countries. But Phipps was the only ambassador to have done so when in April 1937, after three years in Germany, he came once again to France.

Small, and rather un-English in appearance, he was a man of great charm and intelligence, clever, amusing, cynical, proficient at his job and knowing all about France. His wife was delightful and extremely intelligent, the friend of all the most interesting people in Paris. They entertained very well in a French fashion, as might be expected of two people who had lived there so much, and the embassy took on a correct atmosphere reminiscent of the Boulevard St Germain or the Haut Bourgeoisie, almost excelling these in the *comme-il-faut* approach to life.

The house was none too large for a family of six children. They filled the second floor; even the entresol, which had been the pleasant perquisite of junior members of the chancery, had to be vacated. The upper entresol became known as Belloc's Room, for Hilaire Belloc was a frequent visitor. Lady Phipps was a convert to Roman Catholicism.

Phipps ran his embassy with immense efficiency. He had a great sense of humour. As minister under Crewe he was once called upon by his vis-à-vis from another embassy, whom he was obliged to leave alone in the room for a few minutes. He returned to surprise him at his desk looking through his papers. '*Mon cher,*' Phipps reassured his visitor, '*je vous approuve, je vous approuve, mais il ne faut pas que je vous voie!*'

While the champagne of George Clerk flowed, clouds were building up. The France of the 1920s had, in large majority, been more determined than England to frustrate German designs but, by the 1930s, she had become weakened and disunited. In March 1936 Germany marched into the Rhineland unopposed. England failed to give moral support to France for, despite the efforts of those alive to the coming danger, the mood of the country was such that a strong policy could not be adopted. It was a shaming period on both sides of the Channel and in France right-wingers were saying, '*Plûtot Hitler que Blum*.' In March 1938 Germany seized Austria and France immediately renewed her pledge of 1922 to come to the aid of Czechoslovakia were she to be attacked. The challenge came that summer and France and England did not meet it.

Grim prospects were set aside for a happy interlude in glorious July weather when King George VI and Queen Elizabeth came to Paris on a state visit. It proved how greatly the French valued the Entente Cordiale and also established the popularity abroad of the newly-crowned royal couple who so admirably took over after the abdication of Edward VIII. The simple dignity of a king dedicated to doing the right thing was held in the highest esteem, while the Queen added to this image of British royalty her happy ease of manner and compelling charm.

Oliver Harvey, able and shrewd, had returned to the Foreign Office in 1936. When Eden resigned in 1938, Harvey kept a vigilant eye on his successor, Halifax. The principal private secretary is supposed to be the chief link between the Foreign Office and the Secretary of State. Some believed that Oliver exceeded this function. There was a precedent. Tyrrell had been even more irregularly influential a quarter of a century earlier.

Defeatism was in the air and nine days before Munich our Ambassador in Paris showed which side he was on. It had for some time been clear that Phipps believed that we should if possible avoid engaging in a war for which we were entirely unprepared without any guarantee of American support. In his famous telegram of 21 September the Ambassador, after strongly criticizing the activities in Paris of Churchill and Spears, went so far as to say that unless 'German aggression' was 'so bloody brutal and prolonged as to infuriate French public opinion to the extent of making it lose its reason, war would be most unpopular in France'. There was great danger in encouraging a 'noisy and corrupt war group'. 'All that is best in France,' he continued, 'is against war almost at any price.' In a follow-up telegram he solemnly added that the notorious pro-German appeaser, Joseph Caillaux, was strongly in favour of putting further pressure on Prague.

Whatever Halifax may have thought, the office was appalled, most of all the Ambassador's brother-in-law, Vansittart, who had been relegated to what proved to be a post devoid of power as Chief Diplomatic Adviser (an adviser who was never consulted). Indignant enquiries revealed that by a 'corrupt war group' Phipps had meant the Communists who were 'paid by Moscow'. Subsequent enquiries about French public opinion were then addressed to various consular officers who were requested to reply directly to the Foreign Office so as to avoid their views being 'doctored' by the embassy. Not since Normanby had the Foreign Office felt such lack of confidence in their envoy and there was a strong feeling that he should be replaced.

The agreement with Hitler was signed by Chamberlain at Munich on 30 September. At the end of November the Prime Minister was to visit Paris and, a few days earlier, Oliver Harvey wrote in his diary how anxious he was to get the retirement of Phipps fixed. In this he was backed by the Promotions Board who, for fear of blocking promotion, recommended against any extension of his term beyond April 1939 when he would be well past retiring age. Halifax had agreed to appoint in his place Sir Ronald Campbell, Minister in Belgrade, when he received a letter from the former secretary to the cabinet, Lord Hankey, so highly praising Sir Eric as 'the best Ambassador ever' that he wavered. It was now hoped that the retirement would be fixed for the following autumn.

The visit of Chamberlain was greeted with mixed feelings and it was fortunate that he was prevented from driving through the streets of Paris in an open car as he had proposed. At the embassy reception so few people accepted that the chancery wives were made to resort to the old stage trick of appearing in a new guise, changing their hats and being announced two or three times, so as to give the Prime Minister the impression that the party was crowded.

On the very day that Sir Eric had denounced the war group, he had begun to harbour a viper in the bosom of the Embassy. A new third secretary was transferred from London to Paris, an immensely tall Highlander, intelligent, interesting, attractive, the son of an esteemed Liberal. This powerful young man promised to be the ideal type for the service, deceiving even the astute Willie Tyrrell, who thought it splendid when he heard, in October 1935, that Donald Maclean had passed the Foreign Office exam.

In March 1939, when the Nazis entered Prague, Oliver Harvey thought that the Government were alive to the situation at last but, by early May, he noted, 'Appeasement is raising its ugly head again. I keep hearing that No. 10 is at it again behind our backs . . . Phipps continues to intrigue against Daladier through Bonnet and to send us patently one-sided accounts of French opinion.' Not only did Harvey miss the close collaboration he had had with his great friend Anthony Eden but he was now no longer even a confidential political adviser. This in no way deterred him from acting in an unusual manner by still dedicating himself to the interests of the ex-Secretary of State.

Eden had received many invitations to speak in Paris which he had been obliged to turn down for various reasons, but in May he asked Oliver Harvey to enquire of the embassy when and where he could give a lecture in June. The reply from Sir Eric, which Harvey dismissed as 'nonsense and intended as sabotage', was that 'June was a bad month for lectures and it would be better to consider it in the autumn.' Ignoring this advice, Oliver, aided by Charles

Peake, now in the Foreign Office News Department, conspired to arrange the lecture independently of the embassy through the *Figaro* correspondent in London. The occasion was to be one of prime importance preceded by a banquet given by the French Cabinet. The Ambassador, backed strongly by his press attaché, was furious at the announcement of this event without his pre-knowledge. 'Propaganda for prolonging Phipps is beginning to work heavily and obviously from all sides,' Harvey puts in his diary in the end of May. However, a change was made later in the year, and at this point Sir Eric cannot have been sorry to leave.

He seemed eminently suitable for the Paris Embassy. But the stresses and strains of the battle between Chamberlain and Eden, the mounting unpopularity of his brilliant, vituperative brother-in-law, Vansittart, whose warnings people preferred not to heed, together with the appeasing advice of those close at hand, including Sir Charles Mendl, probably affected his judgment. His reputation has suffered as a result.

He died in 1945.

XXVII

Sir Ronald Campbell
1939—1940

Sir Ronald was the son of Sir Francis Campbell, Assistant Under-Secretary of State for Foreign Affairs in the Governments of Balfour, Campbell-Bannerman and Asquith. Born in 1883, he entered the service and married the following year. He was the invaluable private secretary to two heads of the Foreign Office in succession, Nicolson and Hardinge, and afterwards to Curzon. Posted abroad for the first time in 1929 as Minister under Tyrrell and then Clerk, he was given the legation in Belgrade in 1935, from where he returned to Paris to succeed Phipps.

He was now 57 and nearly all his career had been spent in the Foreign Office, which he had joined as a clerk in 1907. Indeed he could be described as a very great clerk. Shrewd, quiet, self-contained, firm, the soul of integrity, trusted by all, he was hard to beat from the point of view of work. Insisting that everything be done absolutely right, he himself wrote with such meticulous care that he never needed to correct a draft telegram. The embassy was further strengthened by the appointment of Oliver Harvey as Minister just before the new year of 1940.

Knowing the country, Campbell had a good feeling of what was going on, and soon after his arrival he sized up the weakness of the French, foreseeing how a large number of defeatist politicians would be ready to do a deal with the Germans. It has been said that the interim period known as *une drôle de guerre* was a brilliant strategic move on the part of Germany since it gave France time to relax. With inactivity the garden from where, when she was needed, a footman fetched her by whistling below.

She was delightfully vague and the amusing stories about her accumulated. On the arm of the President she once led the procession for dinner in the direction of the ballroom so that everyone was obliged to about turn. At one of her dinner-parties she sat next to Lord Birkenhead, then Secretary of State for India, and talked to him the whole evening under the impression that he was the Turkish Ambassador. She apologized to a guest for the delay in going to dinner, explaining that they were waiting for the King of Sweden, to whom she was in fact speaking. On another royal occasion she was said to have asked a young man standing near her if he would be so kind as to open the window, unaware that she was addressing the guest of honour, the Duke of York. During this same visit she ran into a figure in the passage and asked anxiously, 'Am I doing all right, Bill?' 'Very well indeed, Lady Tyrrell,' kindly replied the future George VI, whom she had mistaken for the private secretary, Cavendish-Bentinck.

Lady Mendl was not the only chancery wife who thought she could run the embassy, since virtually there was no ambassadress, but Tyrrell was too shrewd to allow this. Nevertheless, as he had few links with the *monde*, she was of use to him in providing something of the glittering side of life. He was a shy man who shunned society, sometimes retiring to the Salon Vert during the King's Birthday Garden Party, yet he was fascinated by people in all walks of life. He made friends with Coco Chanel, the well-known dressmaker then at her zenith, he liked trades unionists and had a certain fleeting interest in extremely rich industrialists. He got on well with Mendl, valuing the sort of continuity he gave the embassy, and he was good with journalists. Thomas Cadett (later BBC representative in France) arrived in Paris in 1929 as a third correspondent of *The Times* and remembers the kindness and interest he showed him. They shared an apprehension for the future, fearing defeatism in certain of the French politicians. He was a great ambassador in the sense that he wanted to do as much as possible for France as well as for England.

The embassy was a happy one under Tyrrell. Provided he liked his staff he was always kind to them and continually invited them to the house. But he had a streak of naughtiness in him and a certain malice, nor did he forget an injury. Soon after his arrival in Paris, Derrick Hoyer-Millar ventured to criticize some odd arrangement which struck him as unsuitable by suggesting that Lady Crewe would have done it differently. Within a very short time he was transferred from Paris and never forgiven.

At the age of 67 his long career came to an end. He retired to London, still watched over by Mad (Lady Tyrrell died in 1939) and was appointed film censor, a suitable post for one to whom the cinema had always been a relaxation. Created a peer in 1929 (with the lilies of France figuring prominently in his coat of arms) he took little advantage of the House of Lords in which to air his views. Oratory was not his means of expression and he preferred intrigue behind the scenes.

In the critical years immediately before the Second World War his advice was continually sought by the Government, TUC leaders, the Foreign Office, and particularly by Oliver Harvey, who became private secretary to Anthony Eden and then to Lord Halifax. In his diaries, Harvey tells how, after the Anschluss, his old chief was obsessed by the shortness of time before Germany became too strong for us. The Prime Minister, Neville Chamberlain, whom Tyrrell said was 'a man without a spark of imagination', consulted him before going to Munich. Tyrrell thought he was right to go but, of course, not that he should have signed the Anglo-German Declaration. No one knew better than W.T. the value of not committing oneself in writing. By the end of March 1940 he was convinced that we never could win the war with Chamberlain but, curiously enough, thought that his successor should be Halifax. He died in 1947.

Crewe will always be remembered for his reforms and his famous memorandum whereas Tyrrell, who criticized more

Lady Diana Cooper on the Lit de Parade
The State Bed-room showing the Lit de Parade and the psyché, 1957

The Library, 1957
Sir Alfred Duff Cooper in the
Library

the fighting spirit of the autumn of 1939 began to deteriorate.

On 10 May 1940, the day Winston Churchill became Prime Minister, the enemy invaded the Low Countries, and by the 16th, after they had broken through on the Meuse, Paul Reynaud warned the Ambassador that German tanks were advancing so rapidly that they could reach Paris in twenty-four hours. Forthwith plans were made in the embassy preparatory to evacuation. The secret archives were burnt in the stoke-hole, the female staff in the Chancery were sent off to England that evening and the Prime Minister himself arrived in the late afternoon, 'Full of fire and fury' according to Harvey. Immediately he went to the Quai d'Orsay, where he learnt from General Gamelin, the Commander-in-Chief, that France had no strategic reserve. Of this blow Churchill wrote: 'It must be remembered that this was the first realization we had of the magnitude of the disaster or of the apparent French despair.'

Back at the embassy he told General Ismay (later Lord Ismay), Head of the Military Wing of the War Cabinet Secretariat, who had accompanied him, to telephone to his office in London asking for more squadrons of fighters and more bombers to assist the French. The consent of the Cabinet was received at about 11.30 that night just as the courtyard, where so many grand departures had taken place, was witnessing a strange one. In pitch dark, the Ambassadress and all the other wives, each with one small suitcase, were reluctantly being bundled into cars and packed off to Le Havre escorted by two attachés. Loath to desert their husbands they were hardly encouraged by Winston's prophecying that it was as well they should leave before the place became a charnel house.

With Ismay he then set off to see Paul Reynaud, who had succeeded Daladier as Prime Minister in March. Having done his best 'to revive the spirits of our French friends' Churchill returned to the embassy, getting to bed about 2 a.m., his sleep but little disturbed by air raids. Both the Minister and the Counsellor had moved into the embassy that evening. Oliver's bad night was cut short by the Premier, rising above the gravity of the situation, singing and splashing about in his bath when getting up at six to catch his aeroplane. Little sleep was also had by the second secretary, Roddie Barclay, as he stayed up till four helping to burn archives. These were also being fed into the central heating, and a junior secretary remembers the Ambassador on a particularly warm day sweltering at his desk in his shirt sleeves. The less secret papers, ironically including those of the peace conference, took days to destroy on three enormous bonfires on the lawn.

The evacuation of the women was premature, for Paris was no longer immediately threatened and the Ambassador remained there for nearly three weeks. An entry in Oliver's invaluable diary strikes a familiar note. Charles Peake warned him that there was a plan afoot to send 'some super Englishman' to reside in Paris in addition to the Ambassador. Charles was doing his best to stop this and asked for facts which would impress the Government of the success of Campbell. There was no counterpart of Lord Esher around to irritate Sir Ronald but Winston, on coming into power, had appointed Major General Sir Edward Spears as his personal representative with the French Premier. This disquieted the embassy, for reactions to this unusually gifted man with his energy and his strong, excitable personality were apt to be mixed. However, soon Oliver noted that 'Spears is being very useful after all and is a useful contact to have with the P.M.', whom he was excellent at managing. Moreover, Spears could argue on a military plane, and as the war progressed it was through him that the embassy got to know just how defeatist the French generals were.

On the night of 8 June Roddie Barclay was giving a small bachelor dinner at his flat for Donald Maclean, who had got engaged to an American, Melinda Marling,* when the party was abruptly interrupted by a telephone call from the embassy reporting that the Germans were fast approaching

---

* After he had defected she joined him in Moscow with their children, left him to marry the arch-spy Kim Philby, and later returned to Donald.

Paris. Because of the immediate threat to Rouen the French Government moved a large number of the ministries to Touraine, leaving only a nucleus in Paris. Campbell decided to send an advance party in charge of Barclay to the château which had been allotted to the embassy. They left the morning of the 10th, some of them driving in the Rolls-Royce of Lord Derby, which he kept in Paris and had put at their disposal. Everywhere were streams of refugees, travelling in any conveyance they had been able to find, many stuck for want of petrol, which was now impossible to get, some already utterly worn out.

Meanwhile in Paris the Quai had also left and Oliver began to worry lest the Ambassador was not given sufficient warning of the departure of the Prime Minister. If there were too much delay they might have to get a plane sent from England. By 4 p.m. it was finally settled that they would go that evening, but no sooner had this decision been taken than a telegram announced the intention of our ubiquitous Premier to arrive at 6.15 and stay the night, this in the face of opposition from the Cabinet. He was stopped just in time but still proposed flying over next day to the new headquarters of Weygand at Briare, where he 'displayed the smiling countenance and confident air which are thought suitable when things are very bad'.

Just before nine on the evening of 10 June, for the third time in the history of the embassy, an ambassador drove out of the courtyard to join the French Government in the south-west. When listing later the causes of the collapse of France, Sir Ronald said that one of the cleverest of the German tactics had been the driving of scared civilians before them as they advanced. This seriously interfered with French military plans and demoralized the soldiers. In his opinion the army was vanquished even before the evacuation of Paris. His journey from the capital was a dreadful experience, with chaotic roads choked with three lines of traffic heading for safety. Led by the military attaché it took seven hours to reach their destination, where Barclay was waiting to welcome them.

They awoke next morning to find themselves in a beautiful sixteenth-century moated château surrounded by a wooded park. Delightfully untouched artistically, the plumbing was in keeping with the period. With perfect manners their elderly hostess, the Baronne de Champschevrier, accepted the enormous influx of extra persons which could only have been equalled in the history of the château when Louis XIII had stayed there to hunt.

Purposely ministries and embassies had been scattered widely over the countryside rather than concentrated in Tours, where they would have been an easy target, and as the telephone was completely inadequate the only means of communication was by car. It took Campbell two hours to drive to the headquarters of Reynaud at the Château de Chissay, where he found confusion, discussion, dictation, frantic last moment telephoning to America for help. The drenching rain reflected the general gloom.

Late in the night of 13 June, Sir Ronald heard that, as the Germans were nearing Le Mans, they must leave for Bordeaux early next morning. It was the day the enemy entered Paris. Arriving at Bordeaux that evening they found they had been allotted a château 50 kilometres away. However, Georges Mandel, the Minister of the Interior, arranged for ten rooms at the Hôtel Montré to be put at the disposal of the more important members of the embassy. The Ambassador intended to set up the Chancery in the consulate, but as this was being besieged by British and refugees of all nations clamouring to be evacuated, he had to make do with a sort of lumber room where telegrams were enciphered and deciphered.

By the next day Campbell knew that things were rapidly slipping. He urged that a British warship should be ready to get people away; meanwhile it could be used as a safe means of sending off telegrams.

At Briare, Spears had reported that 'the only calm and intelligent officer left' was Brigadier General Charles de Gaulle. As Under-Secretary of War the latter was on a mission to London on 16 June when Churchill put a special aeroplane at his disposal to go and rally the French. He arrived too late. There are conflicting reports as to how he managed to leave again on 17 June. Spears says bluntly: 'I brought de Gaulle from Bordeaux to England in my plane'.* He gives a vivid description of the General hiding the previous evening in Reynaud's dark hall, and later, at the embassy headquarters, being 'clearly overwrought' – a judgement disputed by the air attaché, later Air Marshal Sir Douglas Collyer, who was also present.

The next morning de Gaulle is represented as coming to the airport under the excuse of seeing off Spears, who at the last moment pulled him on to the aeroplane. In *L'Appel* de Gaulle states, 'I got away without romanticism or difficulty,' a fact confirmed by his faithful aide-de-camp, Geoffroy de Courcel, later Ambassador to London, and by the air attaché who witnessed the departure.

If Spears's account is accepted then he must have some credit for having potentially changed the course of history and indeed he claims it on the grounds that the aircraft, a de Havilland Dragon Rapide, the pilot of which was subsequently killed, was at his disposal. This flight has been confused with that of Wing Commander Fielden piloting a Flamingo on 16 June. Evidence shows, however, that it was still de Gaulle's, but under the authority of the air attaché, representing the Ambassador on the question of passengers and loading. This is supported by Group Captain E. B. Haslam, historian to the R.A.F. Nor does it appear that Churchill actually wanted Spears to leave Bordeaux. It was only after a long argument on the telephone that Churchill gave his permission. It could be argued that it was de Gaulle who brought Spears to England.

The one bright spot in this gloom and chaos was the celebrated restaurant, Le Chapon Fin, where all congregated and came away slightly less depressed. Everybody had their table and much information could be obtained from watch-

* *'Two men who saved France, Pétain and de Gaulle'* by Major General Sir Edward Spears, written after Spears and de Gaulle had quarrelled over policy in the Middle East.

ing who sat with whom. As Mandel, the Jewish politician who had refused an offer of a flight to England from de Gaulle and from Spears, got up to leave the restaurant after lunch, the police, who had been waiting in the corridor, came in and, on a nod from Laval, arrested him. Sir Ronald said, 'That's the end.' There was a frantic rush to the consulate by British subjects and refugees. They nearly all got away, including the Mendls, who were seen crossing the frontier into Spain in a Rolls followed by a station-wagon piled high with Vuitton luggage. The Consul and his staff left and the embassy was now reduced to fourteen, one of their bedrooms being used as the Chancery. The telephone hardly stopped ringing and so exhausted were they that Barclay remembers how they dropped off to sleep the moment they sat in a comfortable chair. Once Campbell came in at 5 a.m. to find four decipherers slumped over their work.

Ministers were still coming out from England. On the 18th the First Lord of the Admiralty and the First Sea Lord arrived to discuss the fate of the French Fleet and the following day Lord Lloyd, the Colonial Minister, came out with a message for the French Government. British ships were taking away the French who were now in danger and those who had responded to de Gaulle's broadcast from England.

At about 8 p.m. on the 22nd the Ambassador came into the Chancery to announce that he had a further telegram to go. He wrote down two words: 'Armistice signed'. The new Government had not even informed him of this event. He had found it out when he went to see Weygand.

They got away at eleven that night, and at about midnight they reached their temporary destination, a villa at Arcachon. After a few hours' sleep they all climbed into an open sardine boat in which they were mercilessly tossed on a rough sea in pouring rain till finally they reached the Canadian destroyer, the *Fraser*, which took them to the cruiser awaiting them at St Jean de Luz. On boarding the *Galatea* they found already established the wife of Spears and her group of nurses, who were turned off and sent home in another ship. As dusk fell the next evening they sailed into Plymouth Sound, a fine sight made even more so in their eyes by the presence of some French warships.

The exhausted embassy party received the highest praise for the way they had carried on till the last possible moment. In his final despatch Sir Ronald describes how greatly he had been encouraged by his loyal staff, who never spared themselves and accepted the long hours under adverse conditions uncomplainingly, while they, in turn, have recorded their devotion and admiration for this quiet, unruffled head of mission. For if, in certain respects, he seemed to fall short of what is generally expected of an ambassador to France in that he was not a dominant personality, nor particularly notable, nor a social success, being outwardly stiff and giving an impression of dullness, yet he was the ideal man for the post in those last months of the 'phoney war'.

Later in 1940 he was appointed to the embassy in Lisbon, from which he retired in 1945. He died in 1953.

XXVIII

The Occupation
1940—1944

When Ronald Campbell drove from the embassy on the evening of 10 June he left it in charge of four trustworthy persons: Spurgeon, the head chancery messenger, an ex-jockey, and his wife, who had been the embassy telephonist, and Christie, the gate porter, and his wife. Everybody else had fled. The dinner of the Ambassador in the private dining-room was not cleared away, the hot plate was still on.

The following morning a representative of the United States Embassy came to affix seals and printed notices, which stated that the premises were under American protection. The ormolu had already been sent to the Louvre, but otherwise everything remained in the deserted house. The Spurgeons went over to the church and carried back in coal bags the chalice, plate and other objects of value to put in the silver room. Every day they did the rounds of the house to see that all was well. They themselves had the small room at the top of the gate house, once occupied by the Charost 'suisse'. They had no heating and lived on the black market with money paid by the British Government.

Goering had his eye on the embassy. He came to inspect it and sent for the Americans to open it up for him, which they refused to do. Then one day a German diplomat, accompanied by an officer and soldiers with bayonets, demanded to search the Chancery. Mrs Spurgeon recognized him as a frequent visitor in peacetime and boldly told him he had no right to be there. The most alarming experience for the four occupants was when the Germans arrested the two husbands and took them to St Denis. Christie remained there five months but the story of the release of Spurgeon is one of the heartwarming incidents of the war. Mrs Spurgeon, a spirited Frenchwoman, had the courage to pester the German Consulate three times a day and, fortunately, the official with whom she so eloquently pleaded was very humane. Herr Johann Leonhard insisted that he was her adversary, not her enemy, and when, finally, she obtained the release of her husband, said that he hoped she would do the same for him should the occasion ever arise. At the time of the invasion, the news of which was whispered through Paris, he even came to ask if they had enough to eat. Leonhard was indeed arrested at the end of the war, and through the Foreign Office Mrs Spurgeon was reminded of her promise. Her recommendation that he was '*un bon Boche*' regained him his freedom.

At last came the great day of liberation and the flag was once more raised above the gateway by the fire brigade, that splendid body of men who are called on to deal with every emergency. When Patrick Reilly, the first member of the embassy to arrive from Algiers, entered the courtyard he was greeted in style by Christie on the steps in a top hat and purple frock coat.

XXIX

Sir Alfred Duff Cooper
1944—1947

More than any other ambassador, Duff Cooper approached the position that Lytton had held. He was a literary figure devoted to France and had that same kindness of heart which inspired immediate response in others. Unlike Lytton, this likeableness did not preclude fierce indignation in the face of injustice, nor the courage of his convictions carried to the point of resignation. He had a strong personality and chose for his motto '*Odi et Amo*' (I hate and love).

Duff was born in 1890. His father was a famous surgeon, his mother a sister of the first Duke of Fife, who married a daughter of Edward VII. At Eton and Oxford he belonged to that group of brilliant young men who promised to be the future leaders of the country, nearly all of whom were killed in the First World War. In 1913 he entered the Foreign Office, from which he was released in 1917 to join the army, and served in the Grenadier Guards, showing great bravery in battle, for which he won the DSO. After the armistice he returned to the Foreign Office in 1919 and married Lady Diana Manners, daughter of the Duke and Duchess of Rutland, famous for her astonishing beauty. She herself has written that she has had three perfect relationships in life: with her mother, her husband and her son.

It was she who enabled him to fulfil his ambition of leaving diplomacy to become a politician, a change of career he could not afford. But Diana devised a scheme to make money which she called 'The Plan'. She went into films, and later acted the part of the Madonna in *The Miracle*. In 1924 Duff was elected Conservative Member for Oldham and for the St George's Division of Westminster in 1931. With the experience of two financial secretaryships he was appointed Secretary of State for War in 1935 and two years later First Lord of the Admiralty, when he and Diana relished living in beautiful Admiralty House with its Fish furniture. He resigned over Munich, the only Cabinet Minister to do so.

Politics had not prevented him from becoming a successful writer, the biographer of Talleyrand and Haig; but when, a year later, war was declared, he minded intensely the inactivity of a back-bencher and his uselessness as a fighting man. The fear that the friends of his youth, 'the noblest of their strain', might have died in vain inspired him to clarify his thoughts in a fine rousing poem which he sent to *The Times*. The editor, an advocate of Chamberlain's policy, neither published nor acknowledged it.

On becoming Premier in May 1940 Churchill offered Duff the Ministry of Information, which proved his least happy post, so he was glad, six months later, to become British Representative in Singapore, where he remained till General Wavell was put in command of all the Far East. He was then made Chancellor of the Duchy of Lancaster till, in the autumn of 1943, Anthony Eden offered him the choice of the embassy in Rome, as soon as that city fell into our hands, or the rank of ambassador in Algiers as British representative to the French Committee of Liberation, and from there eventually to go to the Paris Embassy. He and Diana chose the latter.

Duff liked and admired de Gaulle. He always got on well with him, so well that Churchill, who found the character of the French leader antipathetic and sometimes impossible, had hesitated over the appointment, fearing that the British representative might not carry out his policy. Having put him at rest on this point, Duff found in Algiers that his endeavours to maintain harmony between the two were made even more difficult by the near presence of Spears as minister in Syria and the Lebanon. This close friend of the Premier had now become a definite francophobe.

In August 1944 Paris was liberated and Duff's mission to France, the apex of his career, began. In September the Coopers crossed from England escorted by 48 Spitfires. They went to a hotel till the house was made ready for them. Work in the chancery, by candlelight, could start immediately. Not only had it been kept immaculately by the Christies and Spurgeons, but it contained an abundance of such things as pre-war stationery, which contrasted with the poor quality used in the Foreign Office.

The new Ambassadress was of a goddess-like beauty, which rivalled memories of Pauline. She is one of the most remarkable and original women of our age. Dazzling Anglo-Saxon fairness belies the bohemian in her. Oblivious of convention, indifferent to luxury, her background might have been a race of Romanies rather than an English ducal family. Best of all is the devotion to her friends, deep humility, a refreshing absence of feminine wiles and foibles, and the brave maxim of rising above all adversity.

This last quality was immediately called into action when she surveyed her new home. At the time of the exodus to Touraine, the belongings of all members of the embassy, of the Duke of Windsor and of certain British subjects, had been stored on the ground floor by the Americans, stacked naked but highly professionally up to the ceilings. An incongruous collection of objects met the eye on entering: jumbled together was everything conceivable required for living or travelling in hot or cold climes. Somebody's bottles of red wine had frozen in the cold of winter and burst, leaking from their cases as though a bloody crime had been committed.

When all had been restored to their owners came the task of rearranging the place and this, with her unerring artistic sense, Diana was the ideal person to undertake. It remains very much as she left it. It was this ambassadress who used the candelabra for their original purpose for, judging from old photographs, they had been candle-less ornaments ever since electricity had been installed in Dufferin's time. Now the golden rooms flickered again in the most beautiful of lights. Then the green drawing-room regained its old importance for there she presided over her salon. From six to eight there came *tout Paris*, friends, travellers, politicians and, most essential of all to their hostess, those known as *La Bande*, which comprised her intimates, the artists, musicians and writers. The star of this group was the brilliant Louise de Vilmorin (Comtesse Palfy), who at one time moved into the embassy, while Jean Cocteau was as much of an habitué as he had been in the days of Reggie Bridgeman.

This daily gathering of interesting people had its value, for it was said that one merely had to go to the Salon Vert to find out what was going on in Paris. It was also a haven of warmth in those fuel-less days with not only the bright fire and the candlelight providing heat, but the animated conversation and laughter of *La Bande*. Certain of '*les amis du Salon Vert*' were believed not to have been among the more enthusiastic *résistants*. On the other hand, they had all been passed as worthy of reception by an eminent and kind *gaulliste*.

To Diana, whose love for beauty was intense and who had been disheartened at the prospect of disciplining herself to diplomatic formalities, these artistic friends made life worth while. They left their mark on the embassy, their most important contribution being the conversion of the ambassador's study into a library. On arrival Duff had been astonished to find that no library existed. Even the un-lettered Pauline had a *bibliothèque*, but the want of such a room appears only to have been felt by Stewart.

Duff now made a generous offer to the Ministry of Works that he would donate his own books to the embassy if a library were made to house them. After some hesitation the ministry agreed and the Coopers saw to it that the new project would be worthy of the house. Designed by the architect Georges Geoffroy, with knowledgeable advice given by the well-known dilettante, Charles de Bestegui, and inspired by such a room in one of the Russian palaces, it is grey and gold with tortoiseshell-coloured paint simulating woodwork, shelves fringed with green silk, tall narrow columns supporting a cornice for busts and urns. The green carpet and black-banded green velvet curtains were chosen by the artist, Christian Bérard, who arranged the furniture. Friends donated more books.

Not only is it an ideal room in which a harassed ambassador or Secretary of State can relax, work or confer, it is artistically the most consistent room in the embassy. Elsewhere successive changes of taste have been ruthlessly superimposed, even the Salon Ionien is not flawless because of Victorian encrustation. Knowing how legends fade, the writer suggested that gold lettering should round the cornice stating (in Latin): 'So that readers might be numbered among his friends, Duff Cooper, excellent Ambassador to France, made over this room to the friendly silence of books. Hail, friend, and read.'

Money was scarce so when Christian Bérard designed the bathroom of the Ambassadress, the most economical solution was to convert it into an Empire Marshal's tent, with coarse striped butcher's cloth obtained from America. The bath in its mirrored niche with swan-heads for taps makes it worthy of Pauline's house.

Labour won the election of 1945, and Duff, a Conservative appointment, offered his resignation to Anthony Eden's successor, Ernest Bevin, tough, rugged and sensible, who ranks as one of the great Foreign Secretaries. The offer was ignored for another two years, during which they worked happily together. Although the Ambassador took no part in the negotiation of the various peace treaties in 1946 he did write more than one impressive despatch advocating the formation of some kind of Western European Union. In 1946 and 1947 the emphasis was still on the necessity of somehow bringing the Russians into the post-war settlement and it was not until early 1948 that Duff's dream came true.

Duff and Diana had become too attached to France to

leave it. They retired to an ideal château in the Park of Chantilly leased to them by the Institut de France, and here they continued to hold brilliant court at weekends.

Duff died in 1954.

XXX

Epilogue

The present is best seen through the telescope of time. It is enough to say that Oliver Harvey, who took over early in 1948, was a contrast to his predecessor and much more in sympathy with the philosophy of the Labour Government. He was greeted at the Gare du Nord with fireworks in recognition of the part he had played when France fell. The whole tone of the house sobered down, becoming serious and correct, as has frequently happened in the past following a period of glitter.

Six years later Harvey was succeeded by my husband Gladwyn Jebb, during whose time the political scene underwent a notable change with the return of de Gaulle in the summer of 1958. Called back from the wilderness, this remarkable man now emerged as the badly-needed father figure. He was '*Louis XIV vieilli*', and his presidency took on a regal dignity and splendour. After an agonizing four years he 'liberated' Algeria. Then he evoked visions of renewed glory to the great and gifted nation that had lacked leadership in the crucial years before the war, and which he was determined to make the foremost country in Europe.

Although after Suez in 1956 it was clear that France was going to look towards Germany rather than Britain as her principal partner, our relations were quite happy during the first few years of the new regime. Gladwyn, consequently, had a fairly easy time. But his immediate successors, Pierson Dixon (1960), Patrick Reilly (1965) and Christopher Soames (1967), could hardly enjoy the rather exceptional relationship

Gladwyn had had with de Gaulle, who after 1962 was determined above all to exclude Britain from the Common Market. They were forced to swim against the tide. Christopher Soames, with Churchillian panache, attempted to break the deadlock by obtaining an interview which produced such extraordinary repercussions that it came to be known as *'l'Affaire Soames'*. Nothing, so it seemed, could now retrieve the diplomatic situation. But in 1968 the President, after further, more serious *'événements'*, thought to strengthen his hand by a referendum which went against him and, declaring France to be ungovernable, retired from public life. During Soames's time, Britain at last joined the Common Market in January 1972 and he, like his successor, Edward Tomkins, was able once more to operate through the normal channels. Again we swim with the tide.

Whatever the political situation, a never-failing success has been the visits of our royal family, whose popularity is now almost a tradition in the hearts of the French. There have been two state visits since the war – in 1957 and 1972 – both occasions for magnificent receptions given by the Queen at the embassy. And the immensely popular Queen Elizabeth the Queen Mother has also visited Paris on several occasions.

Duff Cooper described the embassy as 'a perfect example of what a rich gentleman's house should be. Neither palatial nor imposing, but commodious and convenient, central and quiet.' This conception of the way an ambassador should live is increasingly open to question in our democratic age, apart from the obvious difficulty of running something so large, though, with ministers coming and going, all the rooms are in almost continual use. There are several ways in which it could be reduced in size, such as leaving the ground floor for official entertainment only and, as with the Gate House (the original chancery), giving accommodation to other members of the staff. (A precedent for this is when La Marck divided the house for the use of himself and the Portuguese Ambassador.) Certainly the embassy, with its valuable furniture and ornaments, is a tremendous responsibility. It is something of a museum, and for that very reason a museum director should have the final say in its upkeep and renovations,* the Ambassadress, of course, deciding on the furnishing of her private rooms.

The formal spaciousness of the house may not have appealed to every châtelaine, but all have appreciated the garden, and many applied themselves energetically to its improvement. It is still the *jardin anglais* of La Marck and has several ancient trees. The bases for sphinxes are probably a relic of the Borgheses, also the important second-century Greco-Roman sacrificial altar which lay forgotten in the bushes. Lady Granville enjoyed the countrified peace of this long garden, flanked by gardens. The illusion remains despite the distant murmur of traffic.

Of the 25 ambassadors who have represented us since the embassy was acquired, Tyrrell, with his subtle flair, probably understood the French best. Lytton was the most loved, Derby the grandest and, with Wellington and Bertie, the most typically British – though across the Channel we are considered to be individualists. They were nearly all, in varying degrees, men of ability. Some of them stirred the atmosphere, which is always respected in France. Some just enjoyed themselves. Inevitably, one or two fitted less well into the scene or had the misfortune to serve at an un-favourable time.

Of the ambassadresses surely no one can rival Lady Granville: not as the perfect wife of a diplomat but for her delight in living, genuineness and perception which shine through her descriptions of life in the house. She was the inspiration for the writer to delve into its history.

Always considered to be our finest diplomatic post, Paris is certainly an intellectual challenge to us slower-thinking islanders. Under the luminous skies the very air is volatile with an exciting quality and the Parisians have been com-pared to the *Chevaux de Marly* (the finely chiselled horses by Coustou which eternally champ and chafe at the foot of the

---

* This plan was actually put into effect in 1959 when Lord Molson was Minister of Works but it lapsed.

Champs-Elysées). 'Always bridled and always restive.'

The Hôtel de Charost has been British territory for over a hundred and sixty years. It has greatly added to our prestige and been a home for a succession of remarkable families. On leaving, nearly all must have echoed the words of Madame de Sévigné: *'On ne guérit pas de Paris.'*

Selected Bibliography

Baring, Maurice, *The Puppet Show of Memory* (London 1922)
Berry, Miss, *Extracts from the Journals and Correspondence of* (London 1865)
Bertie, Lord, *Diary* (London 1924)
Blount, Sir Edward, *Memoirs* (London 1920)
Blunt, Wilfred Scawen, *Diaries* (London 1920)
Broughton, Lord, *Recollections of a Long Life* (London 1916)

Cailliavet, Simonne de, *Miss Howard* (Paris 1956)
Canning, George, *Some Official Correspondence* (London 1887)
Churchill, Randolph, *Lord Derby* (London 1959)
Churchill, Winston, *The Second World War* (London 1948)
Cooper, Alfred Duff, *Old Men Forget* (London 1953)
Cowley, First Earl, *Selections from Papers. The Paris Embassy during the Second Empire* (London 1928)
Craven, Mrs Augustus, *Life of Lady Georgina Fullerton* (London 1888)
Croker, J. W., *Correspondence and Diaries* (London 1884)

Dalling, Lord, *Life of Viscount Palmerston* (London 1870-74)
Dard, Emile, *Un Rival de Fersen, Quentin Craufurd* (Paris 1947)
Detrez, Alfred, *Le Faubourg Saint-Honoré* (Paris 1953)

Esher, Viscount, *Journals and Letters* (London 1934-38)

Goldsmith, Lewis, *Secret History of the Cabinet of Napoleon* (London 1810)
Granville, Harriet, Countess, *Letters* (London 1894)
Greville, Charles, *Memoirs* (London 1938)
Greville, Henry, *Leaves from the Diary of* (London 1883)

Hardinge of Penshurst, Lord, *The Old Diplomacy* (London 1947)
Harvey, Oliver, *Diplomatic Diaries* (London 1970)

Inventaire du Mobilier de l'Hôtel de la Princesse Pauline Borghese, 26 Août 1814

La Marck, Comte de, *Correspondence entre le Comte de Mirabeau et le Comte de la Marck* (Paris 1851)

Lutyens, Lady Emily, *A Blessed Girl* (London 1954)

Lyall, Sir James, *Life of the Marquess of Dufferin and Ava* (London 1905)

Lytton, The Earl of, *Personal and Literary Letters* (London 1906)

Magnus, Sir Philip, *King Edward VII* (London 1964)

Malet, Sir Edward, *Shifting Scenes* (London 1901)

Malmesbury, The Earl of, *Memoirs of an Ex-Minister* (London 1901)

Masson, Frédéric, *Napoléon et sa Famille* (Paris 1899-1901)

Maxwell, Sir Herbert, *Life and Letters of the 4th Earl of Clarendon* (London 1913), *The Duke of Wellington* (London 1899)

Nabonne, Bernard, *Pauline Borghese* (Paris 1960)

Newton, Lord, *Lord Lyons* (London 1935)

Nicolson, Harold, *Helen's Tower* (London 1937)

Paget, Walpurga, Lady, *Embassies of Other Days* (London 1923)

Ponsonby, Sir Frederick, *Three Reigns* (London 1951)

Pope-Hennessy, James, *Lord Crewe* (London 1955)

Ronaldshay, Earl of, *Life of Lord Curzon* (London 1928)

Rose, Kenneth, *Superior Person* (London 1969)

Spears, Maj.-Gen. Sir Edward, *The Fall of France* (London 1954), *Two Men Who Saved France* (London 1966)

Stuart-Wortley, The Hon. Mrs Edward, *Highcliffe and the Stuarts* (London 1927)

Temperley, H. W. V. *Princesse de Lieven, Diaries and Correspondence* (London 1925)

Vansittart, Lord, *The Mist Procession* (London 1958)

Wellington, Duke of, *Supplementary Dispatches* (London 1862)

I have also consulted the Archives du Département de la Seine et de la Ville de Paris and the relevant records of the Foreign Office, the India Office and the Department of the Environment.

Index

DATE DUE

	JAN 12 1983	JAN 2 4 1983	
	201-6503		Printed in USA